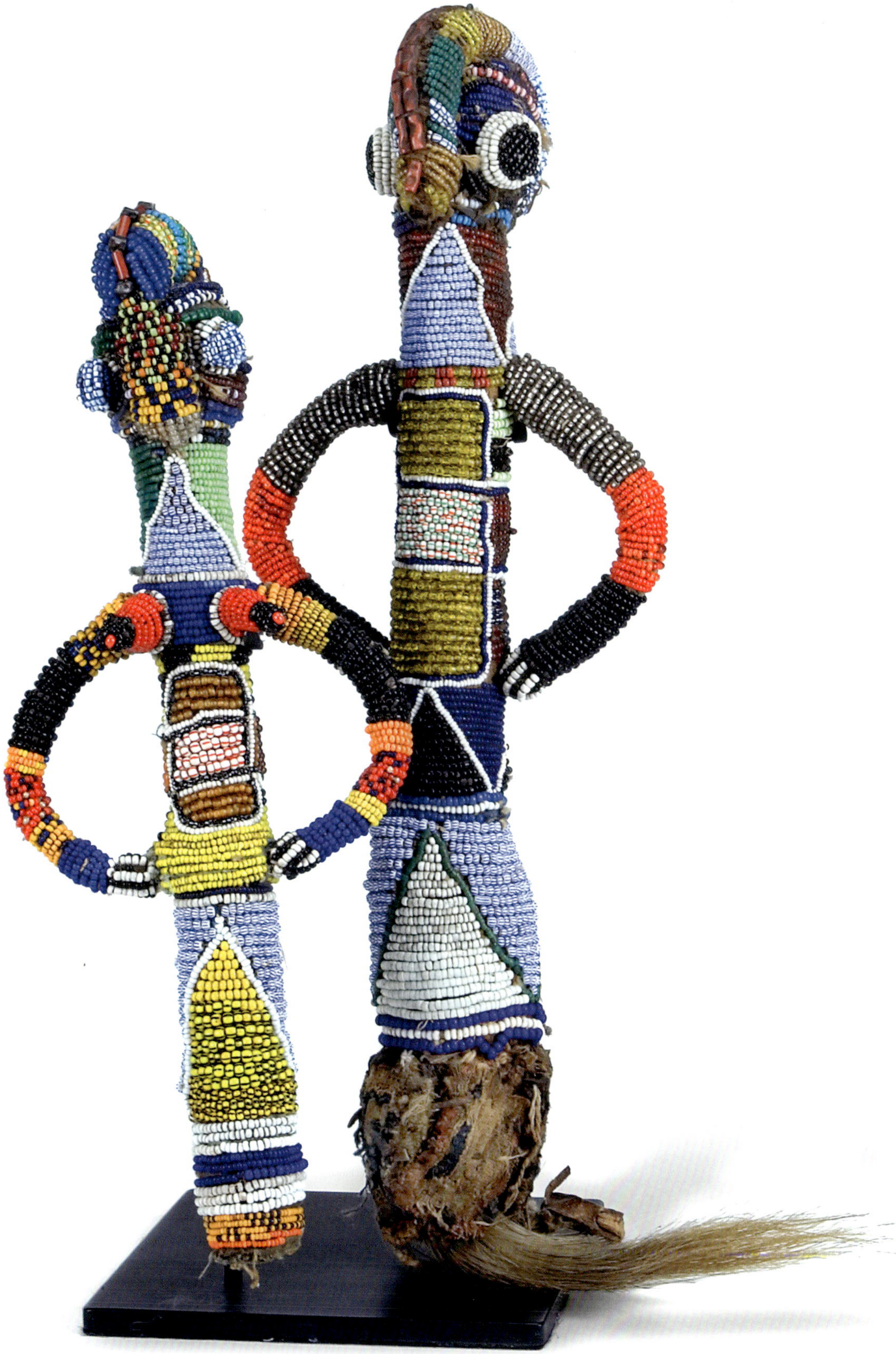

Edited and with an introduction by Joyce Ice

Museum of International Folk Art
Santa Fe, New Mexico

in association with

University of Washington Press
Seattle and London

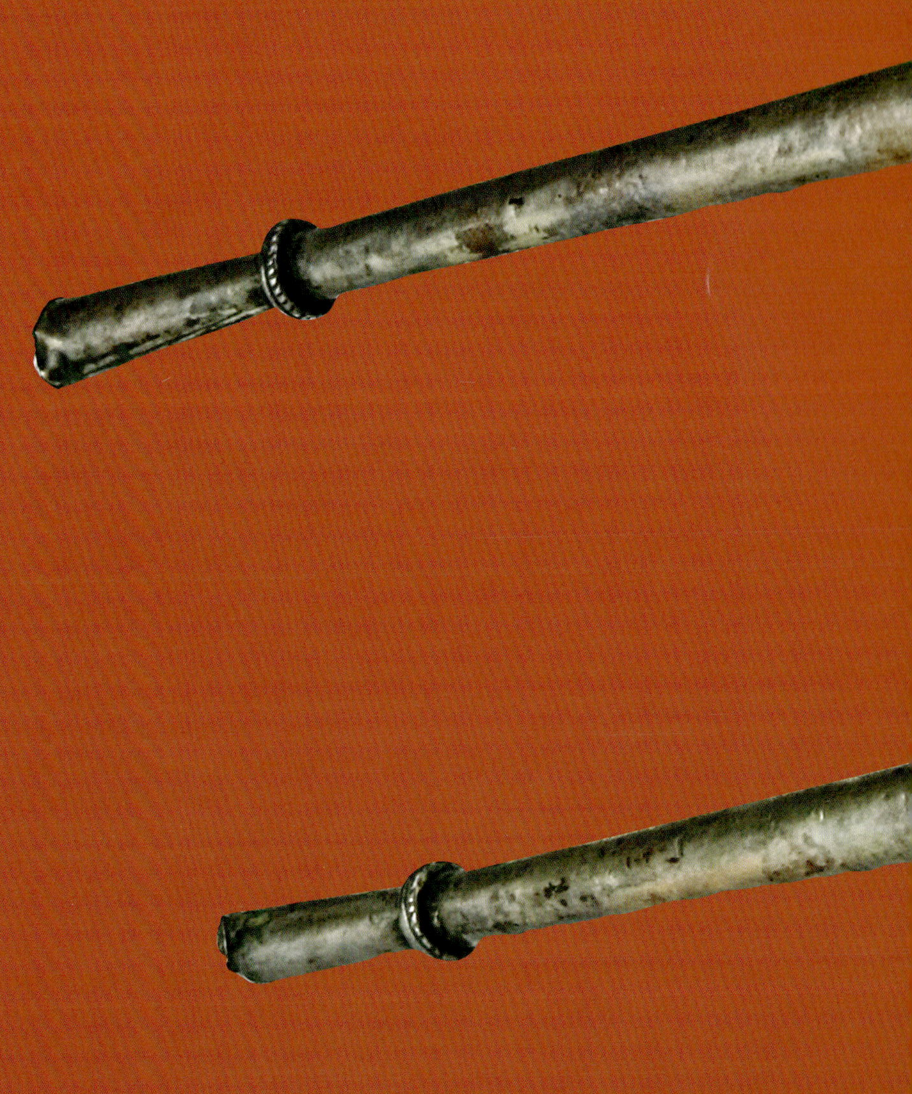

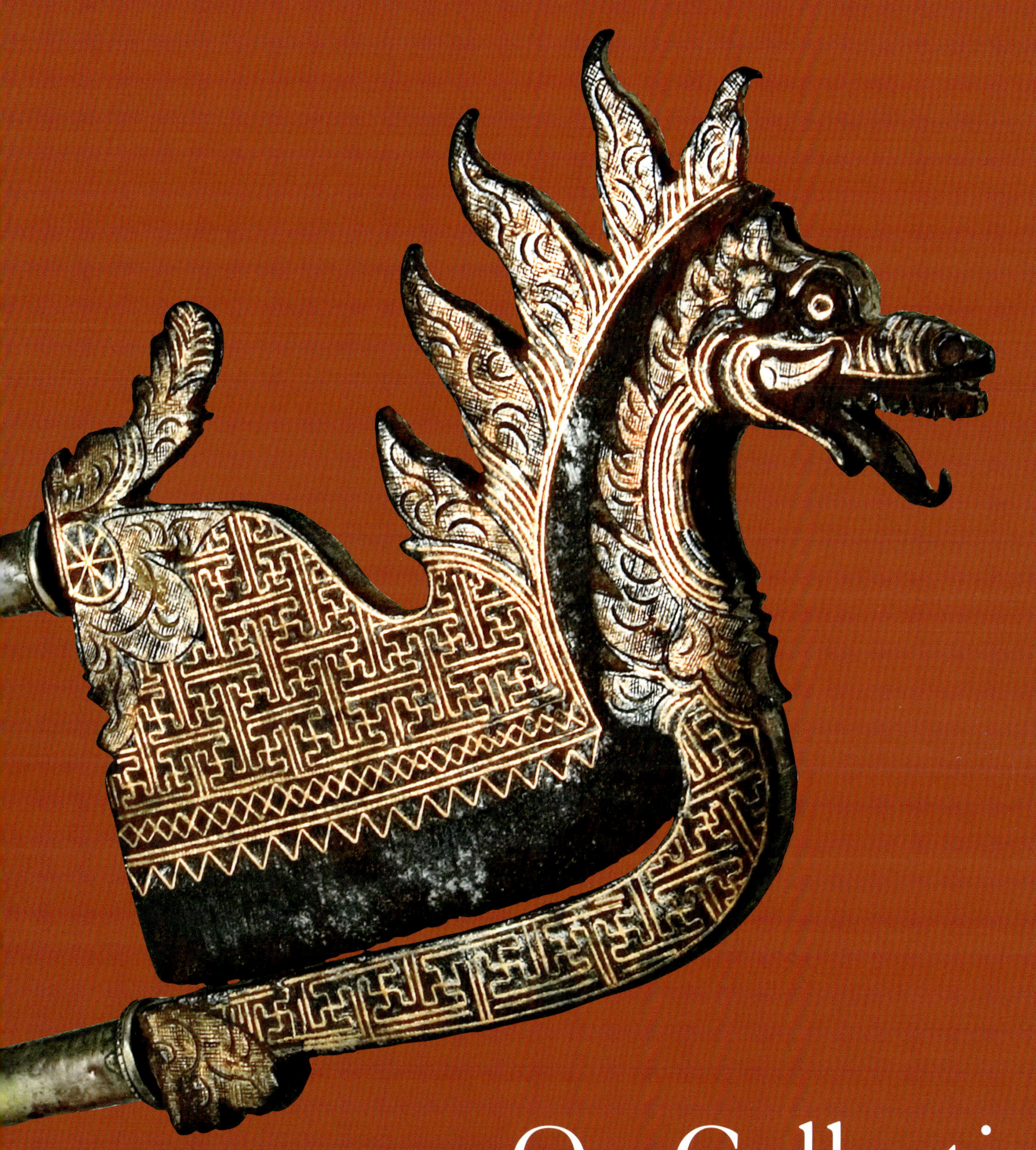

On Collecting

From Private to Public, Featuring Folk and Tribal Art from the Diane and Sandy Besser Collection

Dedicated to a celebration of the life of Diane Besser
by Grant, Matthew, and Sandy Besser

ON PAGE 1:

Figurative fly whisks, 20th century, Yoruba people, Southwest Nigeria, Glass beads, wood, horse hair, cloth. Gift of the Diane and Sandy Besser Collection. IFAF

ON PAGES 2–3:

Betel nut cutter in the shape of a dragon, 19th–20th centuries, Southeast Asia, Metal alloys, IFAF Purchase from the Diane and Sandy Besser Collection

The following abbreviations are used in the photo captions:

IFAF: International Folk Art Foundation Collection in the Museum of International Folk Art, a division of the New Mexico Department of Cultural Affairs

MOIFA: Museum of International Folk Art, a division of the New Mexico Department of Cultural Affairs

MOSCA: Museum of Spanish Colonial Art, Santa Fe

Design by David Skolkin / Skolkin + Chickey, Santa Fe
Typeset by Angela Taormino
Printed in China
14 12 11 10 09 5 4 3 2 1

Distributed by the University of Washington Press
P.O. Box 50096, Seattle, WA 98145 U.S.A.
www.washington.edu/uwpress

Library of Congress Cataloging-in-Publication Data
On collecting : from private to public, featuring folk and tribal art from the Diane and Sandy Besser collection / edited and with an introduction by Joyce Ice. — 1st ed.
p. cm.
Includes index.
ISBN 978-0-295-98888-7 (pbk. : alk. paper)
1. Art—Collectors and collecting. 2. Besser, Sandy—Art collections. 3. Besser, Diane—Art collections. I. Ice, Joyce Ann.
N5200.O5 2009
745.092'2—dc22 2008055995

The paper used in this publication meets the minimum requirements of American National Standard for Information Sciences—Permanence of Paper for Printed Library Materials, ANSI

Contents

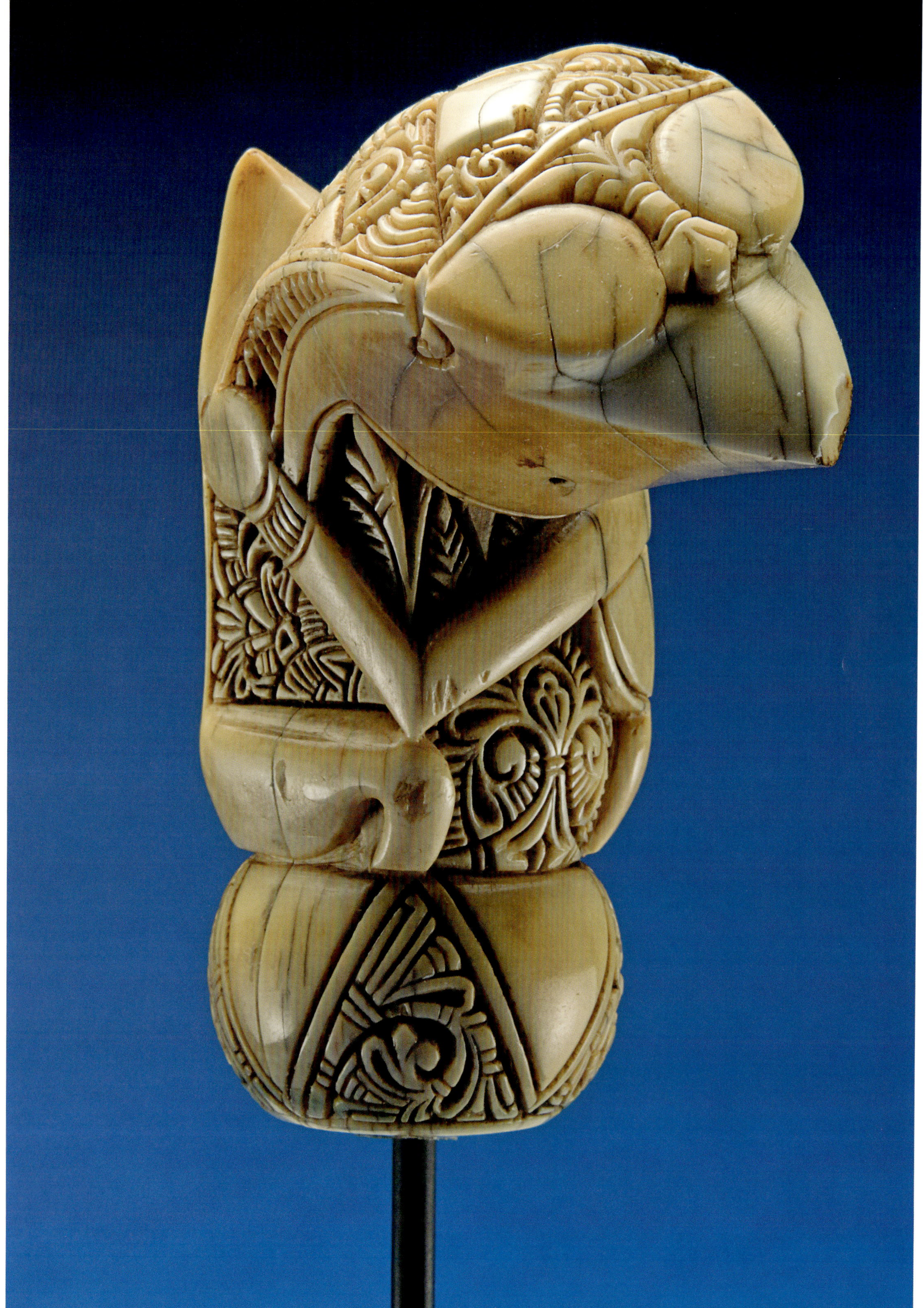

Introduction

GIFTS FROM THE DIANE AND SANDY BESSER COLLECTION of folk and tribal art to the Museum of International Folk Art (MOIFA) led to the creation of this book. To date, the Museum has received more than 850 pieces from the Besser Collection in a series of contributions over several years, with more contributions to come. A major acquisition in both size and scope, the Besser Collection enhances and strengthens many areas of the existing collection at the Museum of International Folk Art in Santa Fe, New Mexico.

The Besser collection includes *bultos* (three-dimensional wood-carvings of saints) and *retablos* (painted devotional images) from New Mexico, as well as intricately carved *keris* (dagger) handles, slingshots, ceremonial objects, curing dolls, jewelry, ceramics, textiles, beadwork, miniature bronzes, and masks from around the globe. Within each category, the objects exemplify some of the finest examples of their kind, inviting study and appreciation of their variety, use, and form.

Over the years, Sandy Besser, together with his late wife, Diane, hosted many people in their home, sharing their collection with curators, museum groups, scholars, artists, and others who enjoyed the opportunity to see the works of art that fill every room of the house. Named one of the top one hundred collectors in America in 2002 by *Art and Antiques* magazine, Sandy Besser works

OPPOSITE:

Kris handle in the form of a Jawa Demam figure, 19th–20th centuries

Sumatra, Indonesia

Ivory

IFAF Purchase from the Diane and Sandy Besser Collection

Kuna curing dolls, 2006
Displayed in the Besser home, Santa Fe, New Mexico

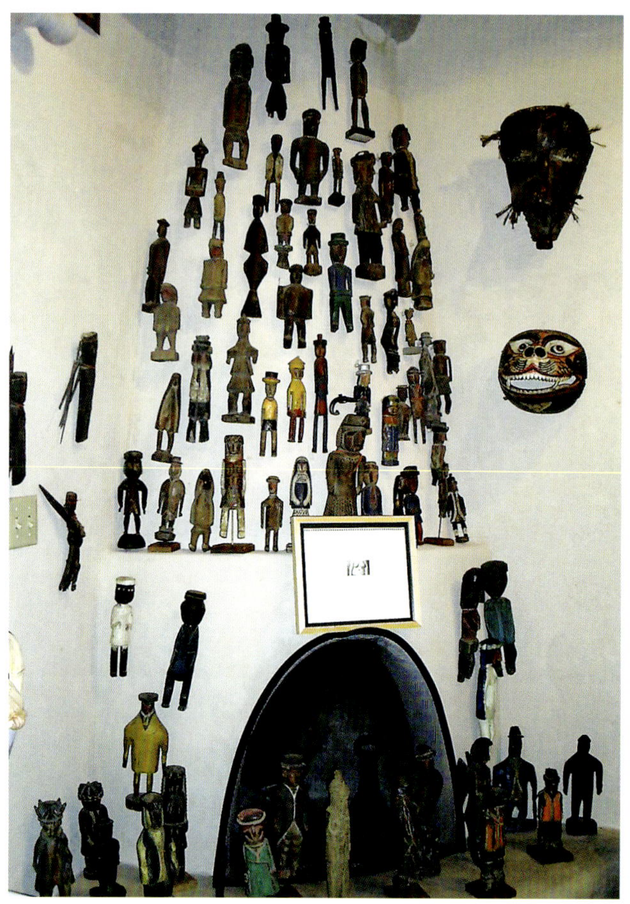

from a collecting philosophy that "one of anything doesn't look right." In building his collection, he seeks works of art for their aesthetic quality and artistic variation—works that speak to him personally—and his intention is eventually to donate the pieces to museums. At MOIFA, works of art from the Besser Collection are made available to researchers, displayed in exhibitions organized by MOIFA, and loaned to other museums. In the future, professional colleagues, students, and the general public will be able to view images from this collection on the Internet, as part of a digitization project that will assist art researchers at MOIFA and in the broader art world and that will provide online access to the collection database.

Each object in the Besser Collection exemplifies the journey of an artwork from its place of origin to a private collection, and finally to a museum that conserves, presents, and interprets its collections for the benefit of the public. This publication contributes to a greater understanding of the collecting process and the

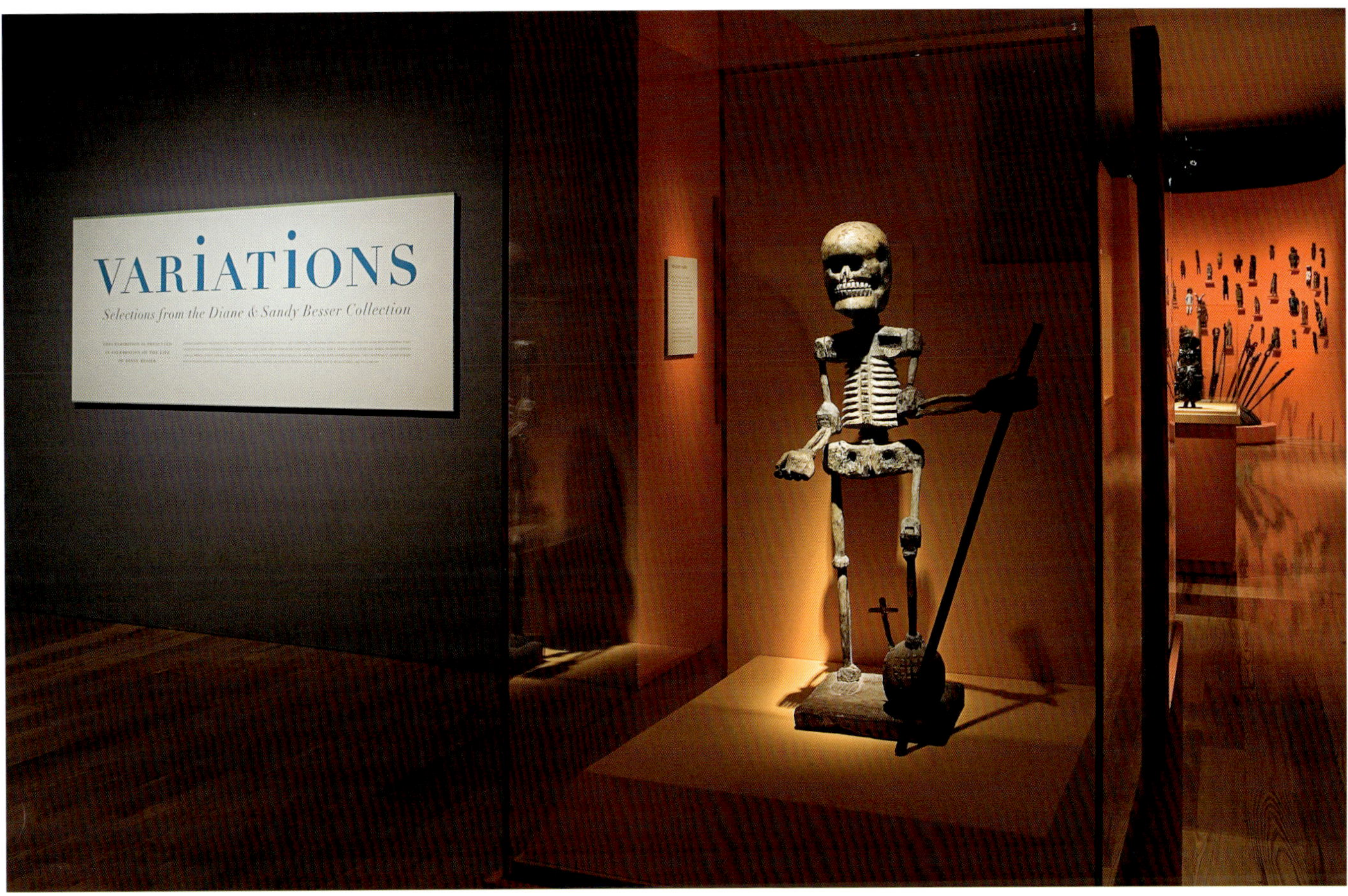

Exhibition title panel for the *Variations* exhibition, October 2006 through April 2007

Bartlett Wing, Museum of International Folk Art

challenges faced by museums of all sizes. The generous donation of the Besser Collection to MOIFA provides a point of departure for the essays in this book, although the discussion is not limited to this specific collection or to a single collector.

The process of transferring a private collection to a public institution is similar to many other transactions involving different kinds of museums and various types of collections. The movement of a work of art from artist's studio to gallery, to collector, and to curator—from private hands to a public museum—sometimes follows a clear and distinct route, easily discernible from start to finish. In other cases, the trail twists and turns, traveling a number of byways before arriving at its destination.

This collection of essays grew out of many conversations about art and collecting, including panel discussions and interviews at the Museum of International Folk Art that were presented in conjunction with several exhibitions featuring the Besser Collection. Taken together, these exchanges were the impe-

Exhibition installation of curing dolls and authority staffs, 20th century

Kuna people, San Blas Islands, Panama

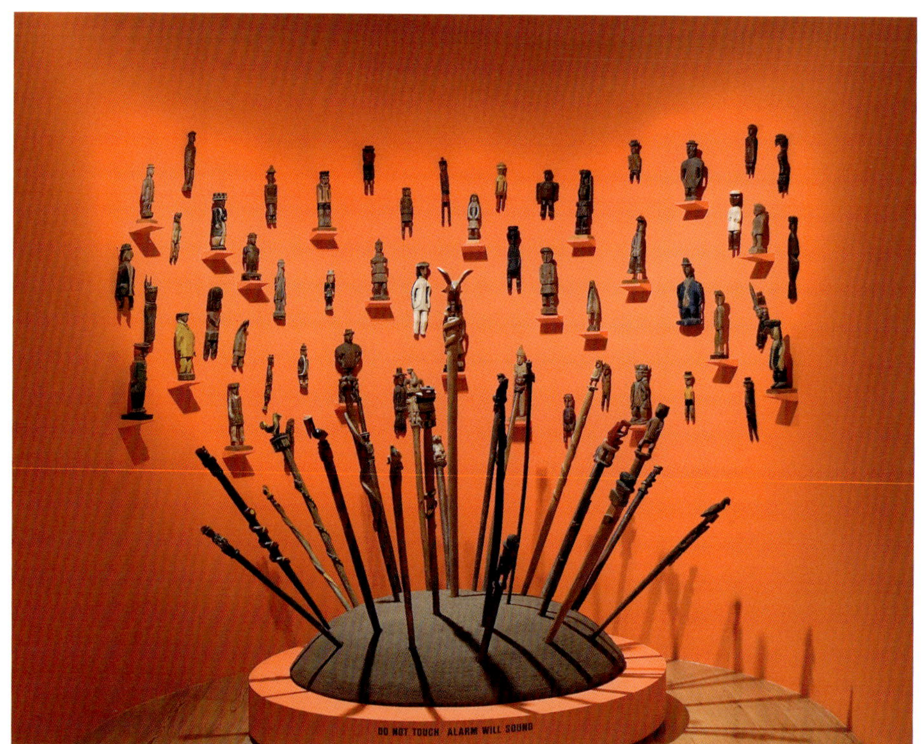

tus for a book that would examine the collecting process from a number of different perspectives: collector, dealer, artist, curator, museum director, and lawyer. *On Collecting* focuses on the themes and relationships that define the world of art collectors and donors, art purchasers and art dealers, artists who themselves create and sell works, and museum curators and directors who acquire and care for art collections. In addition, myriad legal issues must be considered in the present-day art world and in the public arena, contexts that require greater transparency and accountability than ever before. Writing from these varied viewpoints, the authors share their experiences, using examples drawn from their personal and professional lives. Their essays reveal the intersecting roles of the players and the diverse, intertwined aspects of art collecting today.

The authors address issues surrounding collecting by individuals, the transfer of privately held collections to public institutions, and the complex ethical, legal, emotional, and intellectual questions involved. This book explores the process of developing a collection over years of dedicated (some might say obsessive) searching, researching, expanding, and refining. Our contributors also offer insights into the difficult, occasionally painful, and oftentimes joyful, decision-making process about a collection's future, and they discuss the resulting sepa-

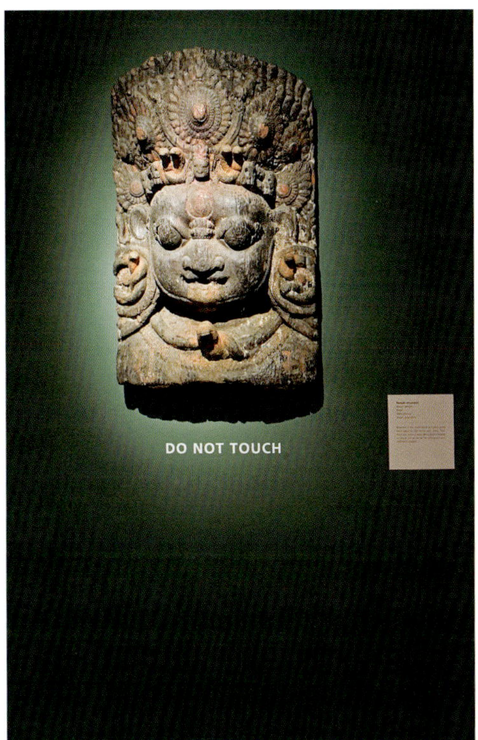

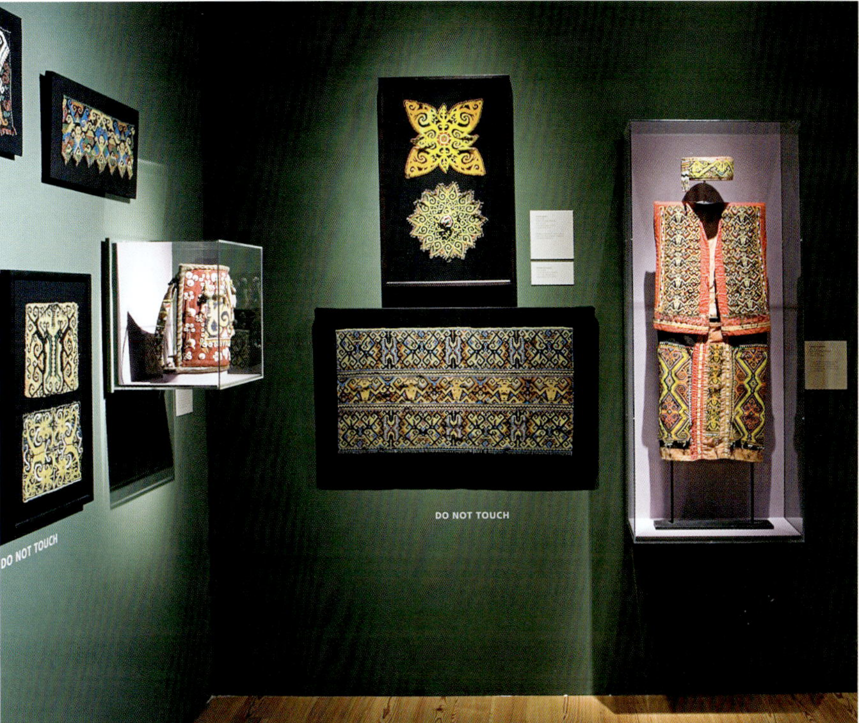

LEFT:
Exhibition installation of Bhairava carving, 16th century

Newar people, Nepal

RIGHT:
Exhibition installation of Asian beaded pieces

ration anxiety and the sometimes conflicting agendas of the parties involved. These convoluted courtship rituals involve collectors, donors, museum staff, and board members, and, eventually, they will affect museum visitors.

Usually the details of negotiations surrounding the acquisition of a collection, the purchase/commission of art from individual artists, and the sales involving dealers are quietly arranged, out of the public's view. The essays in this volume offer readers a glimpse behind the scenes into the roles and relationships that influence the transfer of collections from private ownership to the public trust.

The International Folk Art Foundation has generously provided funds in support of this project, as has the Diane Besser Memorial Fund. Without the encouragement and cooperation of Sandy Besser, this publication would not have been possible.

Joyce Ice
Director, Museum of International Folk Art
Santa Fe, 2008

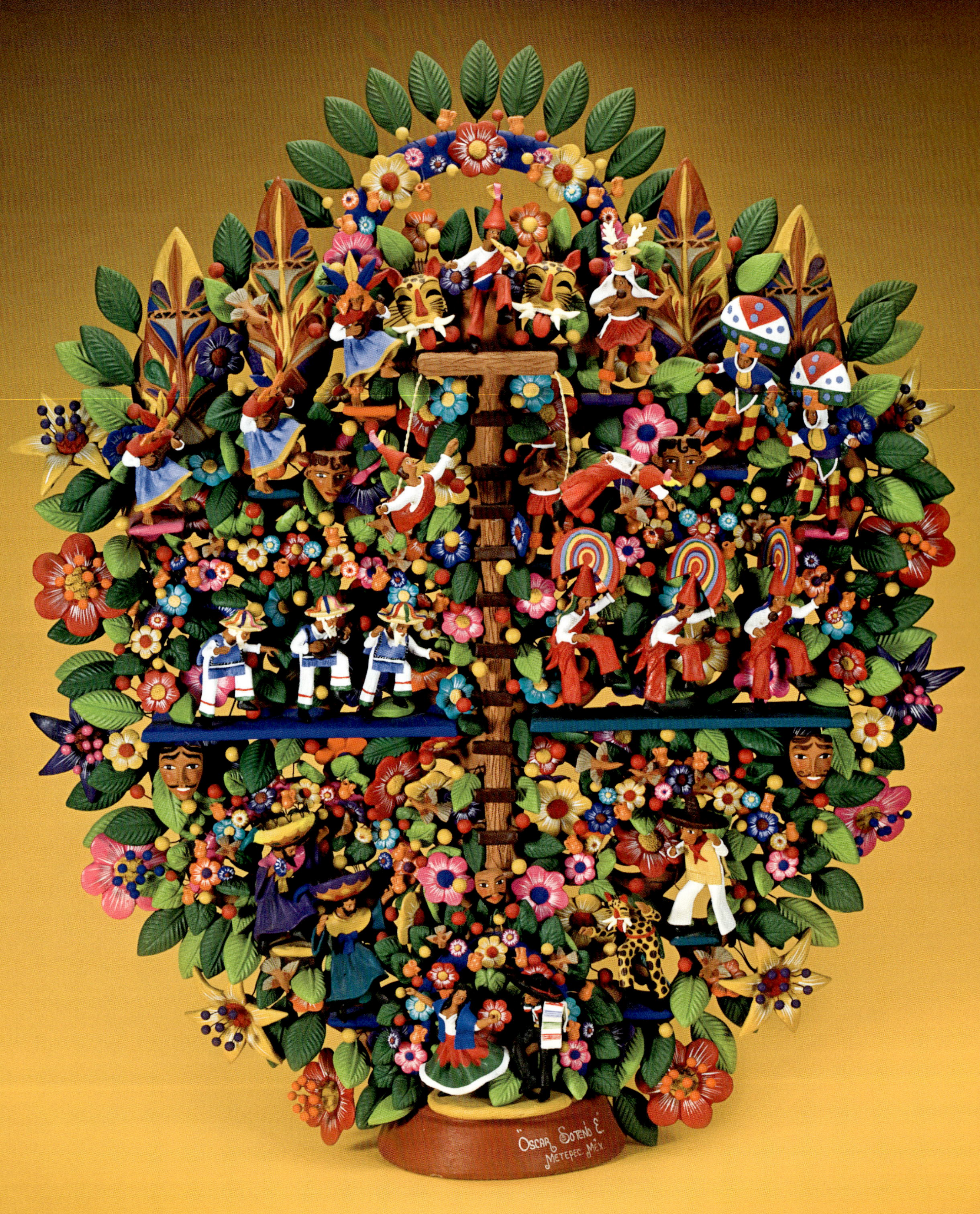
"Oscar Soteno E.
Metepec, Mex.

How Do I Collect?

To "L" with the Norm

Sandy Besser

LEARN AND LOOK. Look lots. Listen less . . . listen little. Locate. Love. Limit lingering . . . Leap.

That is how I have collected art for more than forty years. That is all there is to it. Why complicate what should be a simple sequence of steps? For those who need to go beyond the L's, I suggest considering the following definition of what makes a good collector, from Glenn Lowry, director of New York's Museum of Modern Art: "Someone who's passionate, knowledgeable, thoughtful, who has a clear sense of what he or she wants to do, has a clear sense of the artists who interest them, and who is dedicated to the effort."[1] I must confess that that is who I think I am. But I would add to that definition that collectors like me have to be more than a little nuts. James Michener said, "The typical collector is a male, usually unbalanced in some direction, who, if he were normal, would not need to collect odd bits and pieces. I believe that any collector of anything suffers from some kind of mental or psychological aberration, and that his collecting is a therapy which may run into a great deal of expense but which protects his sanity and allows him to operate in other fields fairly normally."[2] Michener's reputation validates my belief that we collectors are a little, or a lot, nuts—and it isn't confined to males.

OPPOSITE:

Tree of Dances, by Oscar Soteno Elías, ca. 2000

Metepec, Mexico

Clay, wire, paint

IFAF Purchase from the Diane and Sandy Besser Collection

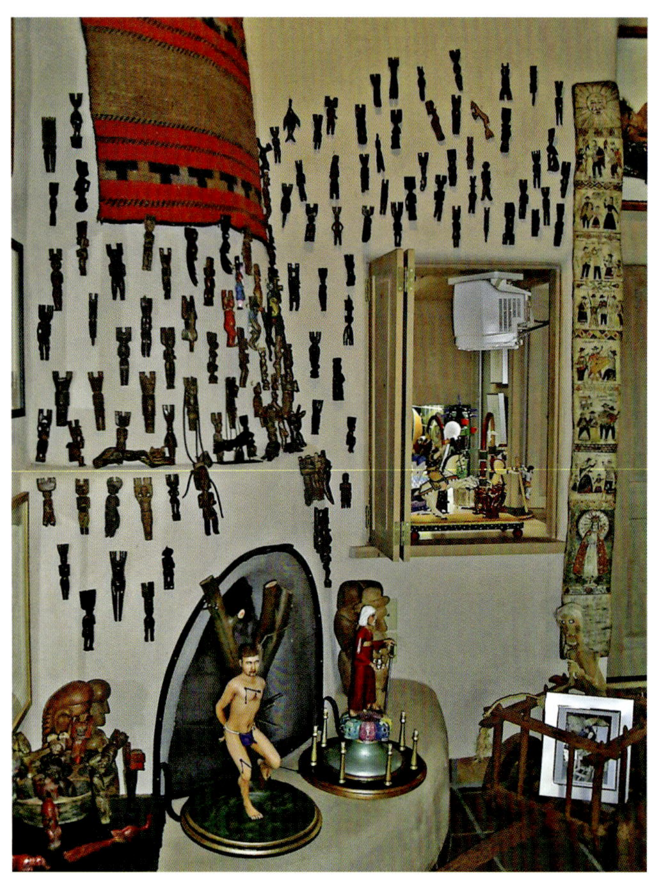

Guatemalan slingshots and other artwork displayed in the Besser home
Santa Fe, New Mexico, 2006

Visitors to my home—and I encourage many visitors, because I want to share the results of my passion—may tell others that I collect fine art, craft, Hispanic religious art, tribal art, ceramic sculpture, folk art, and so forth. But I just tell people that I collect "art." I don't need the nomenclature that segregates art into special categories. I am tired of exhibitions and museums of "women's art" or "black art." Several times I have been asked by members of tour groups what percentage of my collection was done by women. Why is that important, and why would I know? I can't imagine going to a gallery and asking to see art by women or left-handed Lithuanians. I love art and I collect art. I also don't store works from my collection, because storing a work of art was not the intent of the artist. If I am short of display room or if I have fallen out of love with something, I gift it to a museum, which is a great strategy, a win-win-win.

Giving collections to museums is a two-edged sword and can be painfully sharp if not executed properly. It is an act that requires mutual respect. The donor should recognize that the museum must adhere to American Association of Museums standards. If there are additional museum guidelines, one hopes that a decent dose of flexibility goes with them. At the same time, the museum must recognize that donors' egos often need massaging. While donors may state that they don't want much recognition for their generous acts, they really don't mean it. For some, banners flying at every street corner would not be too much!

If the gift is a large and significant one that leads to an exhibition, the wisest choice for museums is to involve a donor in the planning of the project. The donor should be made aware that he or she is a member of the team and clearly *not* the leader of the team. However, the museum should remember that the donor knows the most about the spirit in which the gift came about and may well know more about the material than the museum staff.

Although I never set out to form a charm bracelet of artists, I do enjoy working with some artists whom I describe as under-recognized. The pattern that has evolved is that I collect their work in depth, expose them to other serious collectors, gift their work to museums, and attempt to find a gallery for their

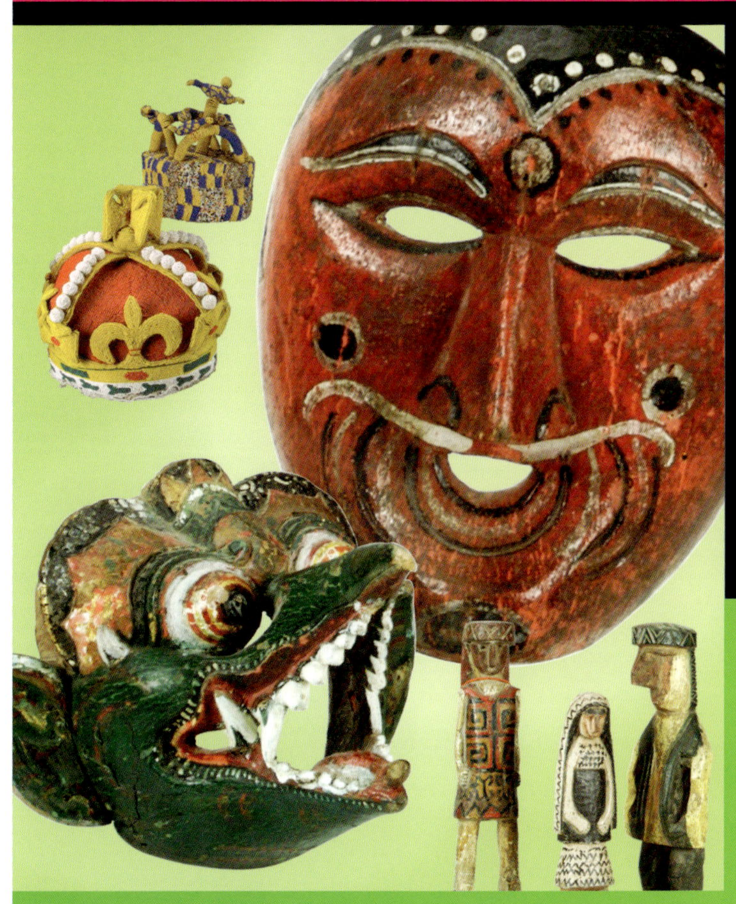

Banner for *Variations* Exhibit, featuring the Diane and Sandy Besser Collection

Museum of International Folk Art, Santa Fe, New Mexico

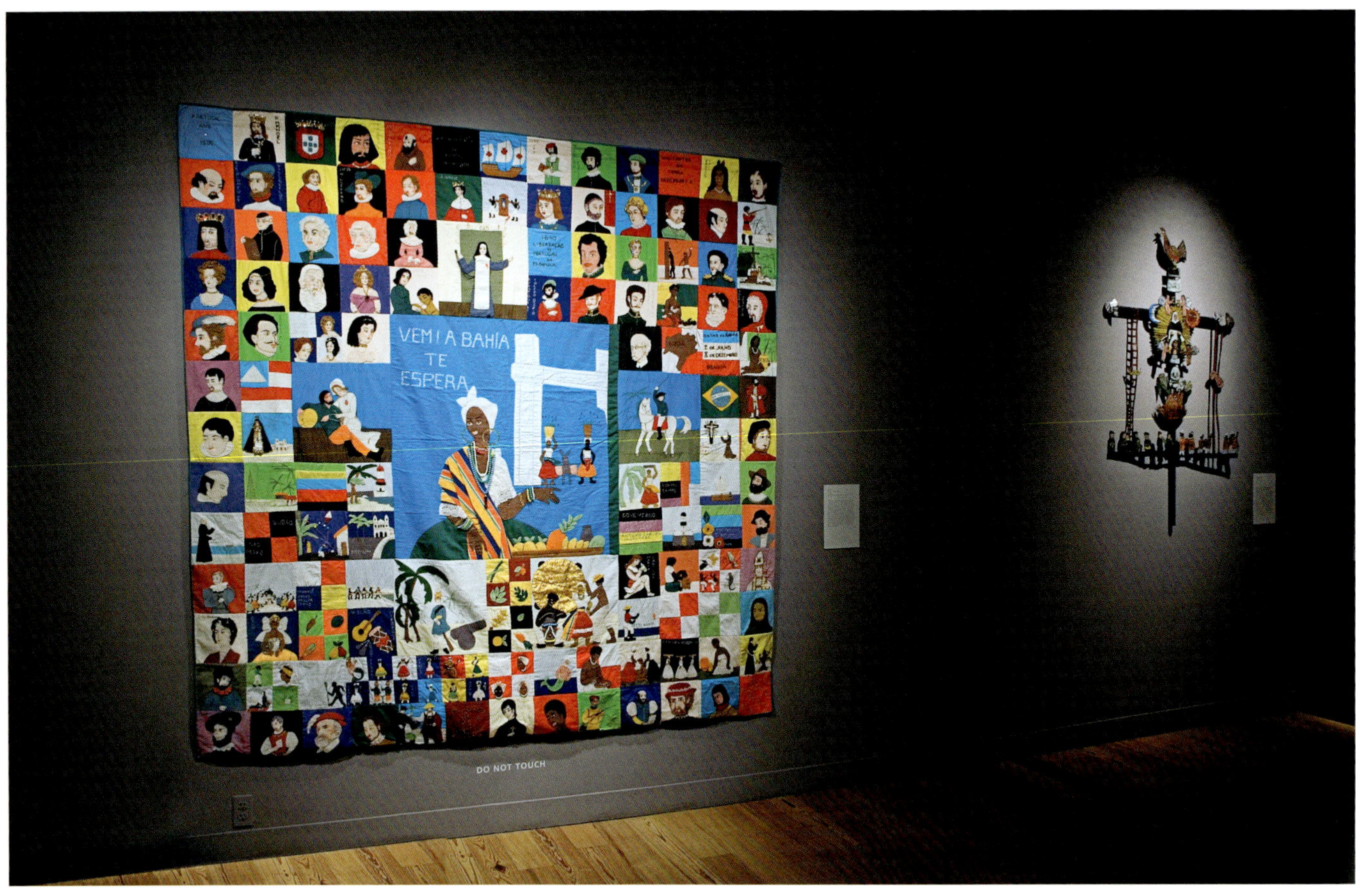

Exhibition installation of quilt from Salvador, Bahia, Brazil, ca. 1960, and festival cross by Claudio Jimenez, Lima, Peru, ca. 1985

work. I am a hands-on patron and, for the most part, this approach has been satisfying. Some artists have deservedly found success, left the nest, and all but forgotten our history. That never feels good. In other cases, I remain their best collector for a time—but maybe not forever. And then there may be instances when either my judgment is wrong or the artist doesn't have the inner drive that it takes to succeed, something I can't give to an artist.

Today, the art market is the place to be for "in" people. Currently, the market is hot, it is chic, it is more important than any other of today's fashions. Table the martini, snub out the cigar, quit snapping the braces. Get to the openings of the fairs and be damned sure to come early (like the day before); art is where it is—but remember that where it is *not* is at many of today's art shows. To me, this doesn't make sense.

This hot art market is on the cusp—in fact, it is almost over, but art-buying lemmings keep marching to the sea. Some dealers feed buyers yesterday's fare, but the initiates often fail to recognize the odor of spoil. If you want, you can go worship at the feet of certain top-name dealers. You may be lucky enough to be put on the waiting list for the latest over-priced, huckterized, here today–gone tomorrow creation. What is wrong with this scene? There are thousands of good artists out there making lots of good art available at very reasonable prices, and here are these buyer-victims trying to get on a dealer's waiting list! I forecast that Humpty-Dumpty is about to receive a royal dumping. In contrast, there are the real collectors such as the Rubells, early buyers willing to take risks on what they see and never buy on just what they hear. Pay attention to the Rubell Collection. Go to the satellite art fairs. It's more fun and less money.

Come back to reality. Go against the norm. Find a few galleries that have an eye for the under-recognized. Visit artist co-ops and play the game of discovery. Maybe you'll like what I like. But remember, look rather than listen.

Notes

1. "Collecting Advice," *ARTnews,* September 2006, 100.

2. James A. Michener, "The Collector: An Informal Memoir," foreword to *The James A. Michener Collection* (Austin: University of Texas, 1977), ix.

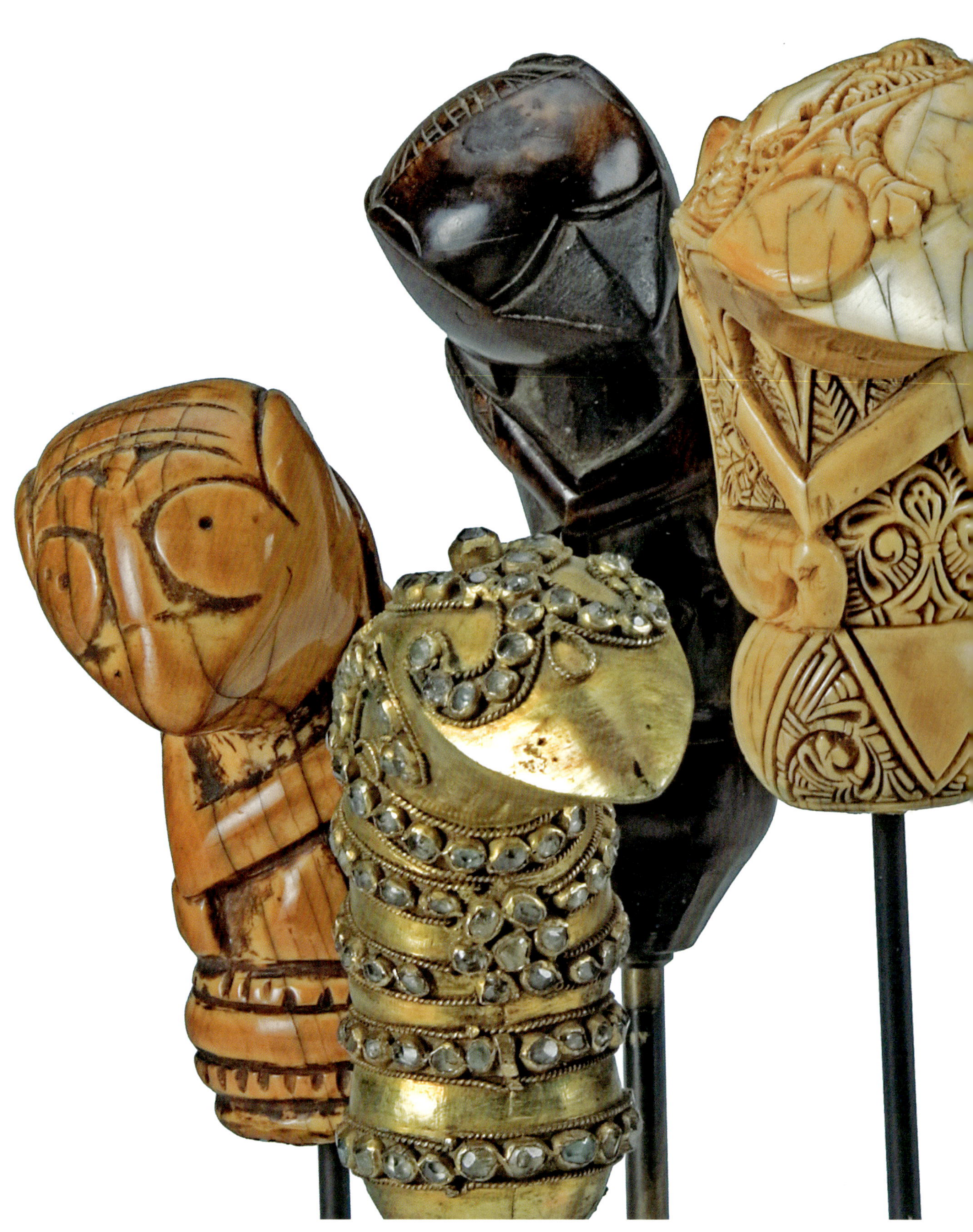

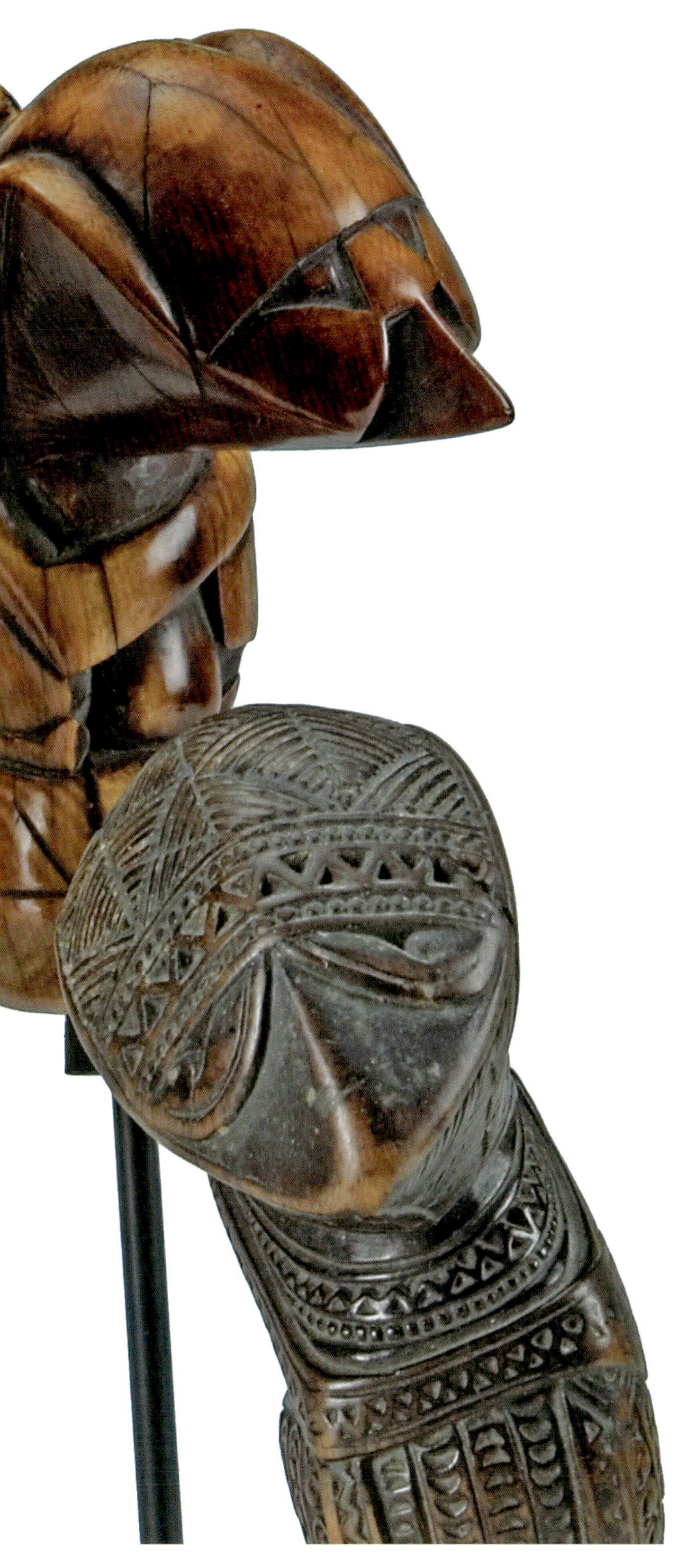

Keris or Kris Handles for ceremonial daggers, 19th-20th centuries

Indo-Malaysian archipelago (Malaysia and Indonesia)

Animal bone, ivory, wood, metal alloys, gemstones

IFAF Purchase from the Diane and Sandy Besser Collection

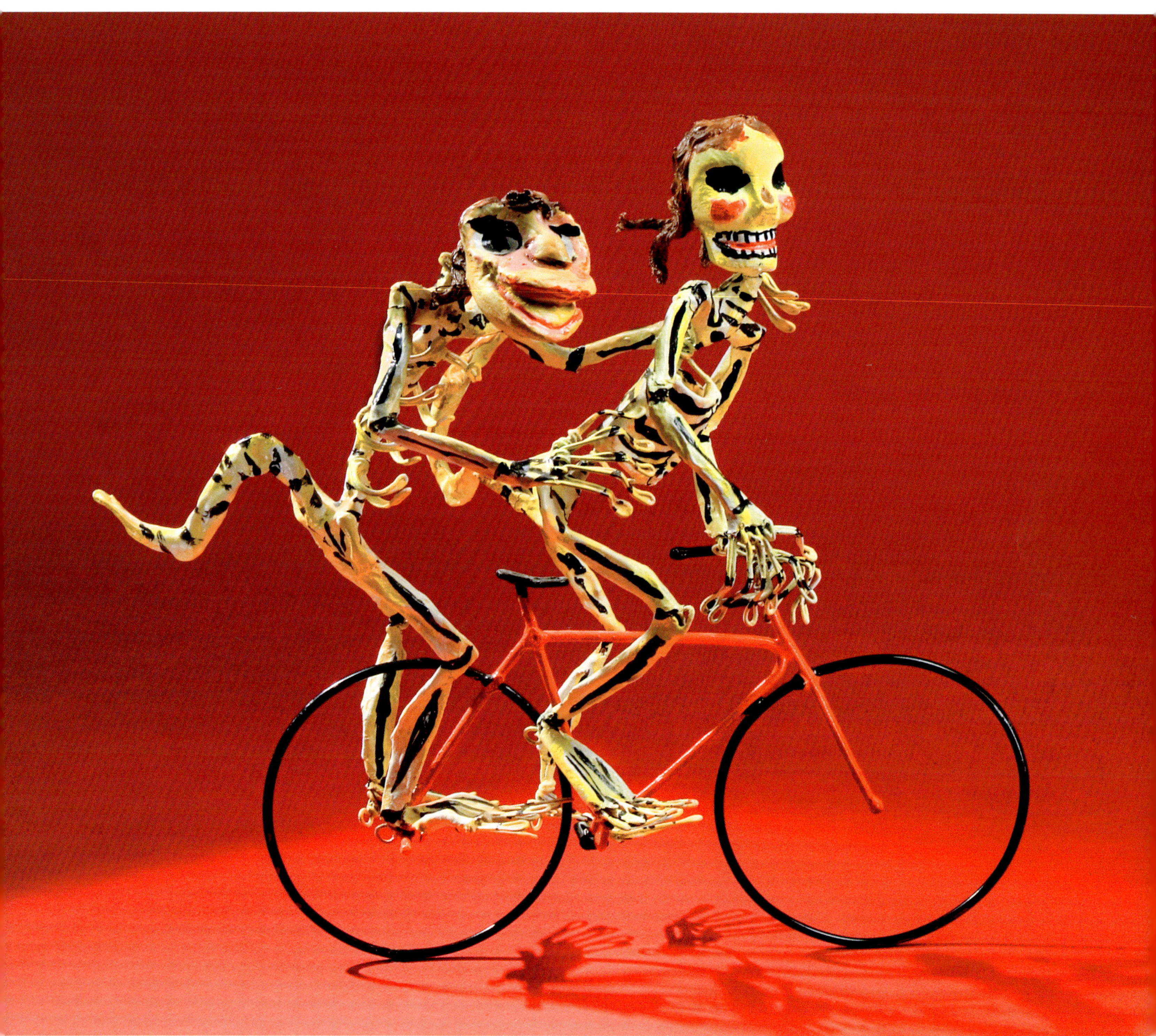

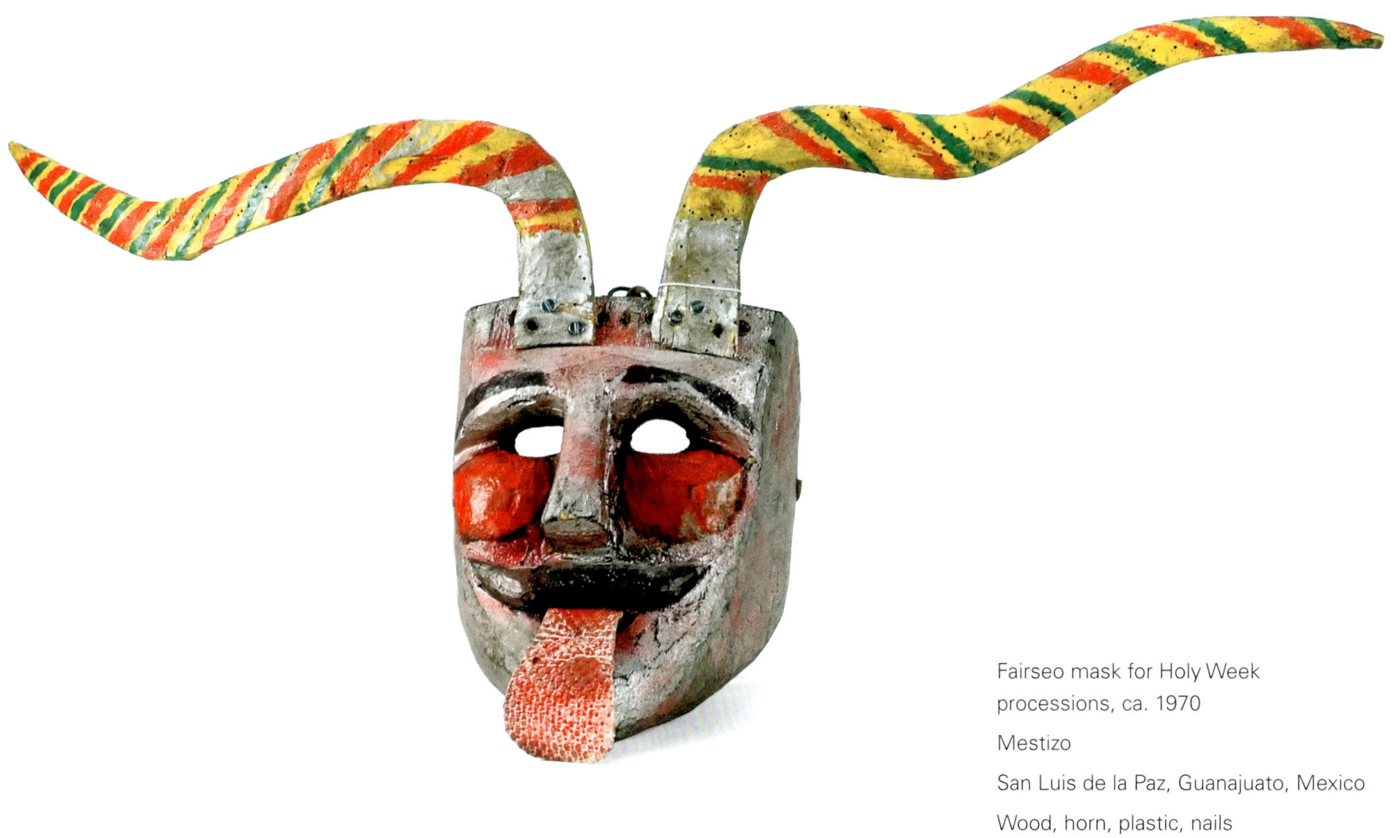

Fairseo mask for Holy Week processions, ca. 1970

Mestizo

San Luis de la Paz, Guanajuato, Mexico

Wood, horn, plastic, nails

IFAF Purchase from the Diane and Sandy Besser Collection

OPPOSITE:

Skeleton couple on a bicycle, by Saulo Moreno, ca 2000

Tlalpujahua, Michoacán, Mexico

Wire, cardboard, paint

IFAF Purchase from the Diane and Sandy Besser Collection

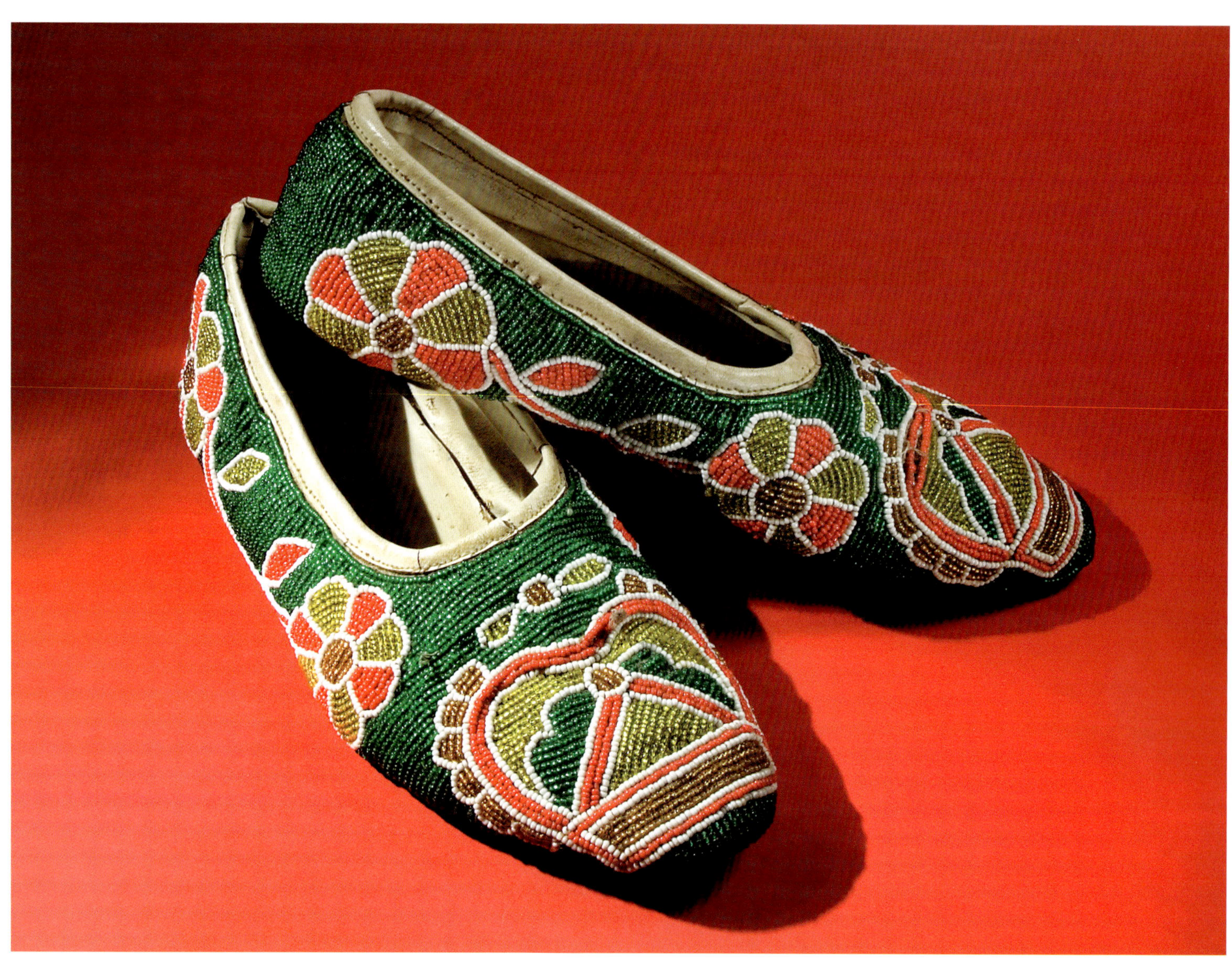

Shoes (*bata ileke*), 20th century
Yoruba people, Southwest Nigeria
Glass beads over shoes
The Diane and Sandy Besser Collection

OPPOSITE:
Necklace, 20th century
Naga people, northeast India and Burma
Glass beads
The Diane and Sandy Besser Collection

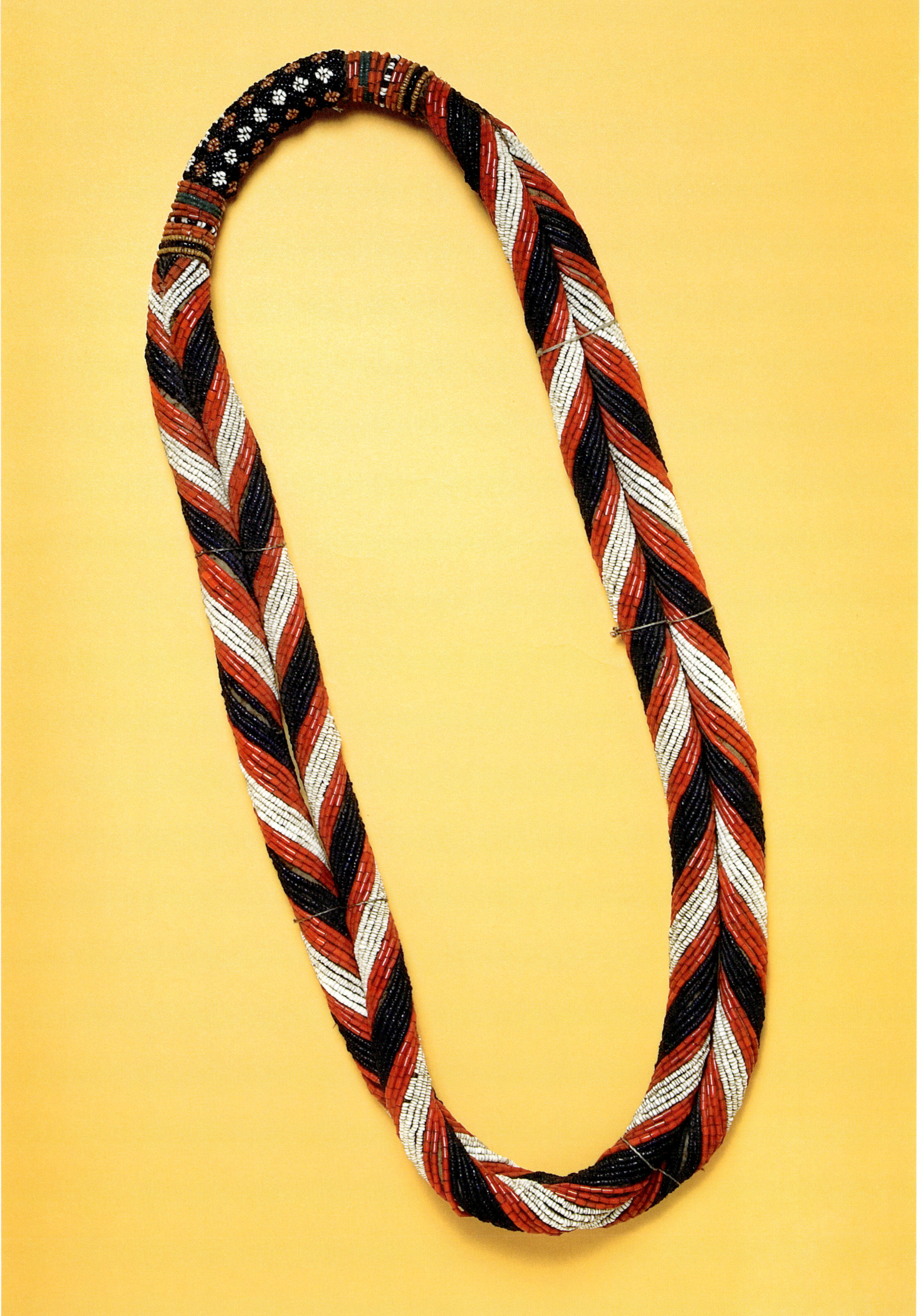

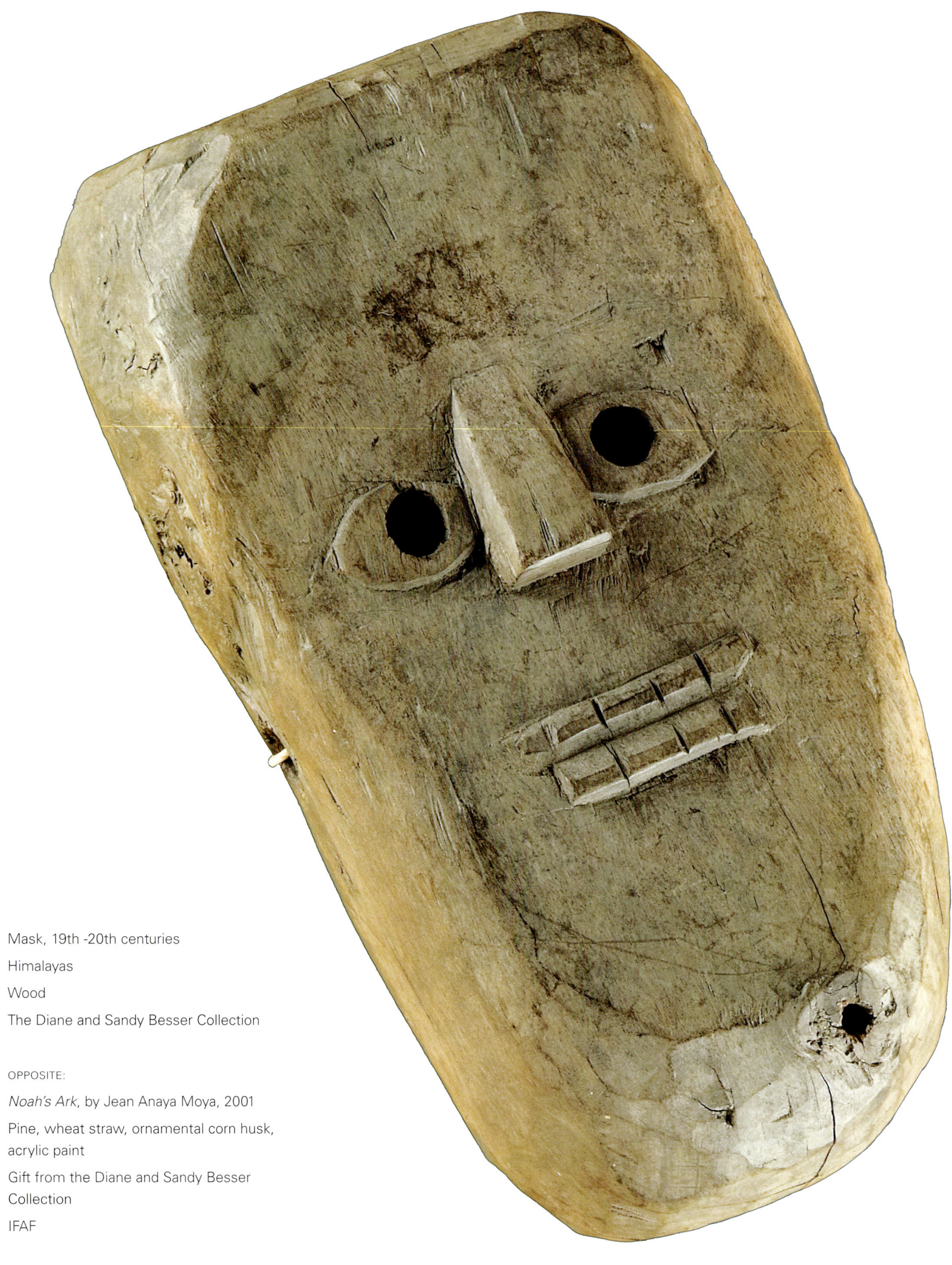

Mask, 19th -20th centuries

Himalayas

Wood

The Diane and Sandy Besser Collection

OPPOSITE:

Noah's Ark, by Jean Anaya Moya, 2001

Pine, wheat straw, ornamental corn husk, acrylic paint

Gift from the Diane and Sandy Besser Collection

IFAF

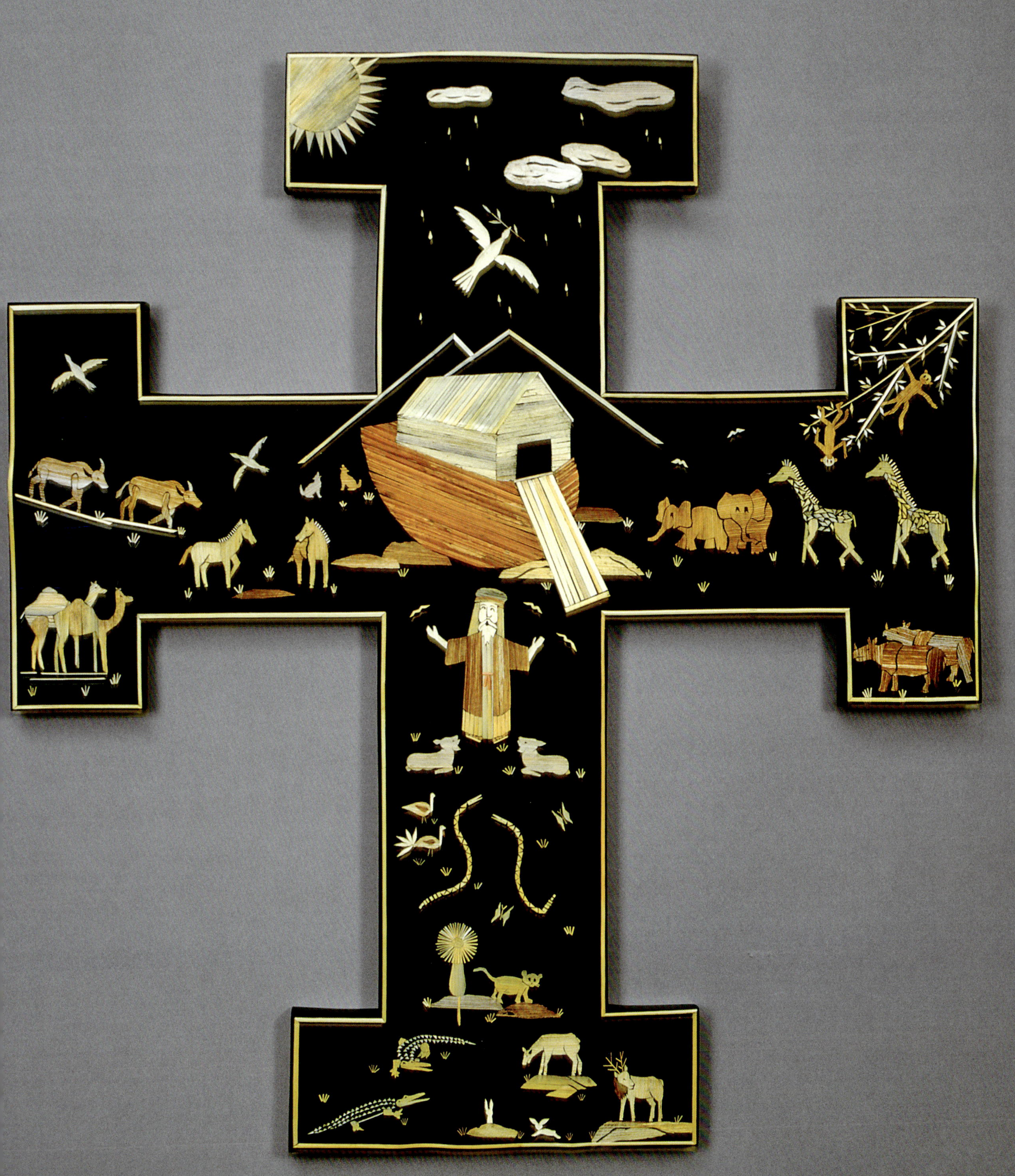

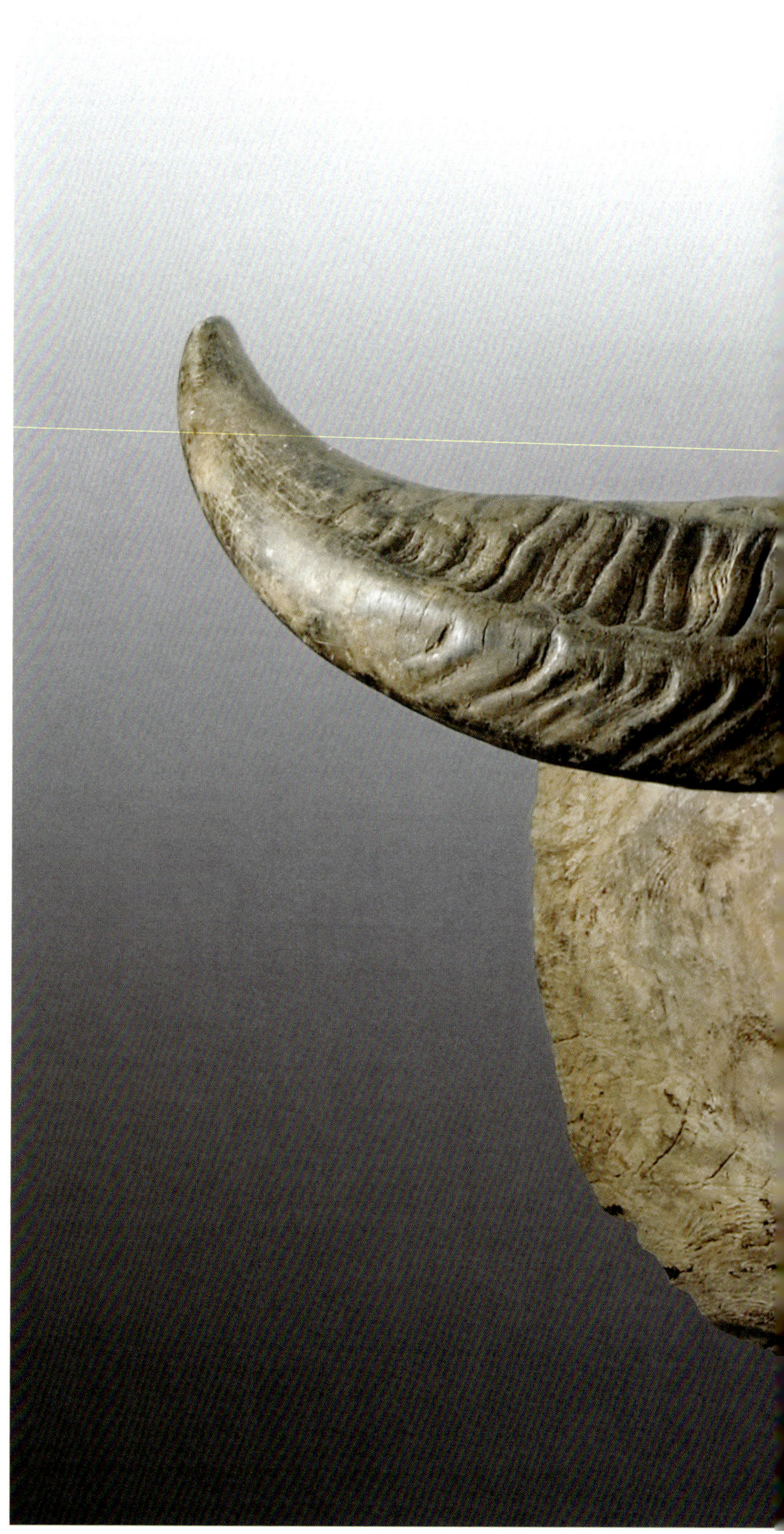

Architectural ornament (*kabongo*),
late 19th–early 20th century

Toraja people, Sulawesi, Indonesia

Wood, water buffalo horns

IFAF Purchase from the Diane and Sandy Besser Collection

During funerals and occasions of celebration, a particular species of buffalo may be sacrificed for the village feast. The host receives the buffalo's horns as a gift of appreciation from the village for the event. The number of horns adorning house posts indicates the homeowner's status and prestige in the village.

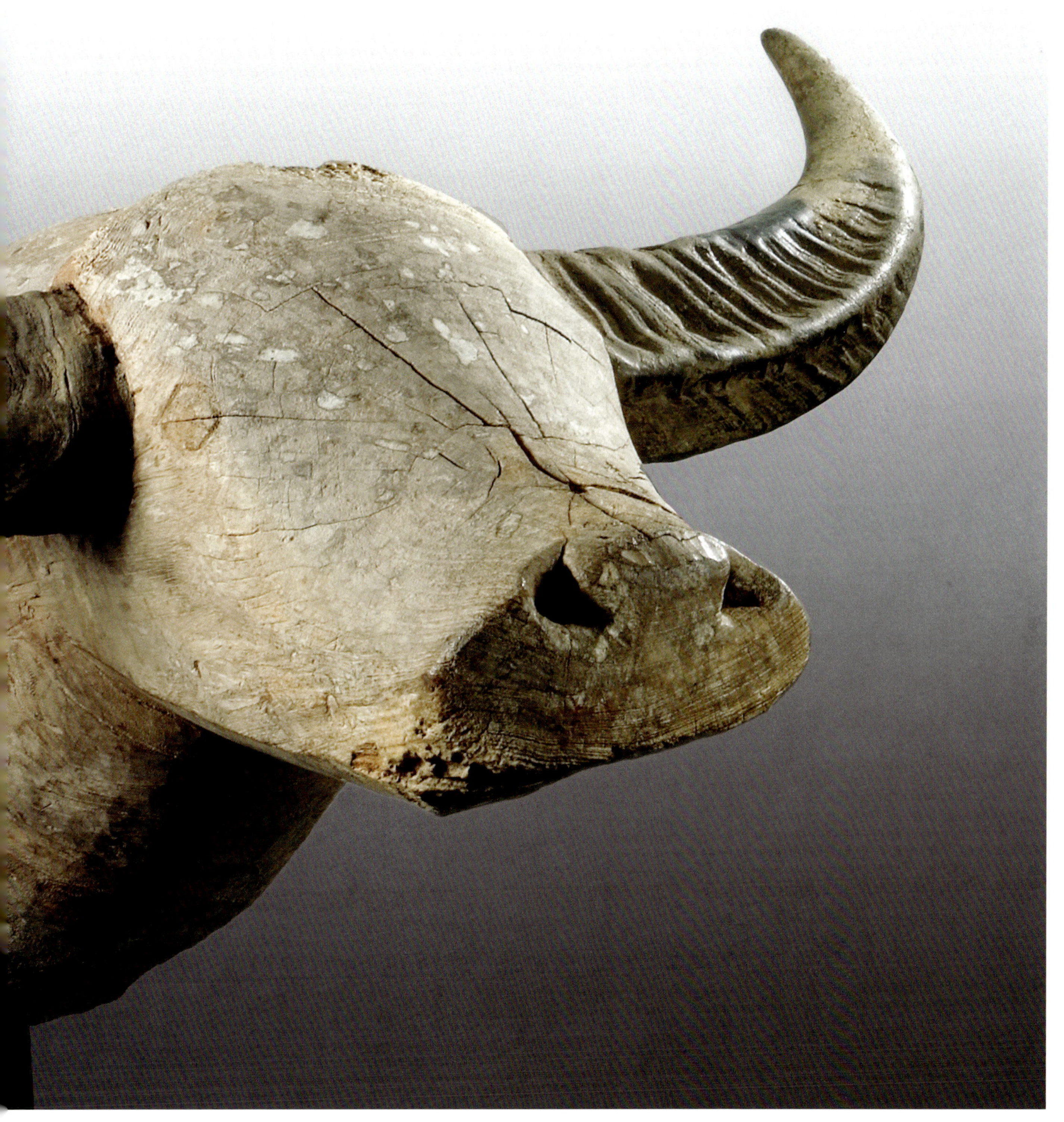

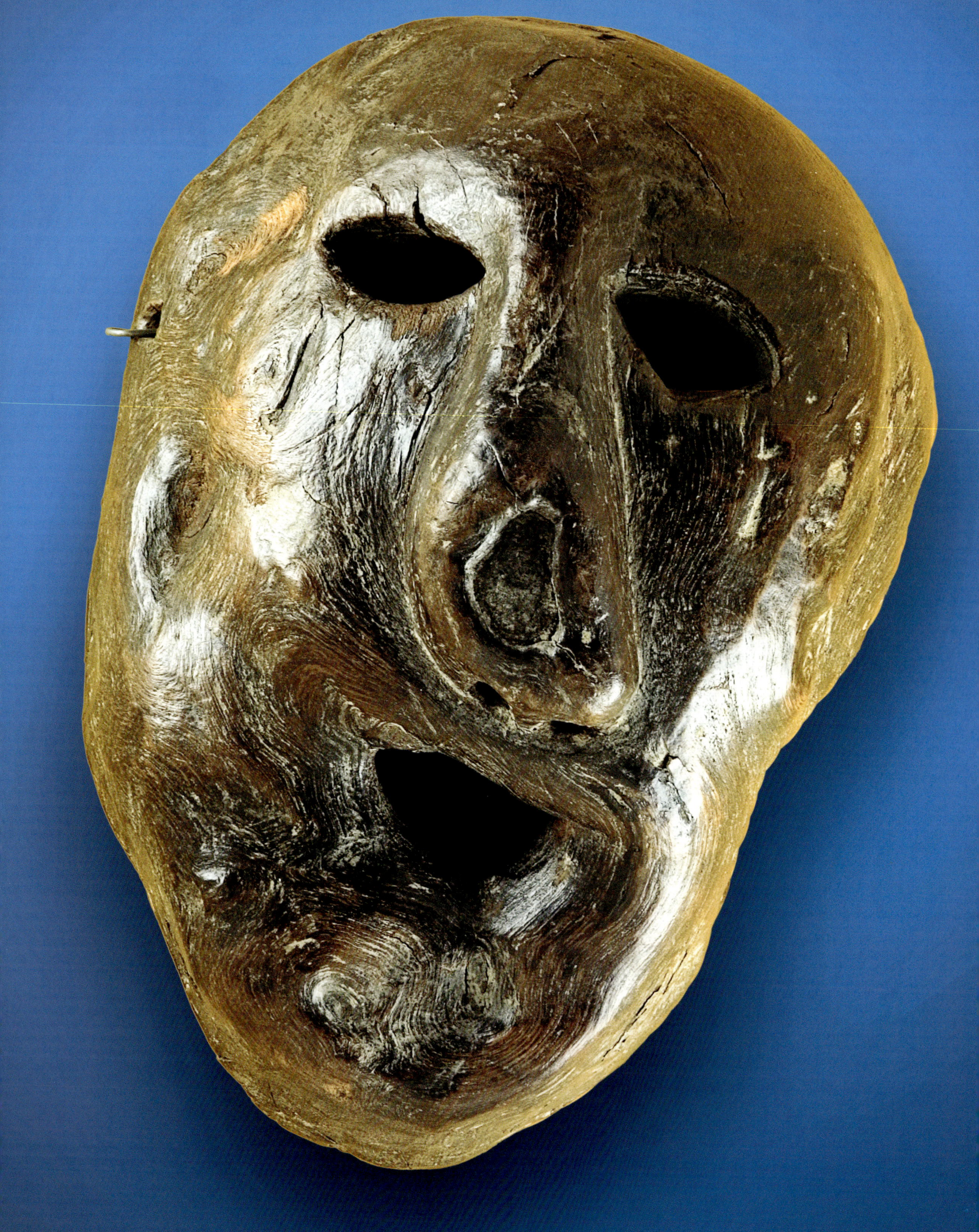

A Perspective on Dealing and Collecting

Indian Miniature Bronzes and Himalayan Masks

Daniel H. Cook

I HAVE BEEN AN ART DEALER AND COLLECTOR FOR THIRTY-FIVE YEARS, ever since Albert Rudolph ("Rudi"), a well-known Asian art dealer and owner of the Rudi Oriental Art Gallery in New York City, inspired and launched my career. In 1971, I opened the Rudi South Gallery in Dallas, Texas, with a container of consigned goods from Rudi. Twice a year I traveled to Asia to look for and buy artifacts in the field. Each trip introduced me to extraordinary cultural experiences that developed my taste and eye for Asian folk and classical art. Delving into the cultures of this region allowed me to spend countless hours discovering the works of ancient artisans who crafted masterful works and captured the power of Eastern philosophies and spiritual traditions in wood, ceramic, metal, and stone.

Fieldwork provided me with opportunities to learn about the diverse arts of indigenous cultures that remained relatively unchanged by the fast-encroaching modern world. Many of the rare objects that I saw were believed by their owners to possess the energy of shamans, spirits, and gods. Himalayan dance masks, dowry textiles, sacred iconic figurines, and sculptures were preserved and utilized for worship and healing, as well as for use in societal rituals that inspired the local people and reminded them of their social commitments and their roots.

OPPOSITE:
Mask, 19th–20th centuries
Himalayas
Wood
The Diane and Sandy Besser Collection

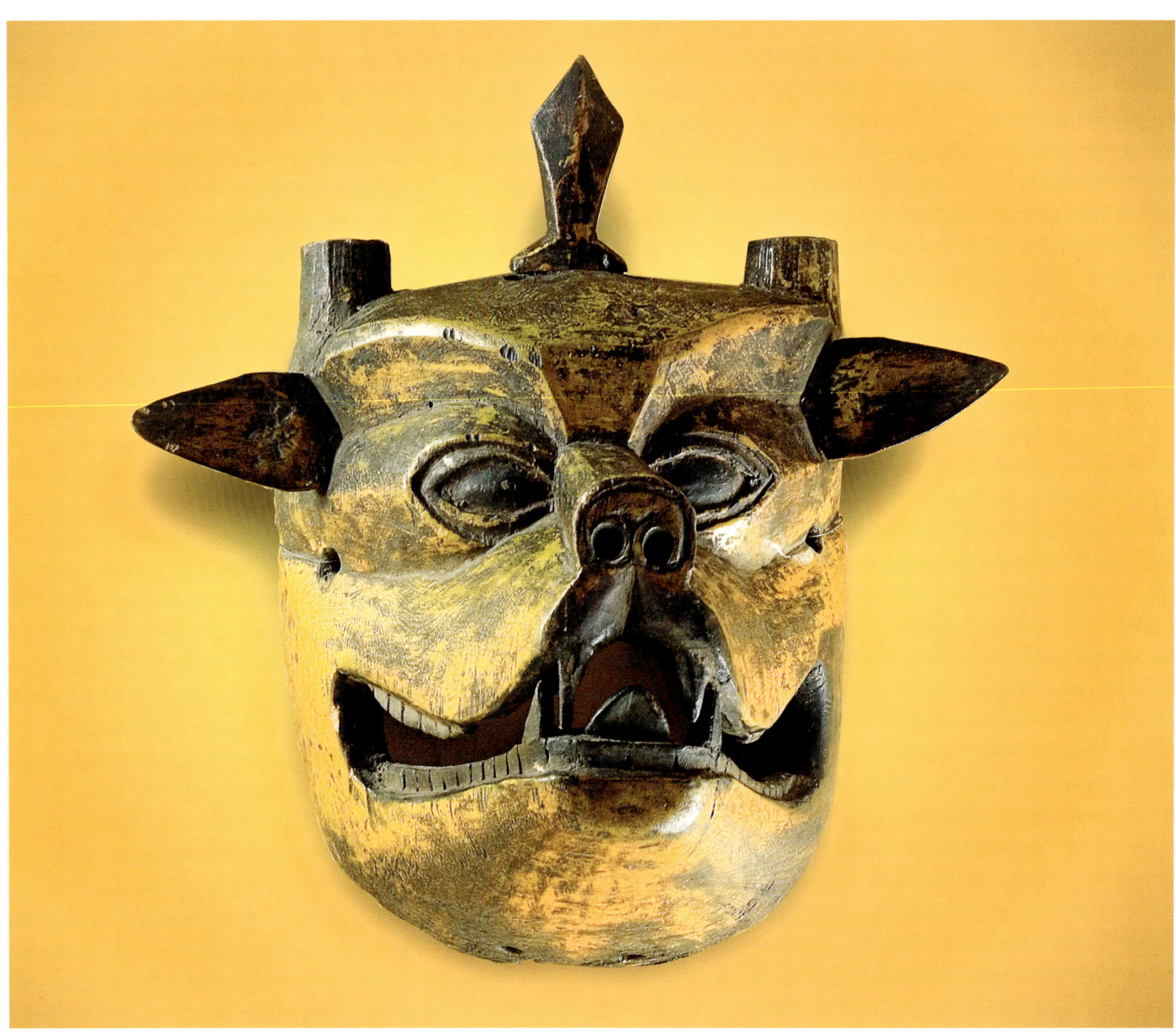

Animal mask, 19th–20th centuries
Himalayas
Wood, pigment
The Diane and Sandy Besser Collection

OPPOSITE:
Sculpture of Vishnu depicted with Lakshmi and attendants, 16th–19th centuries
India
Bronze and metal alloys
Gift from the Diane and Sandy Besser Collection
IFAF

Later, many of the same objects that I saw were replicated for mass production and were sold to handicraft vendors; this, in turn, supported the growing tourist art market in the region, and simultaneously the international art retail market. As an art dealer, I have tried to bring these remarkable experiences to my work, so I can share with collectors the sense that they have the rare privilege of being custodians of world history preserved in art. In short, hunting ethnographic art for collectors has been a personal and professional education that to this day continues to enliven my own walk in time.

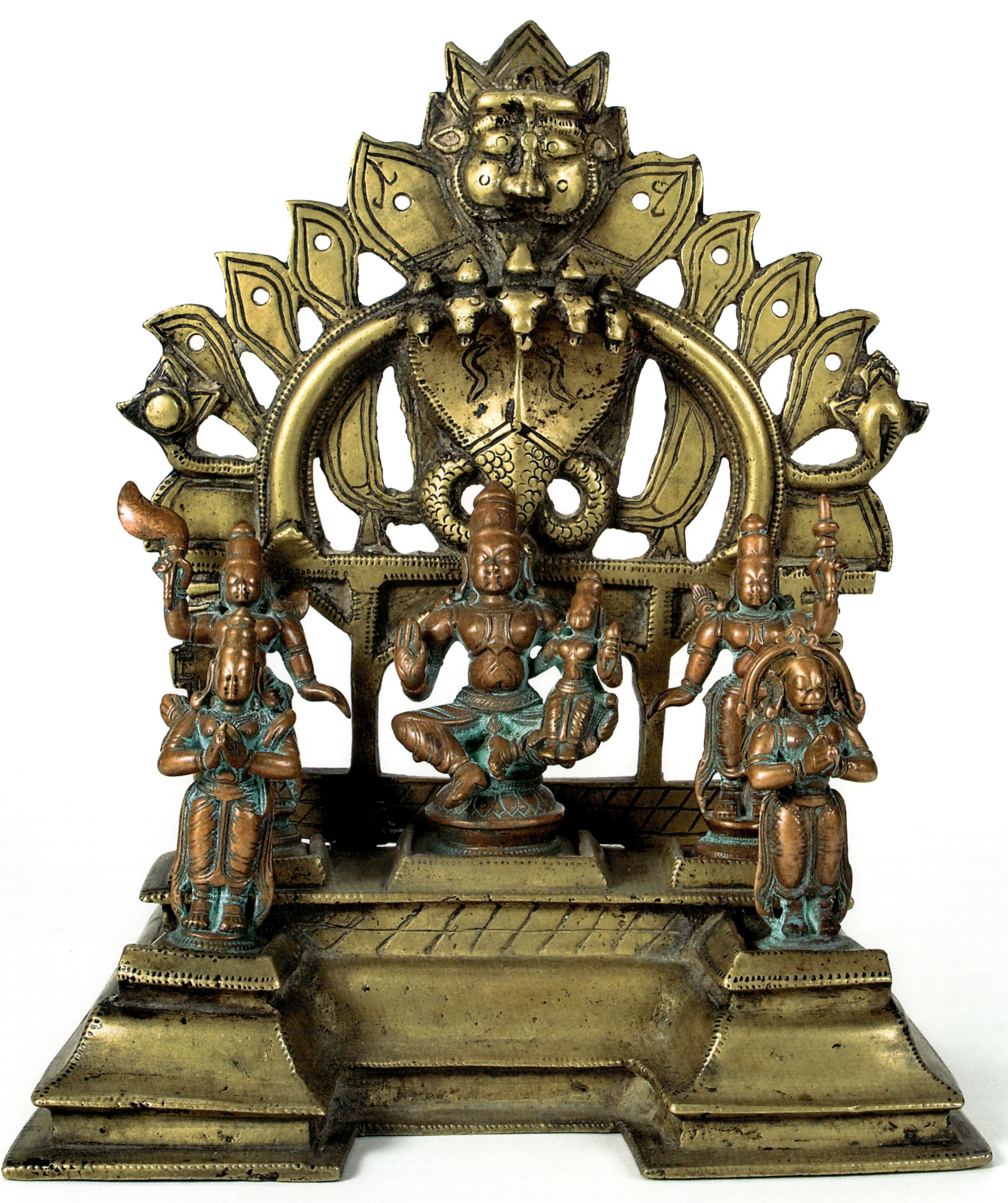

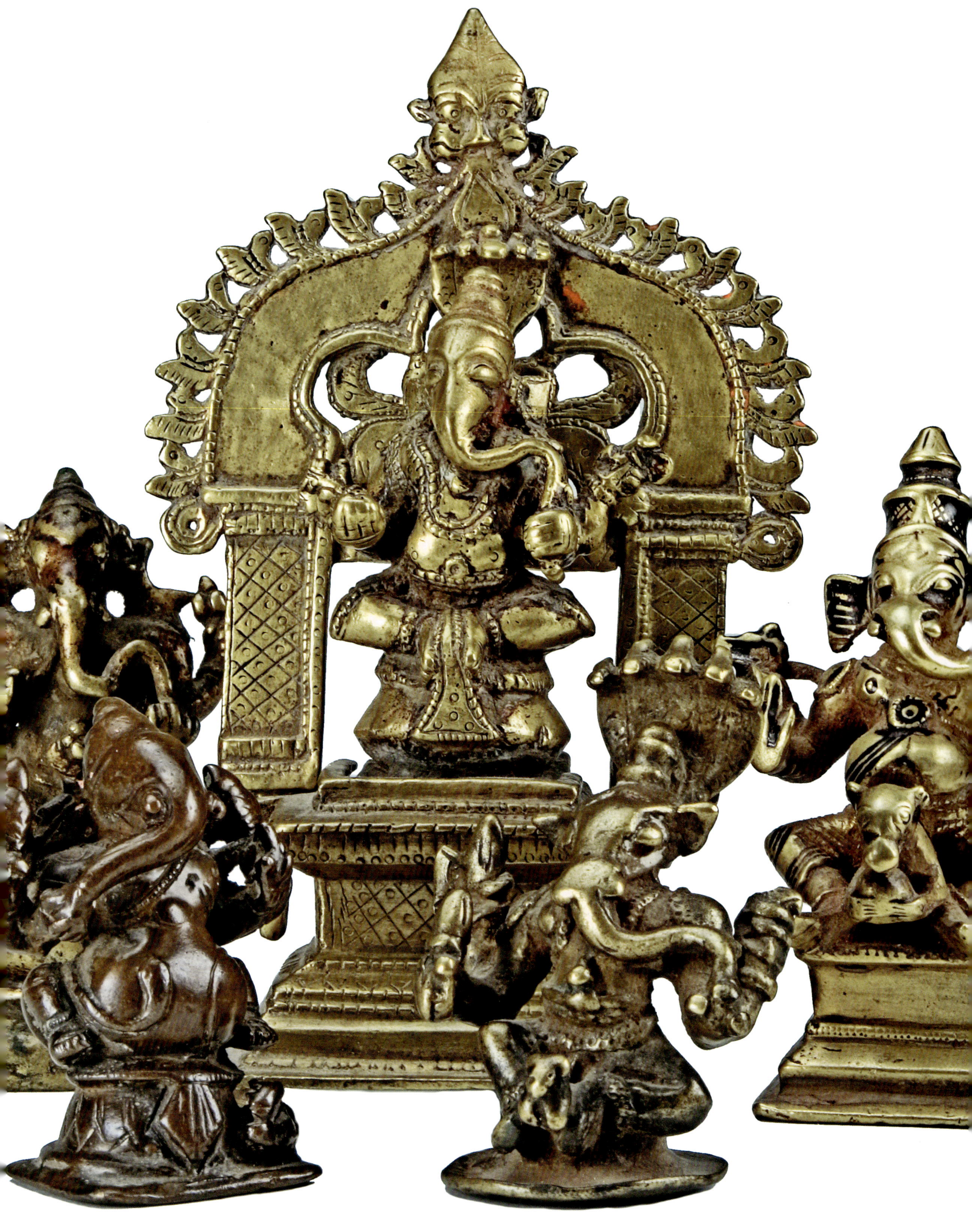

OPPOSITE:

Bronze sculptures of Ganesha, elephant-headed god, 16th–19th centuries

India

Gift from the Diane and Sandy Besser Collection

IFAF

Loved for his association with wisdom, good fortune and new beginnings, Ganesha is the remover of obstacles.

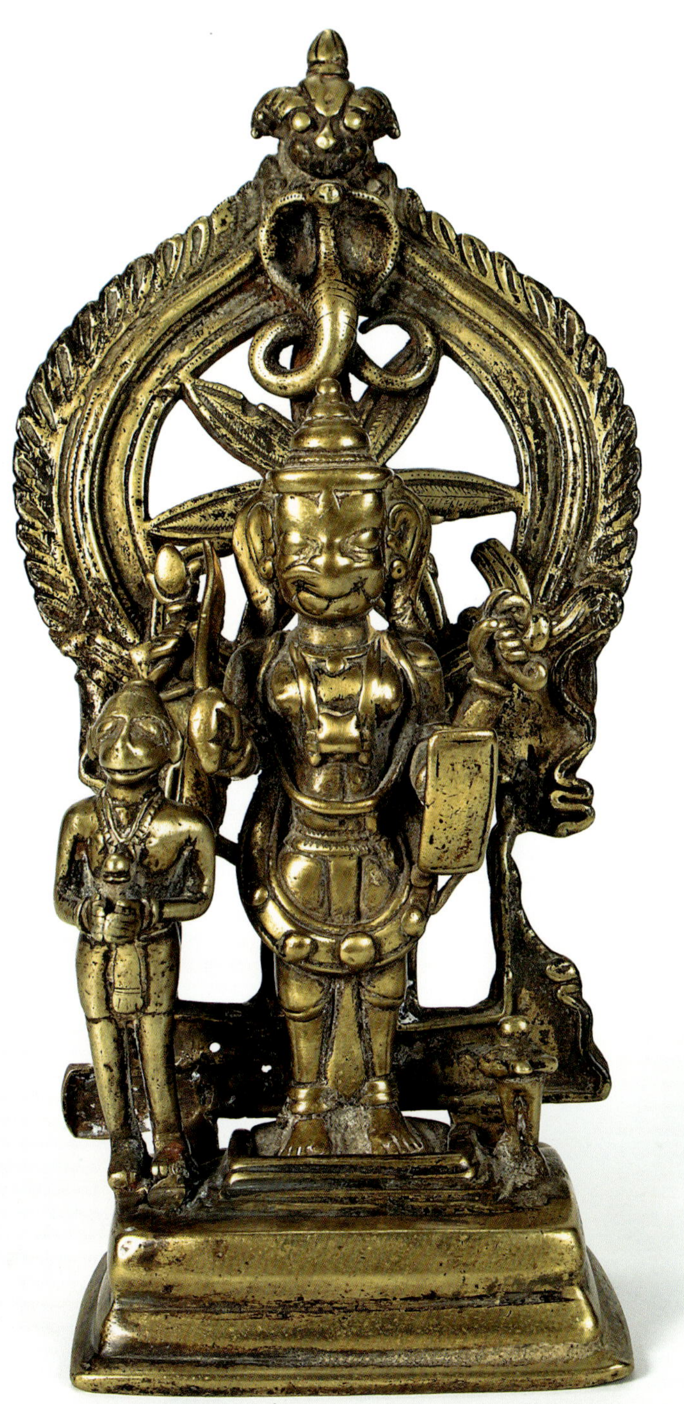

Sculpture of Virabhadra, destructive form of Shiva, 16th–19th centuries

India

Bronze and metal alloys

Gift from the Diane and Sandy Besser Collection

IFAF

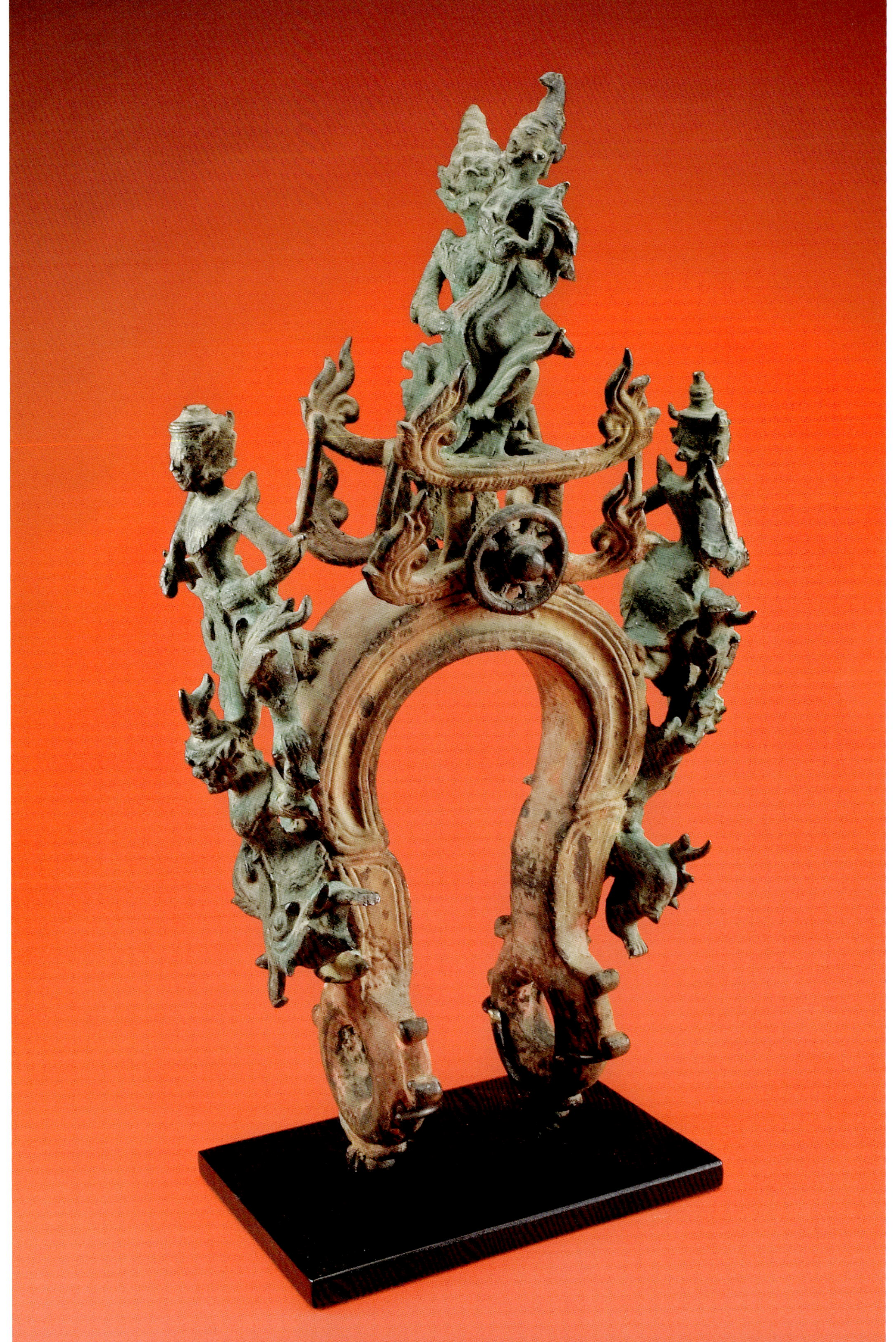

ACQUIRING ART

Early in my career, I spent most of my time in the field in search of collectible artifacts. Collecting good material in the 1970s and 1980s was very different from what it is today. Back then, there were more fine-quality pieces available and many tribal cultures around the world had not yet been affected by modernization and globalization. I remember the day I realized the world had shrunk with the introduction of the fax machine. I was making regular trips to Sarawak, Borneo, collecting early export ceramic vessels called *tampanyan*. At first, I found myself working with only a handful of local traders. Being one of the earliest dealers to bring these ceramics into the U.S. market, I was pleased to have found something that was beautiful and affordable. In September 1979, I traveled up the Rejang River to the longhouse of one of my suppliers, a *Dayak*[1] tribesman. I selected several pieces and started to make payment as usual. With a half-smile, my supplier pulled out a faxed copy from a Sotheby's catalogue and enlightened me on the current values of ceramics from Borneo. Overnight my cost of goods rose substantially. In the long run, I knew this was a healthy trend, but at the time it came as a shock.

With the advent of e-mail and the use of Web sites, art prices have continued to escalate and the world art market has become more competitive. All of this international competition has raised the bar, and even though there is not much left in the field to buy, today's collectors are more informed about quality and availability. Research on once obscure artifacts has suddenly become available. However, with increased market competition and greed for monetary profits has come an increased motivation to make reproductions.

As a young art dealer in the mid 1970s, I brought my portfolio to New York. I walked down Madison Avenue trying to figure out whom I could meet, and who would want to see my art collection. I found William Wolfe's gallery and walked in. I felt intimidated by the scope and variety of the extraordinary pieces of art in his showroom. After a handshake, Mr. Wolfe invited me to show him several small objects that I was carrying in my briefcase. He relieved most of my insecurities when he said that he liked what he saw. We negotiated prices and finally Mr. Wolfe purchased a beautiful *Ban Chiang*[2] bronze bracelet with a green patina. He then asked to see my portfolio of art photos. As we went through each photograph, he shared with me his expert opinion. His brow furrowed when the page opened to a photo of a Chinese stone figure of *Quan Yin*.[3]

OPPOSITE:
Temple bell yoke, 16th century
Burma
Bronze and metal alloys
Gift from the Diane and Sandy Besser Collection
IFAF

He asked, "What do you think of this piece, Dan?" I replied quickly that I would rather hear his opinion about the piece. Wolfe said he thought the stone figure "was not right." I was devastated to think I had a fake in my collection and expressed my disappointment. He looked at me and said, "Danny, if you haven't bought a fake, you haven't bought enough!" This was a great lesson and I found out later, a mantra shared by many dealers.

Another important lesson came in 1973, in a display booth where I was exhibiting at a gun and antiques show in Dallas, and where my sale items included a collection of six Indian miniature bronzes. A man in worn jeans, mud-crusted cowboy boots, and a black cowboy hat walked up to my table and casually looked at my goods. I picked up an Indian bronze sculpture and held it out for him to examine. I said, "This is from India and it's 300 years old." The man looked at the bronze and then handed it back to me, saying "Son, it was ugly 300 years ago and it's still ugly today!" I realized then that just because a piece is ancient, it doesn't mean it is valuable art.

Finally, political developments have influenced the process of acquiring art. For example, the changing political climate in India created an opportunity to obtain artifacts that were otherwise not available. On June 26, 1975, Indira Gandhi, the prime minister of India, declared a state-of-emergency. Because of increased political instability and controversy, the Indian government declared that the security of the country was threatened by internal disturbances. This political unrest became a critical problem for the traditional *Maharajas* and *Maharanis* of India. The Indian government confiscated most of the land and wealth belonging to these royal families, allowing them to retain only a fraction of their original land to surround their grand palaces. Desperate to maintain a level of dignity and a lavish lifestyle, these once-elite families were forced to sell large parts of their estates.

During this period of social upheaval, I received an invitation to meet with a Maharaja, in the state of Gujarat. His plight forced him to sell various collections that were part of his family inheritance. He offered me extraordinary pieces of art and jewelry, including life-size sterling silver lions with crystal eyes, leaping silver panthers, beautiful silver doors, a 1940s Rolls Royce, Purdy shotguns, miniature Indian paintings, emerald carved cups, and a ten-karat diamond. The Maharaja and I negotiated intensely over various items for several days. Finally, I was able to purchase the silver lions and silver doors along with a fine

OPPOSITE:

Pendant, 20th century

Naga people, northeast India and Burma

Leather cord, metal

The Diane and Sandy Besser Collection

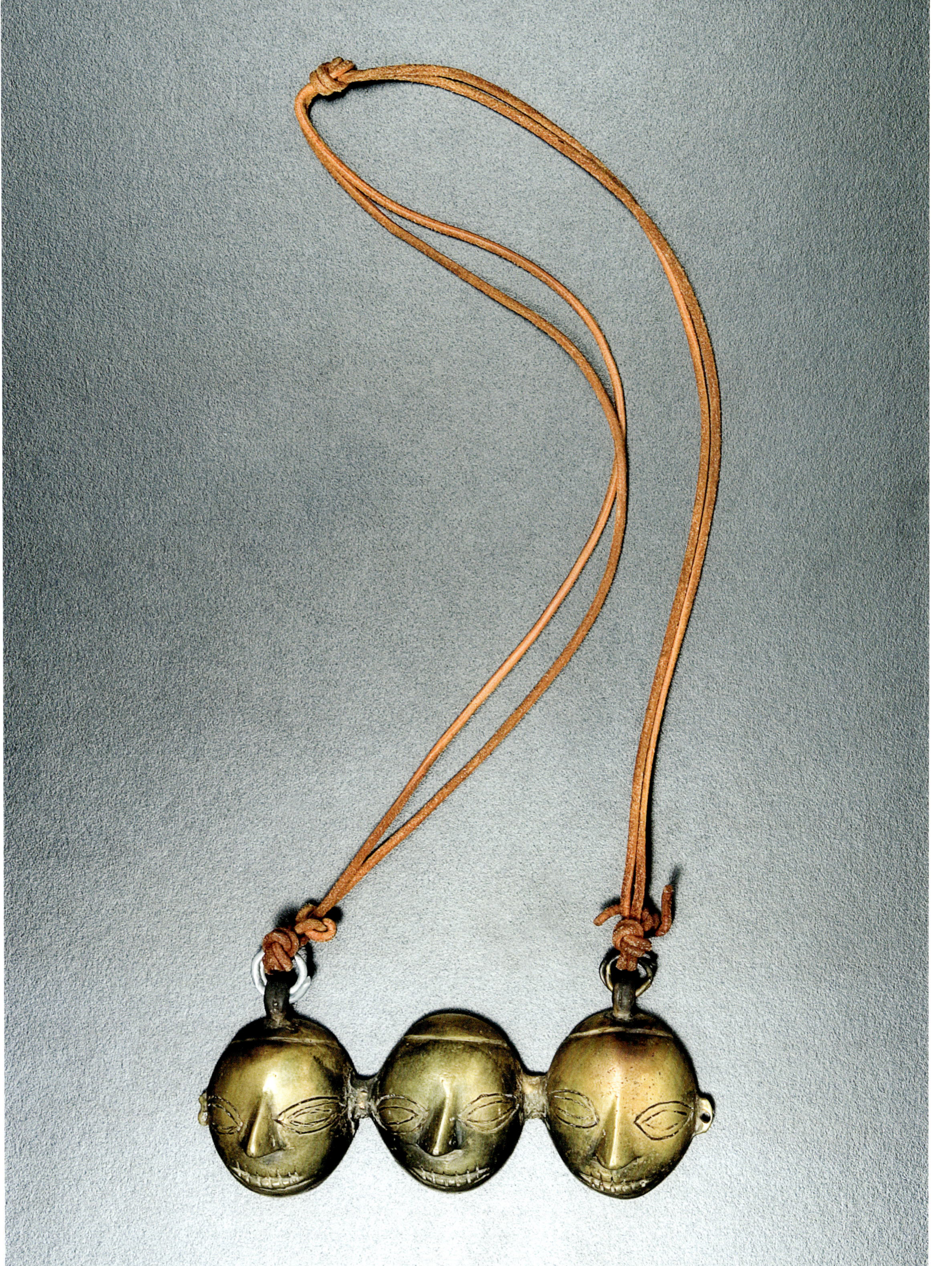

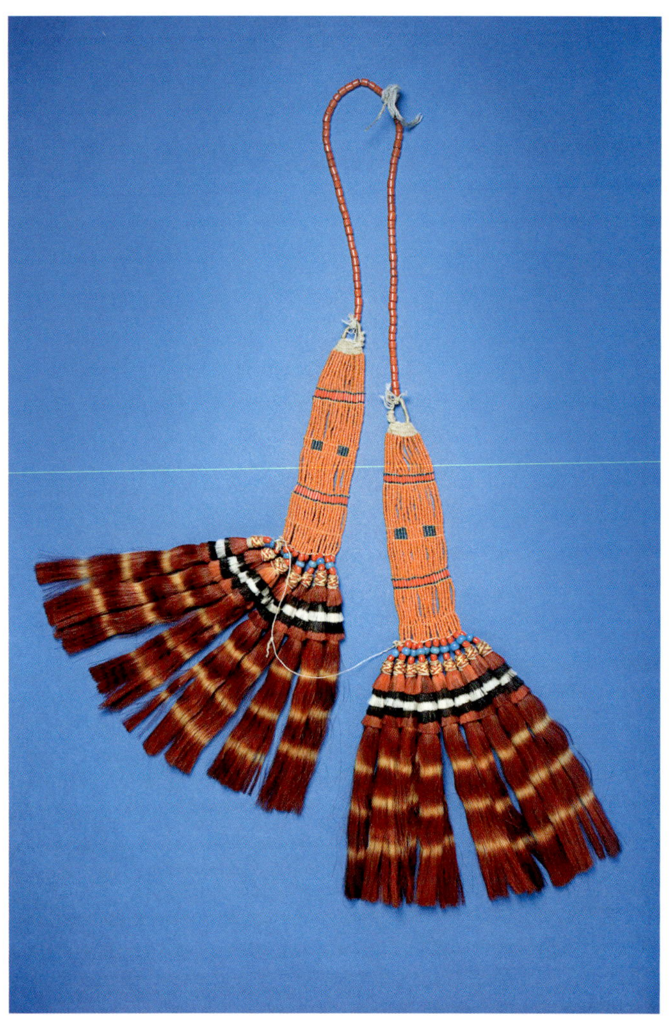

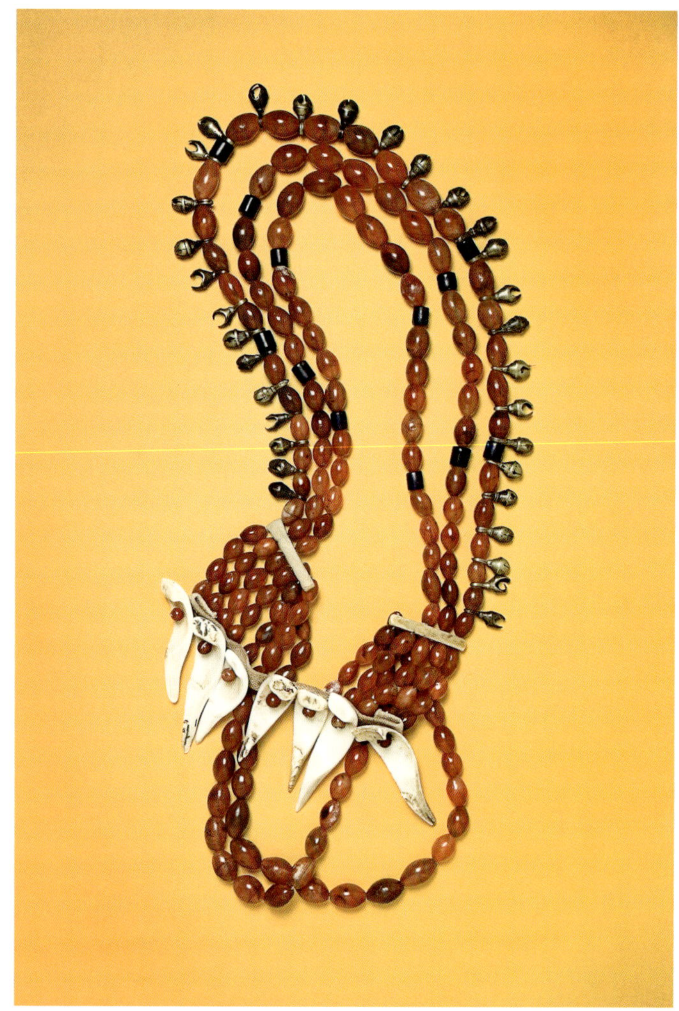

collection of mogul pendants and earrings. Private collectors in the United States now own and preserve these artifacts.

INDIAN MINIATURE BRONZES

The Diane and Sandy Besser Collection at the Museum of International Folk Art in Santa Fe contains Indian miniature bronzes from Maharastra and Gujarat, as well as Karnataka and Tamil Nadu in South India. Understanding how miniature bronzes like these have been obtained can shed light on the collecting process.

I began collecting Indian miniature bronzes in 1973. I found my first collectible pieces in Puri, in the state of Orissa, while walking through a bazaar that sold everything from used car batteries to antique pocket watches. My curiosity

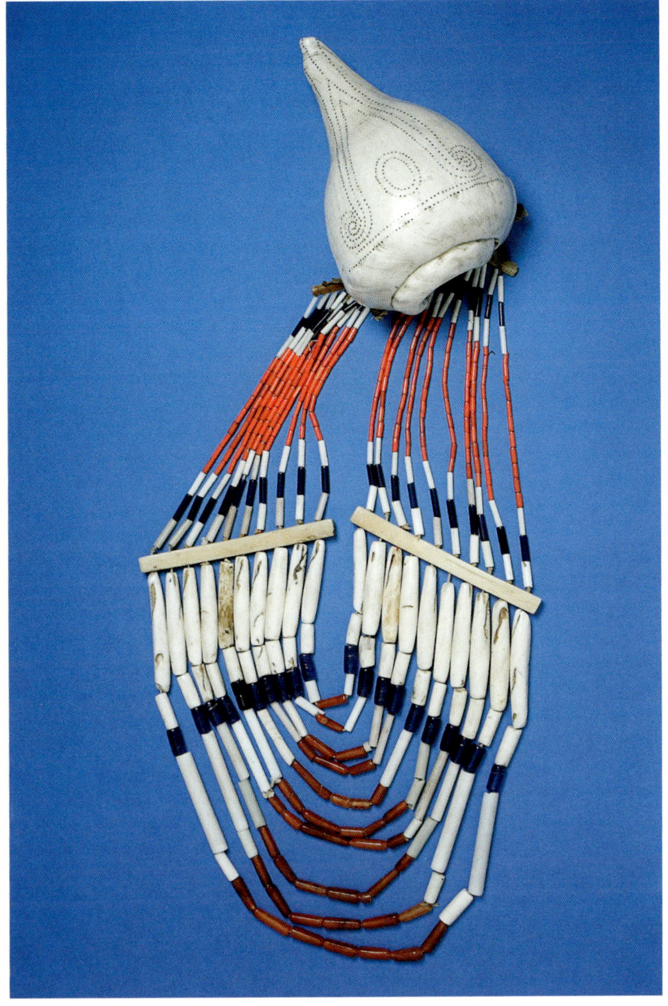

Necklaces, 20th century
Naga people, northeast India and Burma
The Diane and Sandy Besser Collection

pulled me inside one shop, where I saw a man recycling metal. He was dumping scrap metal, which was stuffed in several burlap bags, into a smelting pot. My eye caught sight of an interesting bronze figure in one bag with its arm sticking out. I dug the piece out and was surprised to see a beautiful sculpture of Krishna, dating to the seventeenth century. I asked the shopkeeper why this particular Krishna was to be melted down. He said that the face was so badly worn, rubbed during worship, that it was no longer considered a sacred sculpture. It was worthless for all practical and spiritual purposes.

With the shop owner's permission, I rummaged through each bag and rescued twenty-two more bronze *murties* (religious statues). Each one was well worn and all of the items had wonderful patinas. I paid for my find, and then spent the rest of the day searching through the bazaar for more.

My fascination with miniature bronzes began with this first purchase of the beautiful eight-inch bronze statue of Lord Krishna, the god of music and divine love. I quickly became aware that melting down metal artifacts was common in India and for centuries this practice has probably been responsible for the destruction of important historical metal sculptures. This is one of many stories I could write about that motivated me to rescue items from this genre of religious sculpture. These unique sculptures hold a significant place in Hindu culture and are deeply embedded in Hindu social thought and spiritual teachings. For centuries these small icons have been considered active representatives of gods and goddesses that are capable of bringing divine power to family home-shrines, temple altars in local villages, and city *mandirs* (Hindu temples). Devotees leave flowers and *prasad* (blessed foods), and they wave incense in front of these small sculptures. Supplicants touch, rub, and pray passionately over small Ganeshas, Krishnas, Durgas, Kalis, or Shivas,[4] as well as obscure village deities—seeking help for themselves and their community for needs that can range from protection and healing to problems with fertility. I have been personally most attracted to Ganesha, the elephant God who is renowned as the remover of obstacles.

The artisan's expressions of deities and their mythological stories have been overlooked in this small sculpture medium, primarily because of their physical size and because they have been overshadowed by well known earlier classical-period bronzes such as *Chola*[5] (ninth to thirteenth centuries A.D.) and *Vijayanagar*[6] (fourteenth to seventeenth centuries A.D.). In contrast to classical bronzes, I have sought out miniatures that fall under the folk art category. When I first started collecting bronze miniatures, their historical significance and value was not well known; even today, there are few recorded collections of Indian miniature bronzes.

COLLECTING HIMALAYAN MASKS

Early in the 1990s, collectors became more interested in Himalayan masks from Nepal, India, China, and the autonomous region of Tibet. The Himalayan masks that are part of the Diane and Sandy Besser Collection come from three Himalayan regions. The Nepalese masks are from Middle Hills, Monpa, Tamang, Terai, and Newari. Two Mahakala masks and a Cham tiger mask are Bhutanese. And the Indian Himalayan masks in the collection come from Himachal Pradesh

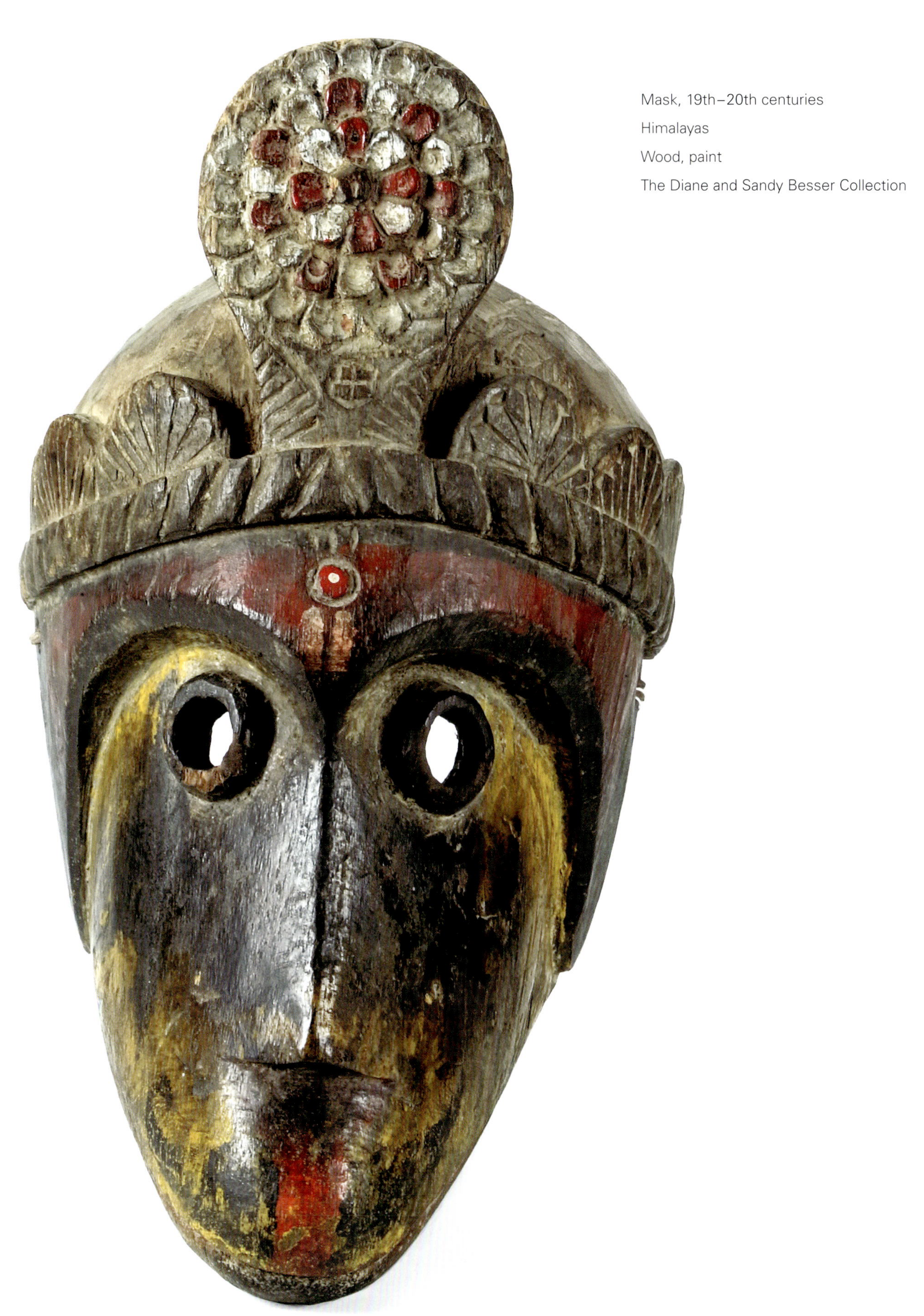

Mask, 19th–20th centuries

Himalayas

Wood, paint

The Diane and Sandy Besser Collection

and Arunachal Pradesh in North India. As in the discussion of Indian miniature bronzes above, it could be helpful for new collectors to learn more about the collection process of these Himalayan masks.

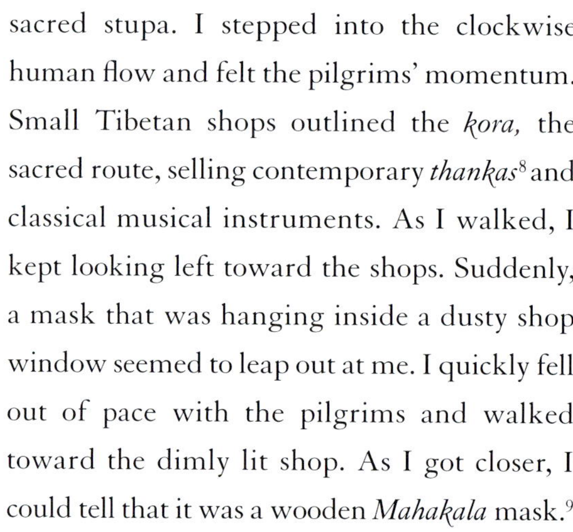

I found my first mask in Katmandu at Bodhinath, the revered fourteenth-century Tibetan Buddhist stupa,[7] which is believed to contain a bone fragment from the Buddha's body. Monks dressed in maroon robes and Tibetan women in long black skirts covered with colorful aprons were circumambulating the sacred stupa. I stepped into the clockwise human flow and felt the pilgrims' momentum. Small Tibetan shops outlined the *kora,* the sacred route, selling contemporary *thankas*[8] and classical musical instruments. As I walked, I kept looking left toward the shops. Suddenly, a mask that was hanging inside a dusty shop window seemed to leap out at me. I quickly fell out of pace with the pilgrims and walked toward the dimly lit shop. As I got closer, I could tell that it was a wooden *Mahakala* mask.[9]

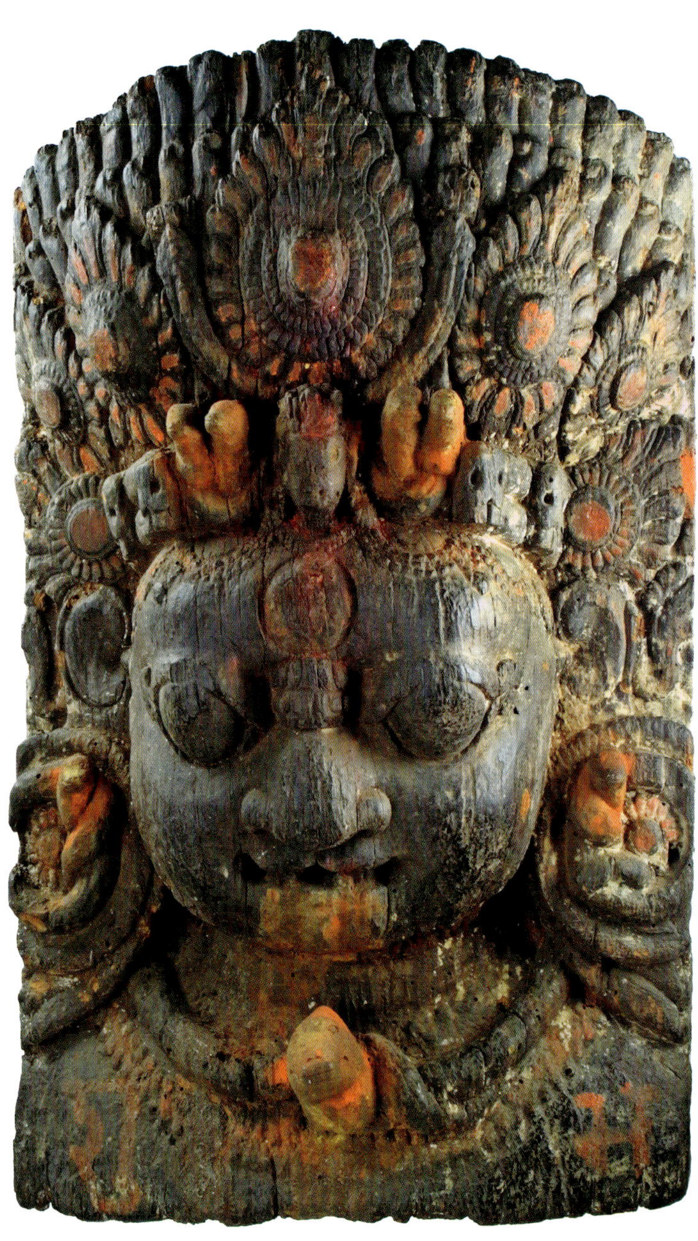

Bhairava temple ornament, 16th century

Newar people, Nepal

Wood, pigmenets

The Diane and Sandy Besser Collection

Bhairava is the most fierce and destructive form taken by the Hindu god, Shiva. This Bhairava carving once decorated a temple in Nepal and protected temple goers who offered it prayers.

When I entered the shop, I could barely see the family that was huddled together, sharing lunch behind the counter. Incense was burning atop an altar, filling the room with opaque smoke. The familiar scent of the incense's earthy fragrance arrested my senses. Then my eyes adjusted to the dark room and I discovered that wooden objects were stashed on multiple shelves in every nook of the tiny space. I turned to the mask hanging in the window that had attracted me, and I rotated it to face me. The carving was fantastic! The warm amber patina covering the smoothed and worn tooled edges around the eyes and nose showed the age of the mask. With controlled excitement, I asked the older man, who was still eating, to tell me about the wooden mask.

Up until that point, I had primarily been taken with the Buddhist images and imagery embodied in traditional Tibetan paintings. This Tibetan mask, in contrast, was a three-dimensional form that deeply stirred my imagination. One is never truly prepared for the spontaneous excitement of first seeing a new art form. When I saw this familiar Buddhist image in three-dimensional form, it "rocked-my-socks." I needed to have this mask and live with it for a while to understand it and to learn more about Himalayan masks in general.

My aesthetic interest in masks grew after this initial purchase. I bought more masks in the field during that trip, and I have bought many masks since then. The shapes, personalities, and mysterious beauty of these masks continue to provoke my imagination. Like the Mahakala mask I bought in Katmandu, I saw that other masks reflect their creator's connection with nature, and belief in animism and supernatural power. The characters depicted in each mask are the individual choices of their specialist-makers. Some masks are sophisticated and ornate, while others have little embellishment. Some are archaic looking and seem to still possess the powers of the supernatural forces that they were meant to embody. Men and women with spiritual power wore such masks to perform magic rites for protection, hunting, healing, and divination.

The Himalayan mask tradition is drawn from shamanism, village life, myths, and the religious traditions of Buddhism and Hinduism. Shamans from Nepal are called *Dhamis-Jhankris* or simply *Jhankris*.[10] The function and religion of the Jhankris synthesize the Tibeto-Siberian and Indo-Shamanic traditions, which derive their symbolism and mythology from Tibeto-Siberian culture but add many Hindu features. Rural Nepalis seek the advice of the Dhamis-Jhankris to give balance and direction to the social and religious life of their communities; and when they are ill, villagers often consult shamans whose medical advice is based on Jhankri traditions. The ancient practice of appeasing demons is still an ongoing practice in Himalayan communities. Theater, dance, and divination rituals throughout the Himalayas incorporate masks that represent demons, animals such as tigers and pigs, and monsters with long teeth, bulging eyes, and crooked faces. Masks are also made to be worn in local village performances and in dances that illustrate domestic and social calamities and the responsibilities and mythic legends related to heroes and deities that function to maintain cultural unity.

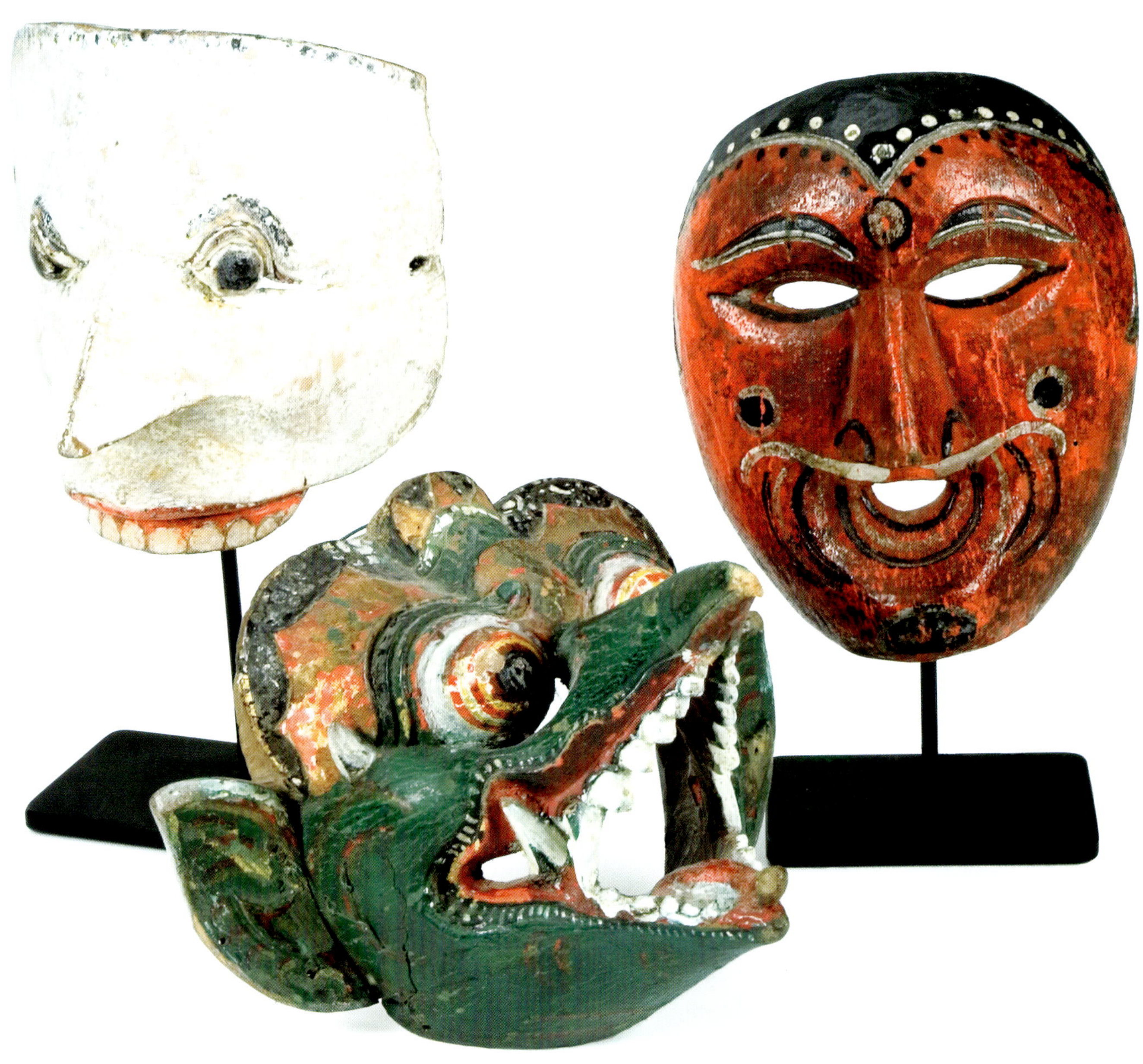

Masks, 19th–20th centuries

Java, Indonesia

Wood, paint

Left, The Diane and Sandy Besser Collection;
Middle & Right, IFAF Purchase from the
Diane and Sandy Besser Collection

SUGGESTIONS FOR COLLECTORS

People most often develop their collections around specific themes, such as shapes, weapons, figures like animals or deities, or unusual objects with varied patinas. Even within one theme or one type of art form, collectors can find many examples in many different cultures that can provide a wealth of materials from which to select. Collections often reflect the collector's love of a particular art form or culture, and, in bringing these artworks into the home, also provide visual subjects that stimulate dynamic conversations and intellectual curiosity among friends and colleagues. Art allows an individual collector to be closely linked with past and present-day fascinations about the human condition, history, and spirituality.

It is important to seek out and purchase art that moves you emotionally and aesthetically. First of all, find local societies and museums that share your interests and become a member or sponsor. Watch for exhibit openings, lectures, and discussion groups, which are good places to meet other collectors, to increase your information about art sellers, and to acquire knowledge about the art collecting process. In addition, you can go to national and international art fairs and shows that are held throughout the year in major cities like Los Angeles, San Francisco, Santa Fe, Phoenix, Chicago, New York, and Seattle. Buy exhibit catalogues and look for art books at booths in each show that sell rare and contemporary books on art and collecting. Building an art book library and subscribing to journals and magazines are also necessary activities for growth and development as a collector.

It is important to keep in mind that there will always be collectible pieces. If you are attracted to a painting, sculpture, or textile, you can probably fit it into your existing collection. However, do not be in a hurry. Amassing large quantities of artifacts, regardless of quality, is not the same thing as building a good collection. In most instances, even seasoned collectors need to convince themselves about a piece before buying it. Just because a piece is old does not necessarily mean it is a good piece of artwork — remember what the man at the Texas gun show told me! But also remember that eventually you will want to upgrade the pieces in your collection.

Other considerations when buying art are the condition of the object and how much restoration has already been done. My approach to these issues is based on the integrity of the restoration: if a piece would be better appreciated and understood with restoration, then restoration is worth pursuing. The process of restoration can enhance or disturb the integrity of any piece, so it must be done well. When buying an art object, ask the dealer to point out any restoration work that has been done. Adding a broken finger or re-attaching a broken arm makes pieces whole once again. It is easy to overlook the value of some pieces because they have some damage. Remember that restoration can add value as easily as it can decrease value.

Also pay attention to provenance. That is, ask the dealer where the piece came from, take photos, and ask for any documented provenance or collection data. Any information is worth obtaining and filing away to help you upgrade or restore your piece or to make it available for exhibits or local interest groups.

WORKING WITH THE SERIOUS COLLECTOR

For an art dealer, working with serious collectors who have established themselves in the art world is both a pleasure and a challenge. Collectors like Sandy Besser know what they like. They are clear about and well-educated in the genres of art and the styles that have captured their eyes. My challenge comes in trying to fill gaps in their collections with examples that they don't have, and to seek out for them examples that are unique. This challenge is what makes art dealing so much fun. In a sense, the dealer must perceive the art acquisition process as a collector would. I have not developed my own collections because I feel that if I did so, there might be a conflict of interest with my clients who are serious collectors and who are seeking to build strong collections.

I set out early on in my career to put together a comprehensive and core group of Indian miniature bronzes and powerful Himalayan masks, with the intention of eventually introducing them to a serious collector. When I introduced my collection to Sandy Besser over two decades ago, he responded with great interest and enthusiasm, and as he learned more and more, his love and knowledge of folk art continually expanded. Serious collectors like this are rare and working with them over time is a real pleasure: they have the unique ability to stay open to art, no matter where it comes from, and they do not restrict collecting to one or two areas. These collectors can see the interconnectedness of art, and they collect across wide ranges of origins, from Hispanic folk art to Himalayan masks. A collector like this can truly be called a patron of the arts.

Notes

1. Dayak are the indigenous people of Borneo. The term *Dayak* is used to describe the interior population of Borneo.

2. Ban Chiang is an archeological site located in Nong Hong District, Udon Thani Province, in Thailand.

3. Quan Yin (sometimes also referred to as Guan Yin or Kuan Yin) is the bodhisattva of compassion in East Asian Buddhism.

4. In Hinduism, Ganesh is known as the elephant god and the son of Shiva and Parvati. His body is human, while his head is that of an elephant. Ganesh represents a solution to logical problems and has the power to remove obstacles. Krishna is the eighth avatar of Vishnu. He is also referred to as the god of divine love and music. Durga is depicted as a female warrior who rides a lion or tiger, with multiple hands carrying weapons. She is probably best known for destroying the buffalo demon Mahisa near the Vyndya Mountains in Uttar Pradesh. Kali is the feminine goddess of creation and destruction and is associated with timekeeping. Shiva is the god of creation and destruction.

5. Chola: This dynasty originated in the fertile valley of the Kaveri River. It was a Tamil dynasty that ruled in south India until the thirteenth century.

6. The Vijayanagar Empire (1336–1646) was based in the Deccan Plateau. The empire was established by Hapihara I and his brother, Bukka Raya.

7. The stupa is the earliest Buddhist religious structure. It was originally a simple mound made up of mud or clay. Stupas evolved into large dramatic monuments and are found across the Asian continent and in the West.

8. Thankas are painted or embroidered Tibetan banners, which are hung in a monastery or in homes and are paraded by lamas in ceremonial processions.

9. Mahakala is the Tibetan protector of Dharma in Vajrayana Buddhism. In Sanskrit, *maha* means "great" and *kala* means "black."

10. Dhamis-Jhankri: Jhankris are shamanic practitioners found in the Himalayan regions of Nepal.

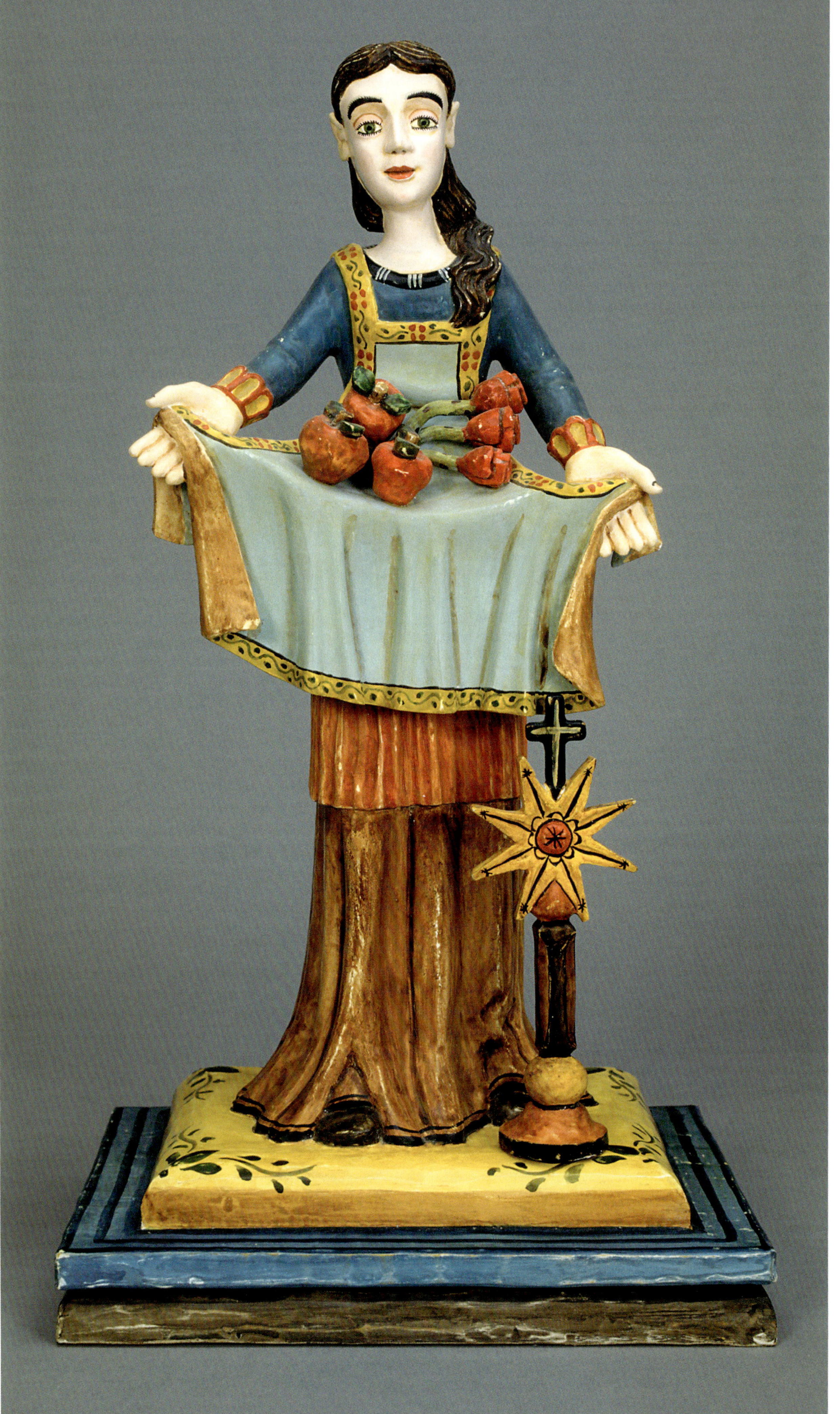

Creating Art, Building Relationships

Arthur López

An artist creates art to be collected and publicly viewed by collectors and museums, and along the way builds relationships with a realm of people, all with different ideas about the artwork that has been created and what it means to them. My first experience with a museum curator and a museum collection was in 1999, when I was doing research on *santos* and *santero* art (the traditional New Mexican genre of religious art forms). I was trying to learn all I could about the subject because I was preparing to submit an entry for the opportunity to participate in the annual traditional Spanish Market, which is put on by the Spanish Colonial Arts Society (SCAS) of Santa Fe. I was told by members of SCAS to contact the Museum of International Folk Art (MOIFA), because at the time the SCAS Collection was housed there.

Tey Marianna Nunn, the curator in charge of the collection, scheduled an appointment so that I could examine the collection. This was my first real contact with a museum professional of any kind. "Dr. Nunn?" I asked when we met. She laughed and said, "Tey is fine." Put at ease by her response, I thought, "She's a real person." Tey showed me cabinet after cabinet of *bultos* (sculptures of saints) and drawer after drawer of *retablos* (paintings of saints), which were created by artists for hundreds of years, up to the present day. I was overwhelmed

Saint Dorothy, by Gustavo Victor Goler, 1999
Sugar pine, handmade gesso, watercolors, piñon sap varnish
Gift from the Diane and Sandy Besser Collection
IFAF

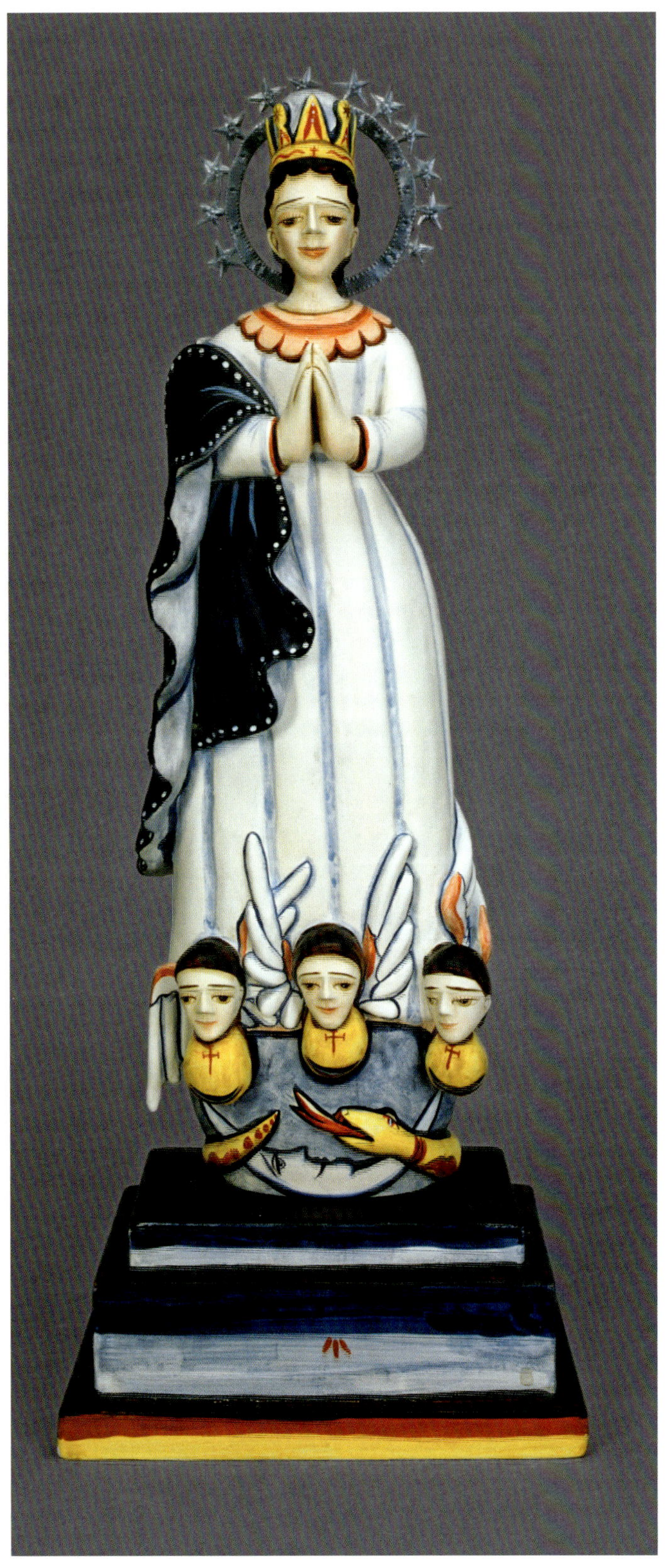

by the collection itself, by the idea of having this kind of collection available to the public, and by seeing it right there in front of me. As Tey showed me the collection, she asked what I was working on. I had just finished my fifth piece, a Santiago (St. James) on horseback. Tey asked to see this figure because she was putting together a show on Santiago. I brought the Santiago to the museum, and she asked if she could include it in the show. I was very excited: my work was going to be in a museum show and I wasn't even in the market yet!

As planning for the Santiago show progressed, Tey called with more good news: the museum wanted to purchase my piece for the permanent collection. I was amazed that not only was my work going to be on display for thousands of people to see, but now could also be seen for generations to come. This was truly my baptism into the art world. In January 2000, I was accepted into SCAS's Spanish Market for the following summer.

An artist has the opportunity to meet many different collectors, but I believe that there are really only two basic types: art collectors who collect for the artist's name behind the art, and those who collect for the art itself. For instance, some collectors love to say, "Did you see my Picasso?" Or, "You have to own a so-and-so." And others buy a piece just because the work touches them, regardless of who the artist is. I believe the first type of collector will buy a particular artist for the security of possession, that is, as an investment, while the second kind of collector will purchase regardless of investment considerations. I have dealt with both types, and both have one thing in common—their love of art and their interest in an artist's work. But no matter what kind of investor you may be, you should only buy art that you truly love.

I remember the excitement of my first sale in the spring of 2000. It was one of the first pieces I created. A

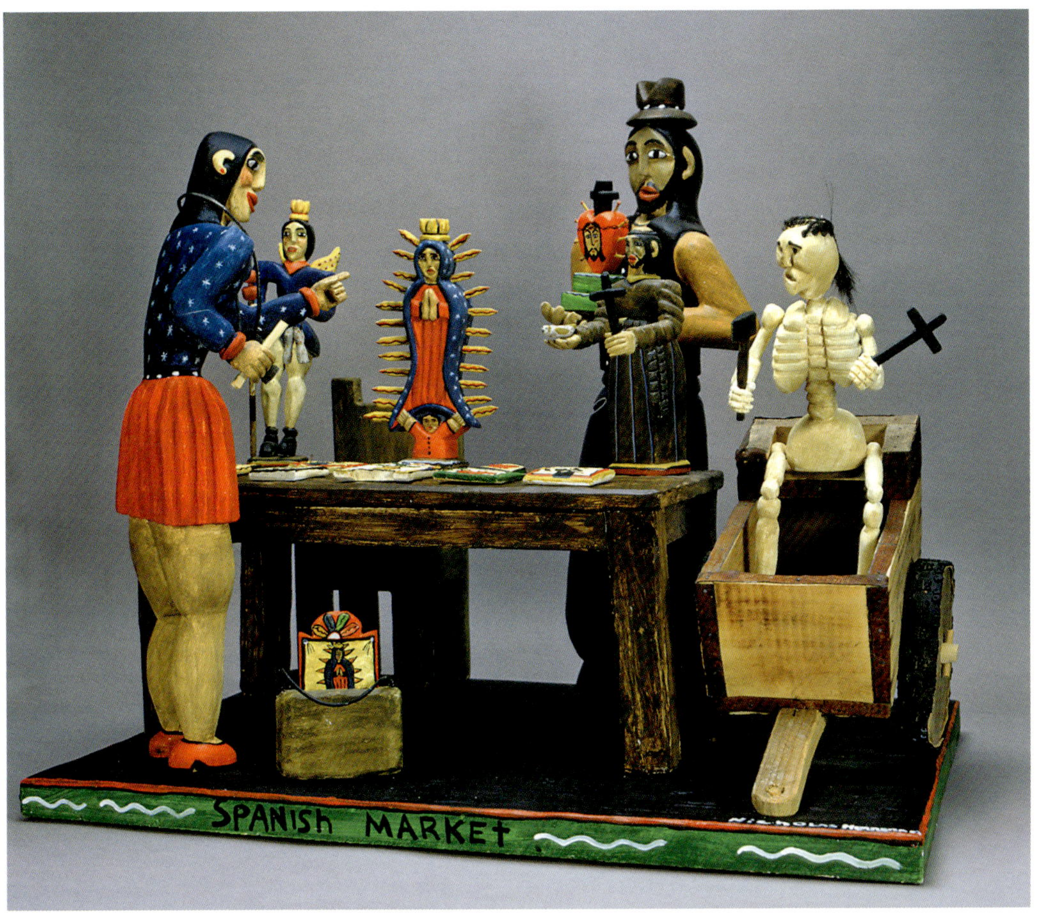

friend put me in contact with a person who had a large collection of santos, as well as many other art objects. I showed him my santo of San Francisco (St. Francis) and felt very nervous because this was one of my first santos and no one other than family and friends had seen it before. The santos collector looked my piece up and down, smiled, and then asked me how much I was asking. "Nine hundred," I said. "I'll take it for eight," he replied. I agreed. At this moment, my work became part of a private collection and a relationship was born. This santos collector has become a repeat buyer and a friend, and since that transaction, I have met with many collectors and have been fortunate in becoming good friends with many of them. At first it was a strange feeling knowing that a piece of me was going to be in someone else's home. When an artist creates a work of art, the energy involved in creating it is left in the piece. But to know that someone enjoys owning and viewing your work as much as you enjoyed creating it is calming.

Spanish Market, by Nicholas Herrera, 2003

Wood and acrylics

Gift from the
Diane and Sandy Besser Collection

IFAF

OPPOSITE:

Our Lady of the Immaculate Conception, by David Nabor Lucero, 1999

Carved wood, natural pigments and tin

Partial Gift of the Diane and Sandy Besser Collections

MOSCA

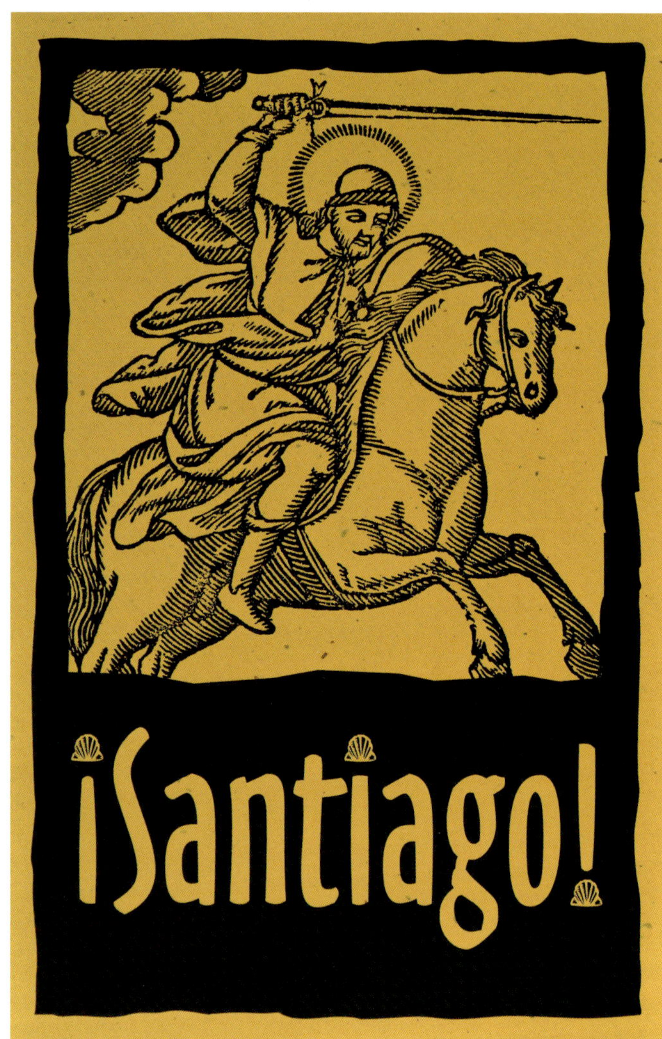

¡Santiago!
Exhibition announcement, 2000;
design by Dawn Manges

OPPOSITE:
Santiago with banner, Arthur López, 2001
Wood, paint, cloth, leather, hair
Gift of the
Diane and Sandy Besser Collection
IFAF

COMMISSIONING ART

When I work on commissioned pieces, I build a close relationship with the people I am making the piece for because these pieces are truly just for them. I always welcome commissions by collectors who have unique ideas: I feel it is the artist's job to interpret the collector's idea and make it his own original creation.

My first commission was in 2000 during the Santiago exhibition at the Museum of International Folk Art. I received a call from Sandy Besser, a collector who had been to the show with his wife, Diane, and he mentioned that they really liked my Santiago and would like to purchase it. I explained that the museum had already purchased it. He told me how happy he was that the museum owned it but that he and his wife wanted to commission one for their own collection. We agreed on a price. I was excited about the opportunity to create a piece for Diane and Sandy Besser's collection. When the Santiago was finished, Sandy asked if I would deliver the piece and if I would like to view his collection. As soon as I drove up the driveway, I was greeted by the works of art that surrounded his home and lined the walkway all the way to the door. "This is my kind of place," I thought as I rang the bell. When Sandy opened the door, I couldn't believe my eyes. There was literally art everywhere—from the floor to the ceiling, in the bathrooms, closets, library, and kitchen. There was art from all over the United States and from many other countries as well—artwork in all media. Now these are some people with an art obsession! I could feel the energy of the work all around me. Once I had a chance to catch my breath, I showed Sandy my Santiago. He loved it and told me he liked it better than the one the museum had bought, although he added that someday this Santiago would go to MOIFA as part of his plan to give his collection to various museums around the country.

POLITICAL ART

I have worked with Sandy Besser on many other commissions since that first one: there was a San Acacio (St. Acacius) in 2003, a multi-figural piece; and a

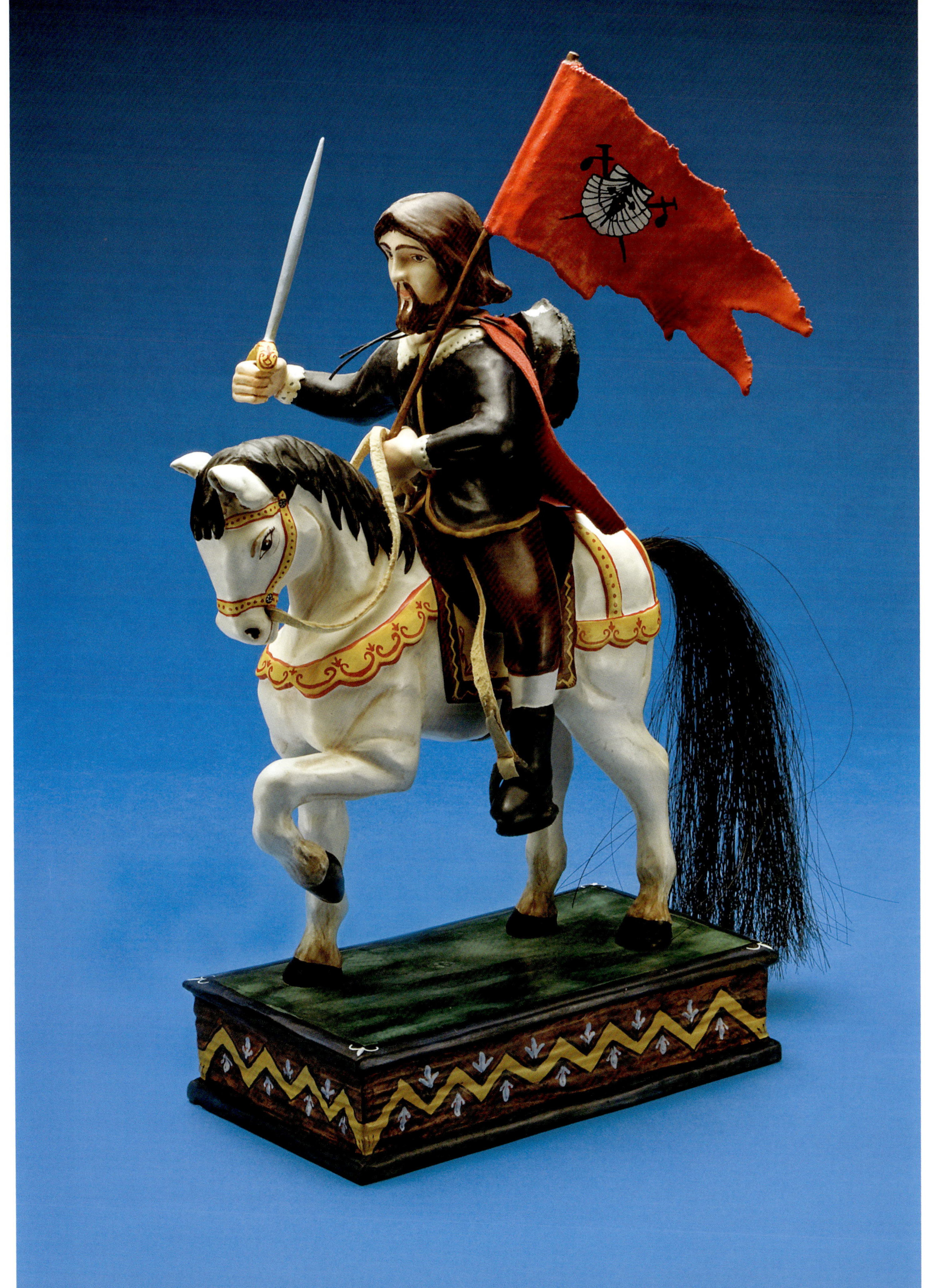

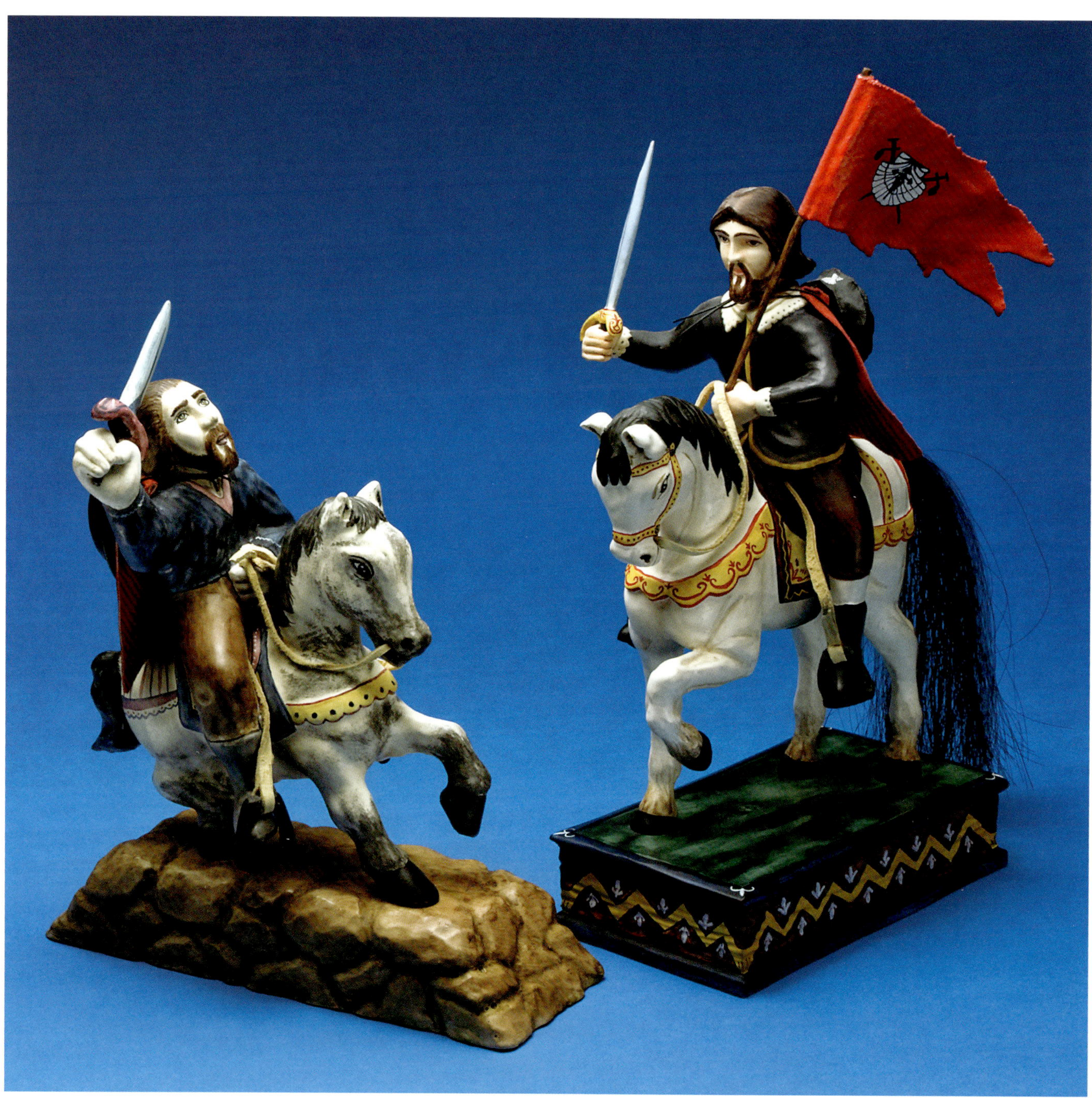

Santiagos, by Arthur López

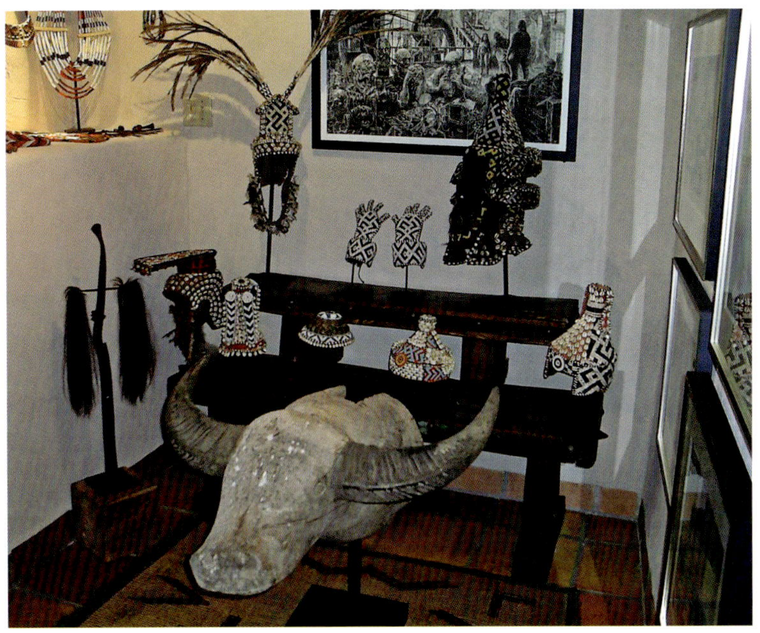

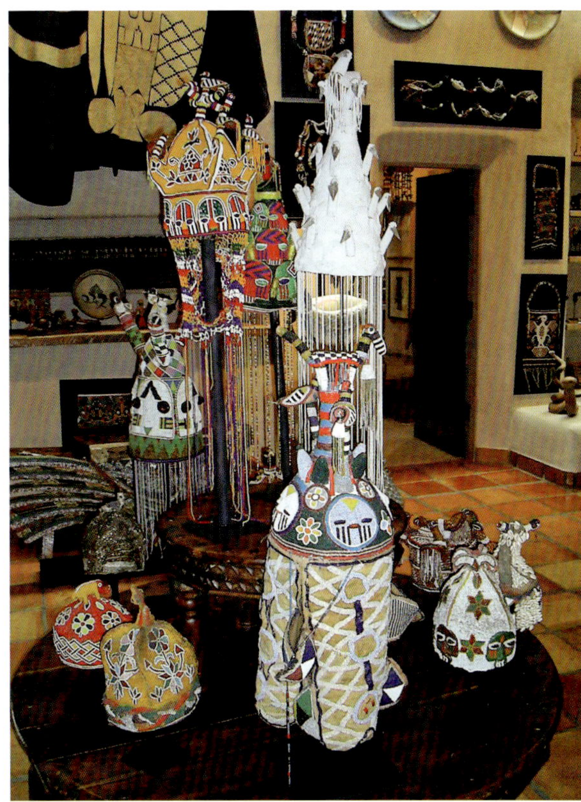

Interior of Sandy Besser's home, 2006

RIGHT:
Beaded Yoruba crowns from Nigeria in foreground

more edgy piece titled "It Is As It Was" that came about because of another piece I had created for my one-man show at the Parks Gallery, titled "Forgive Me, Son, for I Have Sinned." The latter piece was about the recent abuse scandals in the Catholic Church. Sandy wanted that piece but it had been sold to another collector. I told him I had another idea for a piece but that I had been unable to complete it in time for the show. Sandy invited me to lunch to talk about the other ideas I had. I told Sandy my idea of creating a figure of the pope with his back turned to a crowd of faithful outcasts; the work would represent the church turning its back on various groups that are not accepted by the church. The inspiration for this work came from my deep identity as a Catholic and my strong faith and belief in God, and I explained I did not yet have a title for the piece but said that the title would come.

Sandy Besser loved the idea and commissioned the piece, with a request to include a Holocaust victim and to title the piece, "It Is As It Was." (The title comes from a direct quote the pope made when asked to comment on the release of the Mel Gibson movie *The Passion of the Christ.)* My piece is about the

OPPOSITE:

"It Is As It Was," by Arthur López, 2004

Hand-carved wood and mixed media

Partial Gift of the Diane and Sandy Besser Collections

MOSCA

hypocrisy of the Catholic Church and its beliefs. The pope, with his back turned to a crowd of people, represents the church as a whole and is not intended to be a direct attack on the pope as an individual. In the crowd is an altar boy representing the thousands of innocent victims who were affected by the pedophile priests who used the church as a shield to cover up their misdeeds. In the work, there is a Holocaust victim representing the millions who died in World War II; it reflects the belief that the Catholic Church, one of the most powerful organizations in the world, could have stepped in and put a stop to the inhumanity. The work also includes a homosexual couple who, although their faith and belief in God is strong, are turned away by the church because of their love for one another. There is a nun with a picket sign that reads "I can't be a priest so I'll hold out for Sainthood," because the church will not allow a female priest but will allow female saints. There is a pregnant woman with children all around her, in reference to the church's strict stance on birth control.

My work reflects my own beliefs: while the church sometimes turns its back on what it doesn't understand, I believe that if your own faith is strong, no matter what your belief or religion, God will not turn his back on you. For future generations, when things finally change for the better, the piece can also serve as a reflection as to how things were in the church, and a future pope can reflect on the past and say that while it was not right, "It Is As It Was!"

Political pieces like this are often hard to sell, but they are very important in recording events and the history of our ever-changing world. It takes a certain kind of collector to purchase a political piece, for they must also understand the significance of the piece. I have always said that as an artist I do not create the issues, I just comment on them. I will not take a commission for a political piece or any other piece if the piece cannot reflect my own personal view.

For example, at dinner one night with Kirk and Sheila Ellis, friends who collect all types of art, including political pieces, we were having a conversation about the recent Gibson movie, *The Passion of the Christ.* Part of our conversation touched on how some people viewed the movie as another attempt to make money and exploit religion for personal gain. So I told Kirk and Sheila about an idea I had to make a piece about this controversy. My idea involved a couple at a drive-in theater watching the actual crucifixion, and the title of the piece would be "The Extortion of the Christ." They loved the idea especially because both are very much involved in the arts: Kirk is a screen writer/producer himself and

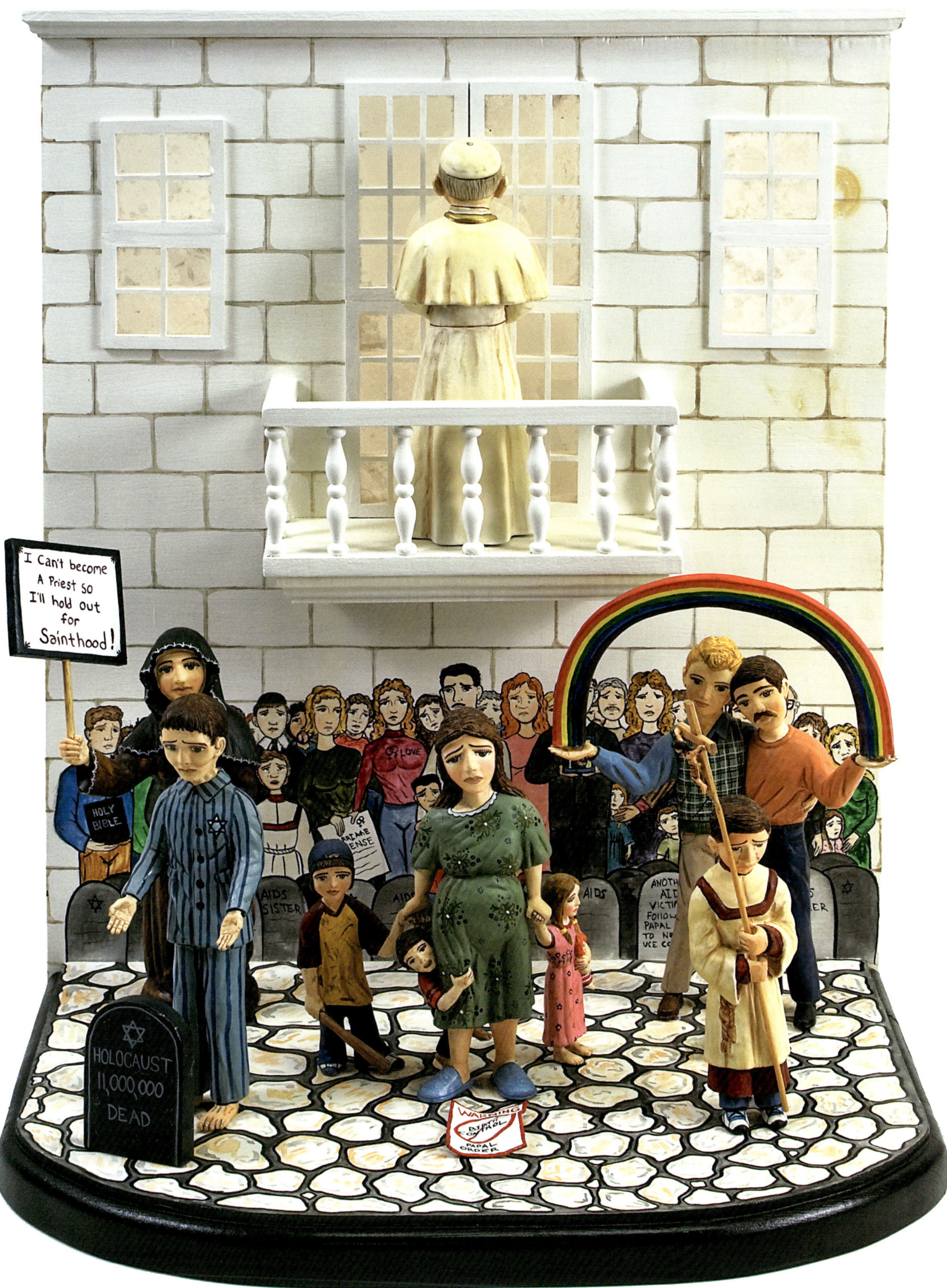
I Can't become A Priest so I'll hold out for Sainthood!
HOLY BIBLE
LOVE
AIDS SISTER
AIDS
HOLOCAUST 11,000,000 DEAD
PAPAL ORDER

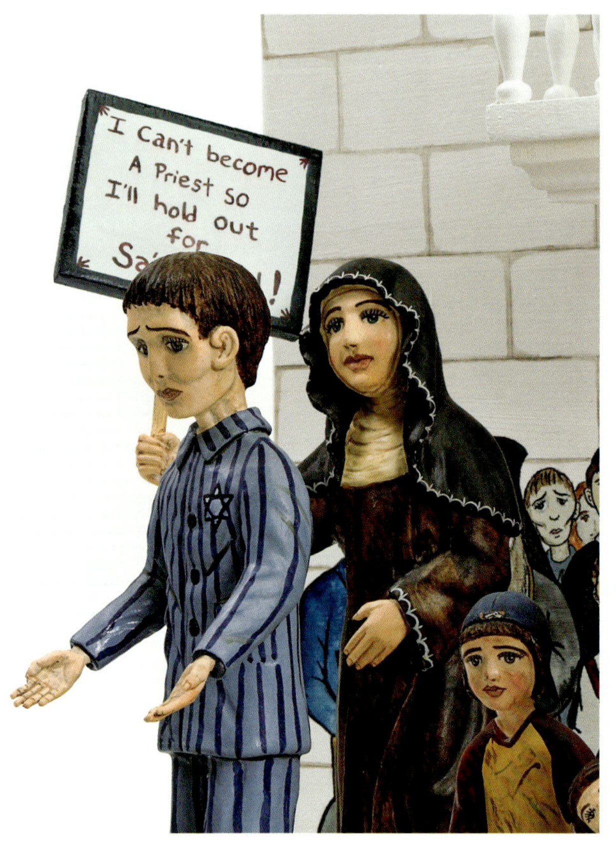

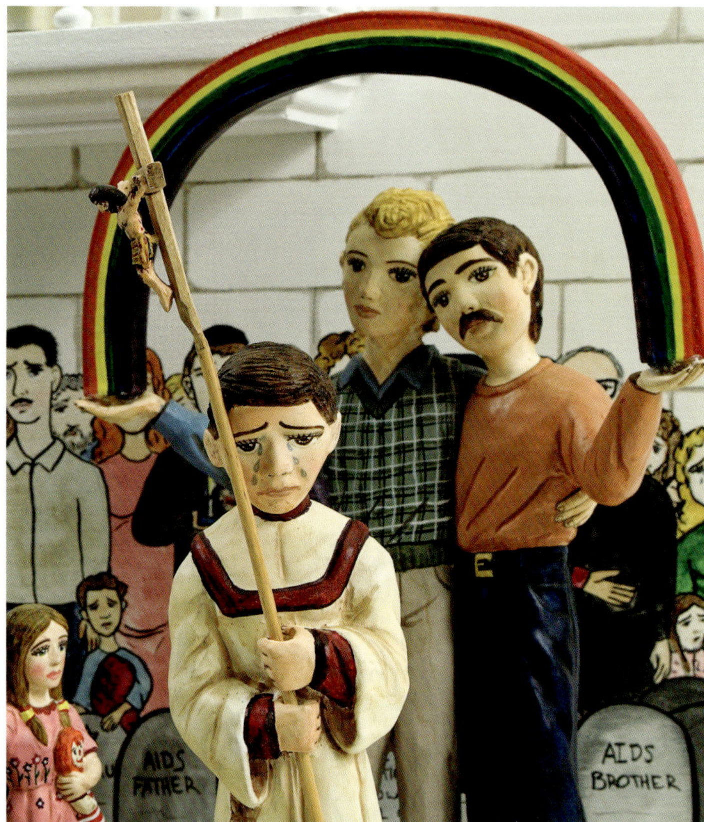

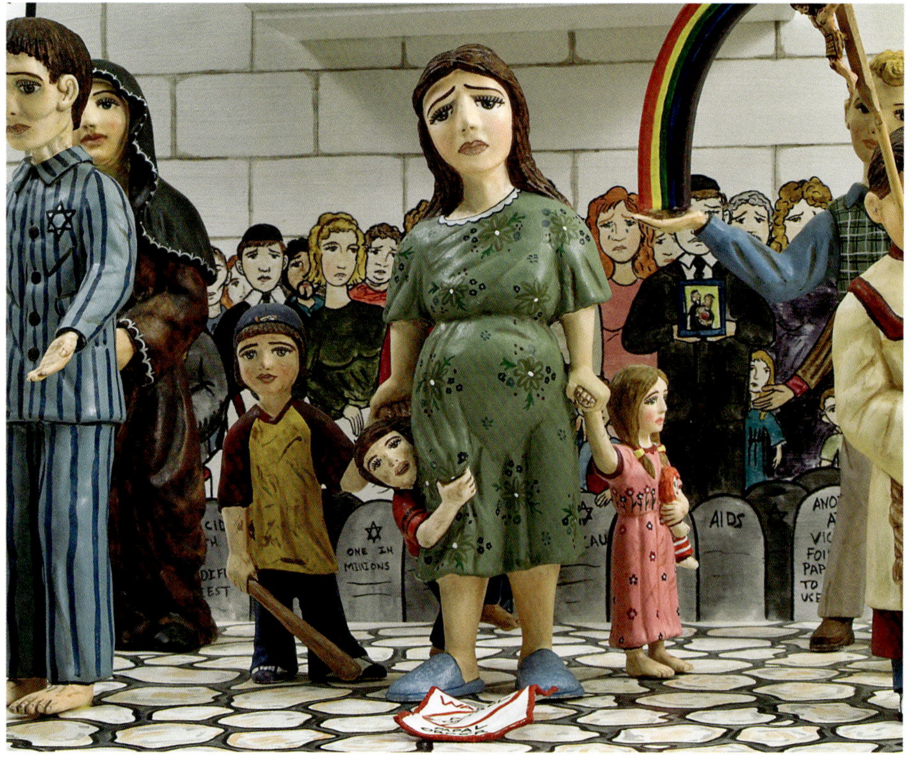

Details of "It Is As It Was," by Arthur López, 2004

Hand-carved wood and mixed-media

Partial Gift of the Diane and Sandy Besser Collections

MOSCA

Sheila is a dealer of tribal art. They commissioned a piece with the request that I include figures of them—along with their custom truck—in the piece. I loved that idea and thought it was a great way to personalize the piece. Kirk and Sheila were very involved in the process, by supplying me with photos of their truck, of themselves, and of the favorite outfits that they would be wearing in the piece—and also by letting me know what they wanted the figures to hold in their hands while watching the movie. When the piece was finished, they were delighted to be included in one of my artworks.

I have always been flexible and willing to work with collectors, and I have since done many personalized commissions—from portraying family pets as Diego Rivera and Frida Kahlo to San Francisco (St. Francis) wearing a 49ers jersey. While some artists may view these as quirky requests and be unwilling to compromise their integrity or vision, for me, as an artist, the smile on a collector's face and the relationship I build with the collector through the process is far more important than worrying about compromising my vision as an Artist.

ARTISTS, BUYERS, AND COLLECTORS

Collectors play a very important role in the marketing of an artist's work because other collectors often view the artwork for the first time in the collections of their friends and families. In one instance, a collector's sister (who is a collector herself) came to visit. The sister saw a Virgin of Guadalupe that the collector had purchased from me and fell in love with the piece. The sister asked to be put in contact with me in hopes of commissioning a Guadalupe of her own. I was more than happy to create a Guadalupe for the sister's collection, but I let her know that I would make it a little different so that each artwork would be unique. When I finished the Guadalupe, I shipped it to the sister in California. After the piece was delivered, she e-mailed me this letter:

> Dear Arthur,
>
> My Lady Guadalupe arrived late last night, and she is beautiful! Lovely! And absolutely perfect!...From the bottom of my heart, thank you. But I will tell you the story of last evening, just after she arrived:
>
> Several hours after Lady Guadalupe arrived, the day become quiet and I made time to sit with her, completely alone. My feelings

were happy and my emotions strong. As I sat gazing at her—my mind quieted and my heart opened fully.... Time had seemed to stop—even my "seeing" was out of time. I felt completely vulnerable—and completely safe. Then quickly—just outside my consciousness—I heard an unfamiliar sound. And for a brief moment I was afraid and my mind quickly re-engaged with a world filled with known and unknown fears and dangers. And in that exact moment, I was surprised I could "see" at all.... I held the image of Guadalupe and let go.... I was with Guadalupe in the home of my heart's spirit. I knew all the shapes and colors and textures that filled it—and each thing held interest and quenched my soul's thirst. I sat this way for a very long time—I know not how long, but it was until I had no need to stay longer. I bid Guadalupe goodnight, went to my bed, fell quickly to sleep, and I dreamed. In my dreams it was a warm day and I sat on a log that had freshly fallen. In the distance children played in a meadow. And near them stood a woman who wore a long glowing robe. Laughter and the sound of birds filled the air and I felt happy to be in this place. After a while, an old and weathered man came walking from beyond the meadow. He didn't stop or pause until he came to where I sat. He stopped and ... look[ed] at the children, and when he did, the woman turned to look back at him. And she smiled. He turned back to me, and in a slow and quiet voice said, "Keep me away from wisdom which does not cry; philosophy which does not laugh; and greatness which does not bow before children" [Kahil Gibran]. And then ... he walked on and was gone. I awoke and felt happy still. I got up and went to greet my home and all the things I know, all the shapes, colors and textures that fill my home.... I was overjoyed to remember Guadalupe was in my home. Here, with the things I know and love and that bring symbolic meaning to my life. This is my home, and now, this Guadalupe's home as well. And it is where we belong—at least for now.

Thank you, Arthur, for your talent and your sight, and for creating this Guadalupe for me, my family and friends....

It is such a great feeling to know that collectors truly love what I have created for them.

Art buyers transform into collectors when they become addicted to or obsessed by an object, whatever that may be. Collectors do not have to come from any economic class, and they don't need to have tons of money. All that is needed is the desire to invest in something that will give visual pleasure and beautify one's surroundings. Most collectors concentrate on one genre in order to gain expertise in one specific area, but others use a broader approach. It is important for collectors to form a bond with the artists and dealers they patronize. It is important to keep up with your chosen genre and to stay current with artists' creations. Artists' work is continually changing from one period to the next, and a collection should contain at least a few examples of the progression of their work from their early career onward.

Both my wife and I are addicted art collectors as well as artists. We love collecting art as much as we love creating it and along the way we have built a great collection in our home. An art collection is an accumulation of art by a private individual or public institution, and the collections of most museums have roots in large private collections. In our collection, my wife and I concentrate on Hispanic northern New Mexico art, but we also collect a variety of Mexican art that we think jells quite well with our basic collection.

I have always loved the energy that is in a piece of original art. The energy of the artist that created it remains even long after the artist has passed. For example, consider the smile of the *Mona Lisa* by Leonardo da Vinci or the intensity of the *Two Fridas* by Frida Kahlo. This energy is what helps to give a home or museum that great visual stimulation that is evident as soon as you enter. Having a home filled with this type of visual stimulation has helped to instill a creative imagination and appreciation for art in both of my sons, Jeremiah and Darean, and both have shared a passion for collecting art from a very young age.

One of my favorite and most special commissions came from my son Darean. When he was five, he came to me one day and asked, "Daddy, can I commission you for a Zozobra for my collection?" Zozobra is a giant puppet that is burned each year in September during the Santa Fe Fiestas. The first Zozobra puppet was created in 1924 by local artist Will Shuster, and a new puppet has been burned nearly every year since, in order to burn away troubles or glooms and to receive a fresh start. My son's birthday is around the time of the Santa Fe

FOLLOWING PAGE:

Nuestra Señora del Carmen, by Arthur López, 2002

Jelutong, pine, gesso, natural and water based pigment

Partial Gift of the Diane and Sandy Besser Collections

MOSCA

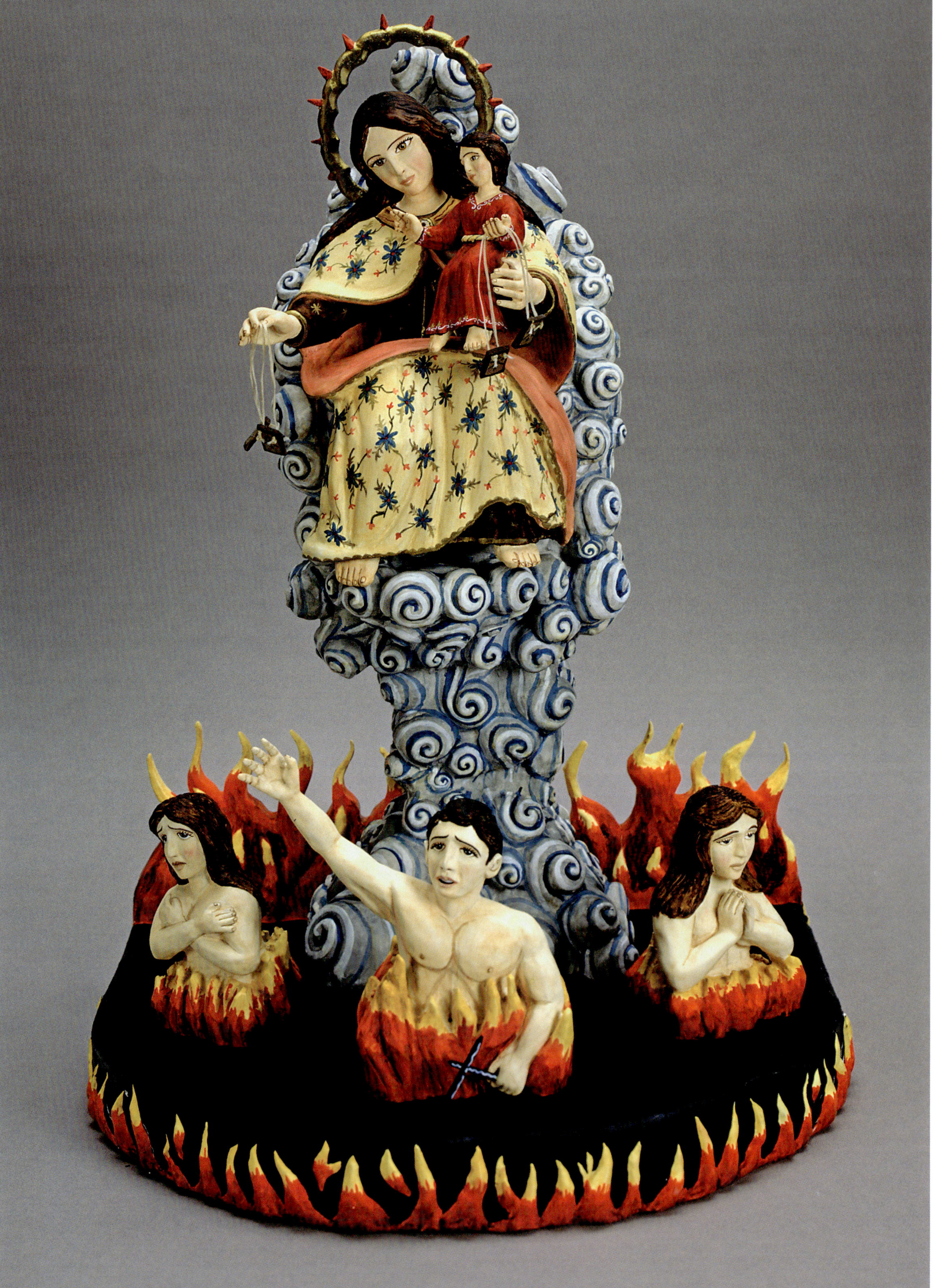

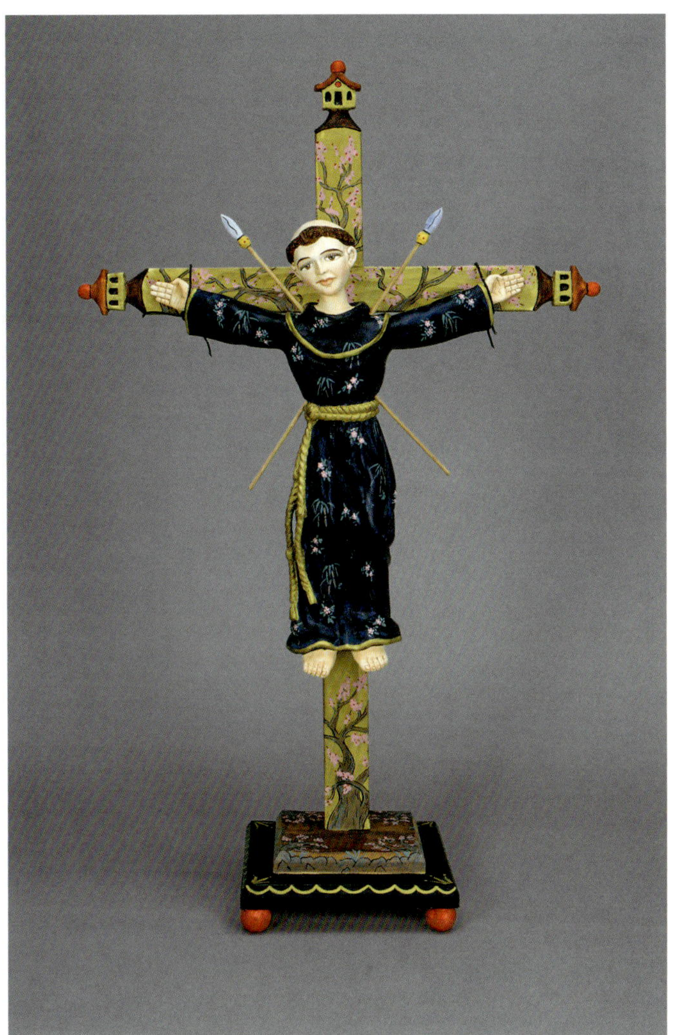

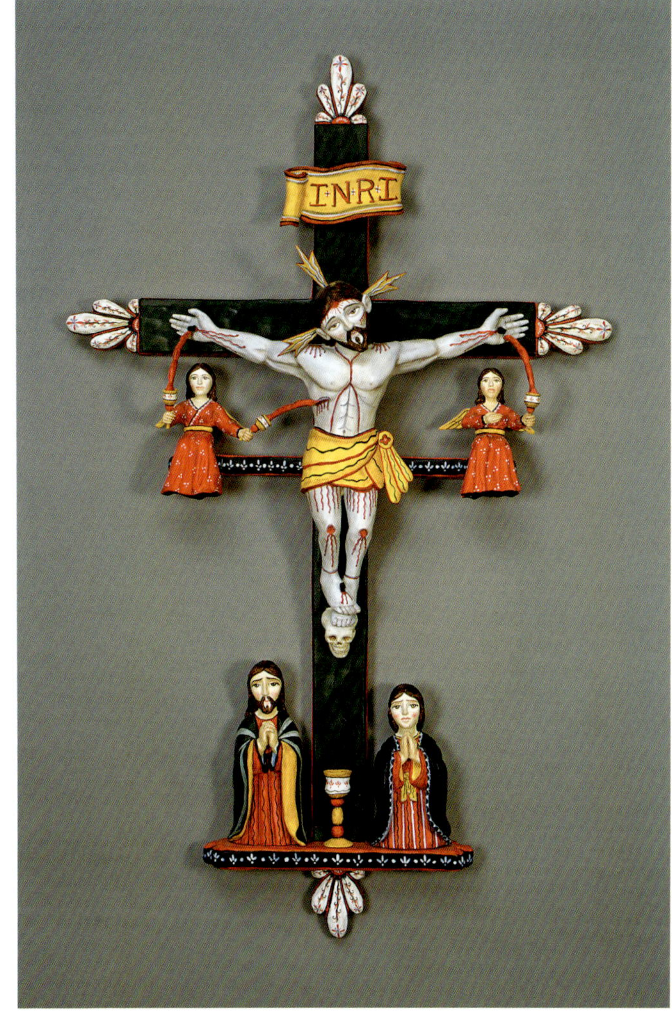

Fiestas and he associates this with his own birthday fiesta. My wife and I have taken him to each burning since he was one year old, telling him that all of the celebration was for him. We have purchased many posters, tee shirts, hats, photos, and art . . . all with the image of Zozobra. So when my son came to me and asked if I would make him one for his collection I got to work right away. Darean helped me the entire way. He picked out the colors he wanted, the way Zozobra's hands would be positioned (Darean even made his own sketches for me to follow), and how Zozobra should look when the figure was finished. It was wonderful to see that Darean knew exactly what he wanted, and he was very insistent that I work on it. It was great to have Darean with me every step of the way and to see the thrill and excitement in his eyes as he watched me carve. As the work progressed, Darean would parade around the house with the unfinished carving

LEFT:

San Felipe de Jesus, by Arthur López, 2003

Jelutong, pine, and natural pigments

Gift from the
Diane and Sandy Besser Collection

IFAF

RIGHT:

Sangre de Cristo Santa Cruz,
by Arthur López, 2002

Jelutong, pine and natural pigments

Partial Gift of the Diane and Sandy Besser Collections

MOSCA

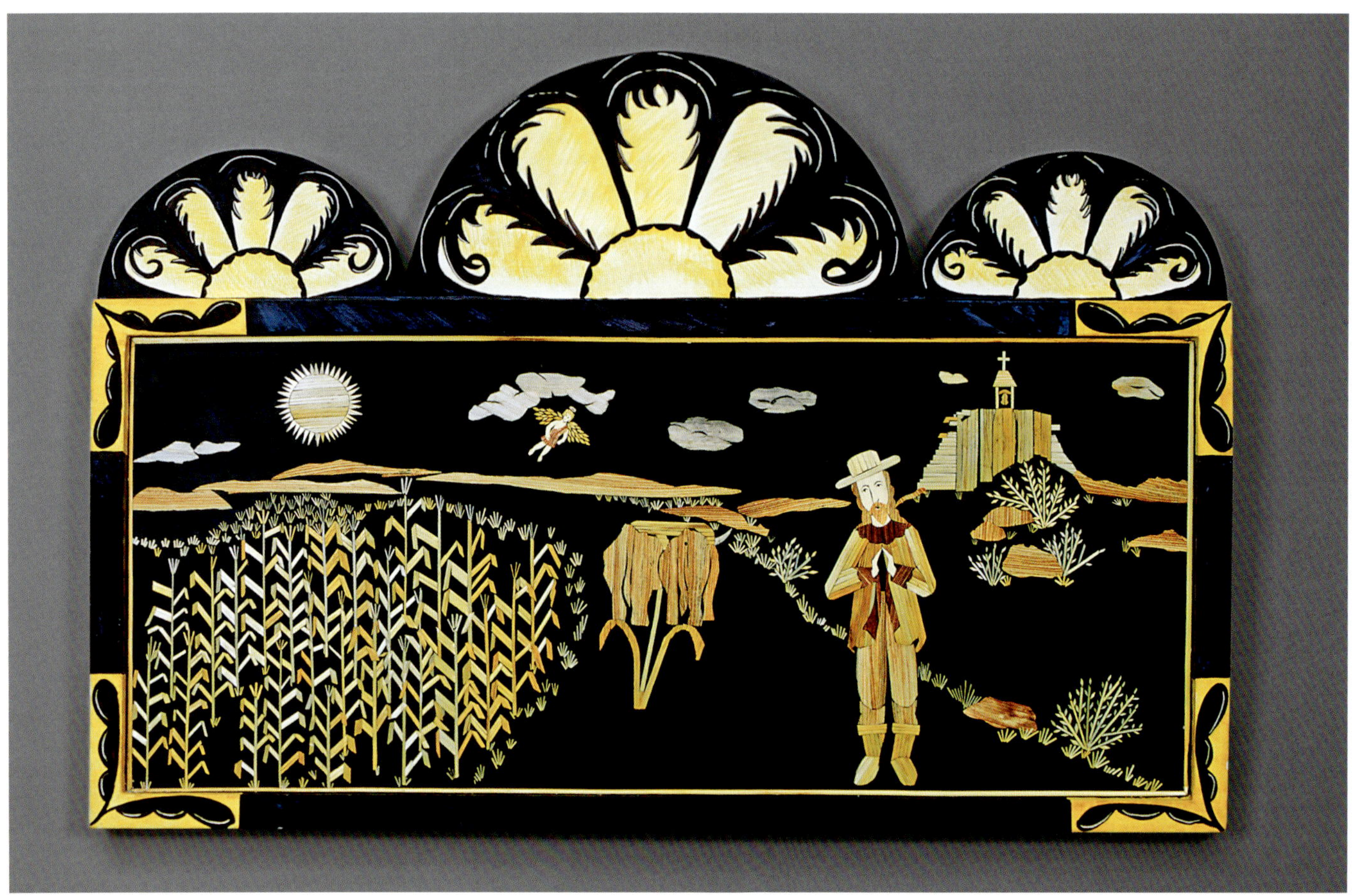

Just Another Day San Isidro Labrador, by Jean Anaya Moya. 2002

Pine, wheat straw, ornamental cornhusk, natural pigments, handmade gesso, acrylic paint and varnish

Gift from the Diane and Sandy Besser Collection

IFAF

at its various stages. He would take pictures of the unfinished carving to his kindergarten class, bragging that I was making him a Zozobra for his collection. Darean tells me the Zozobra is his favorite piece in his collection. Of course, his younger brother Jeremiah, who collects Día de los Muertos (Day of the Dead) items because of its association with his birthday in October, then commissioned me for a skeletal figure: this commission is next on my list. What would I do without my favorite collectors?

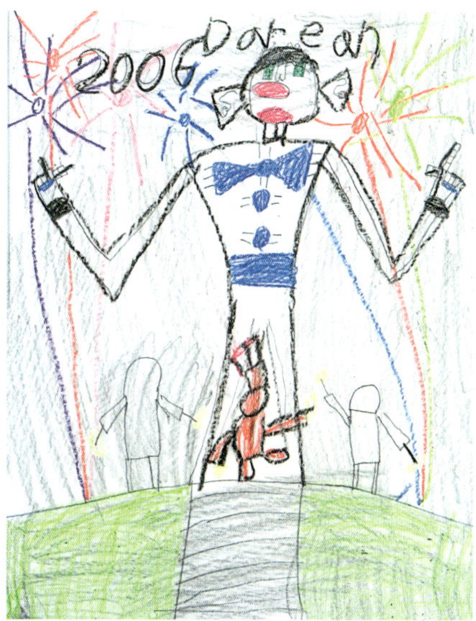

Zozobra sketch, by Darean López, 2006
Collection of the Artist

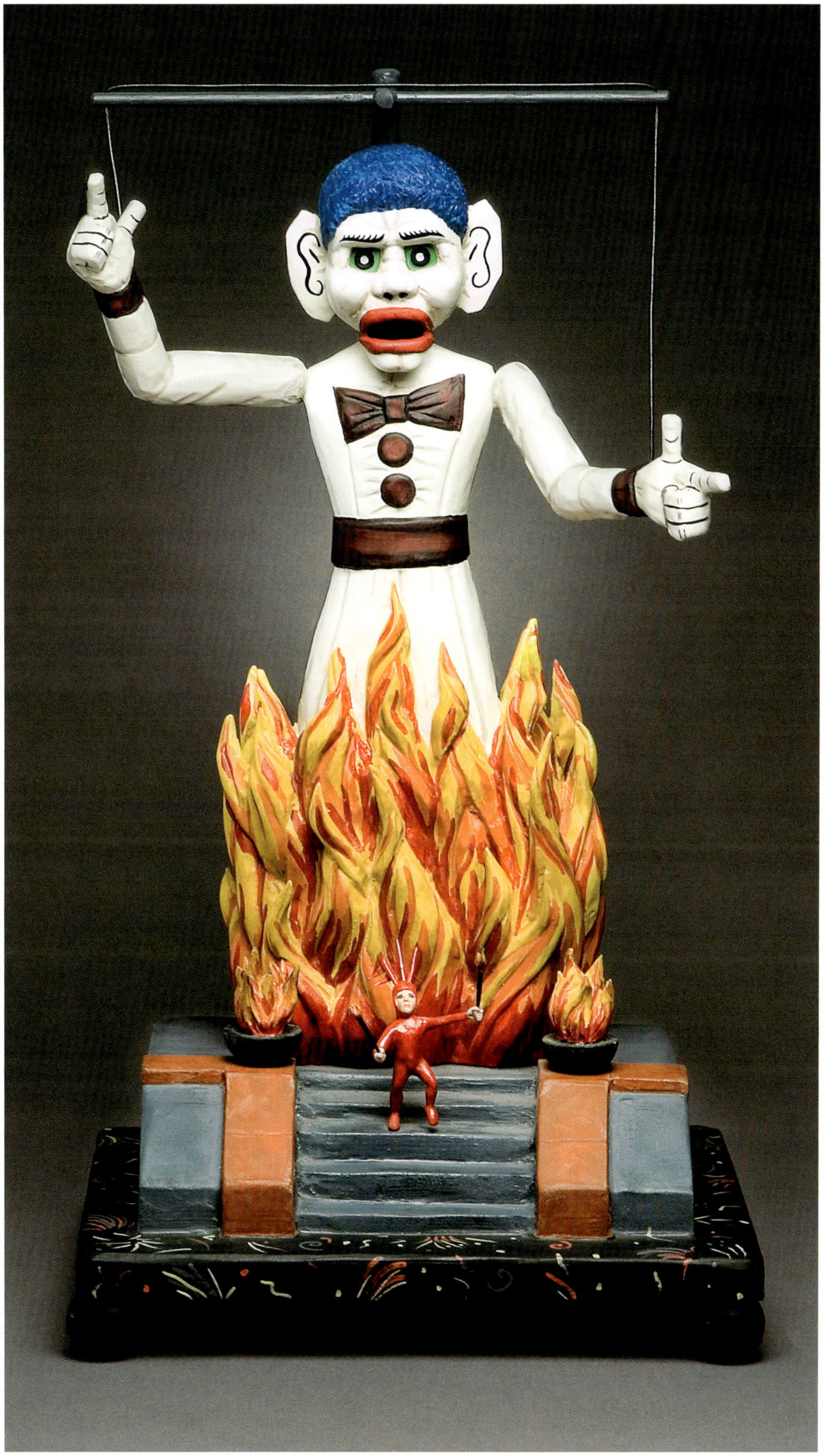

Zozobra, by Arthur López, 2006
Hand-carved wood and mixed media
Collection of Darean López

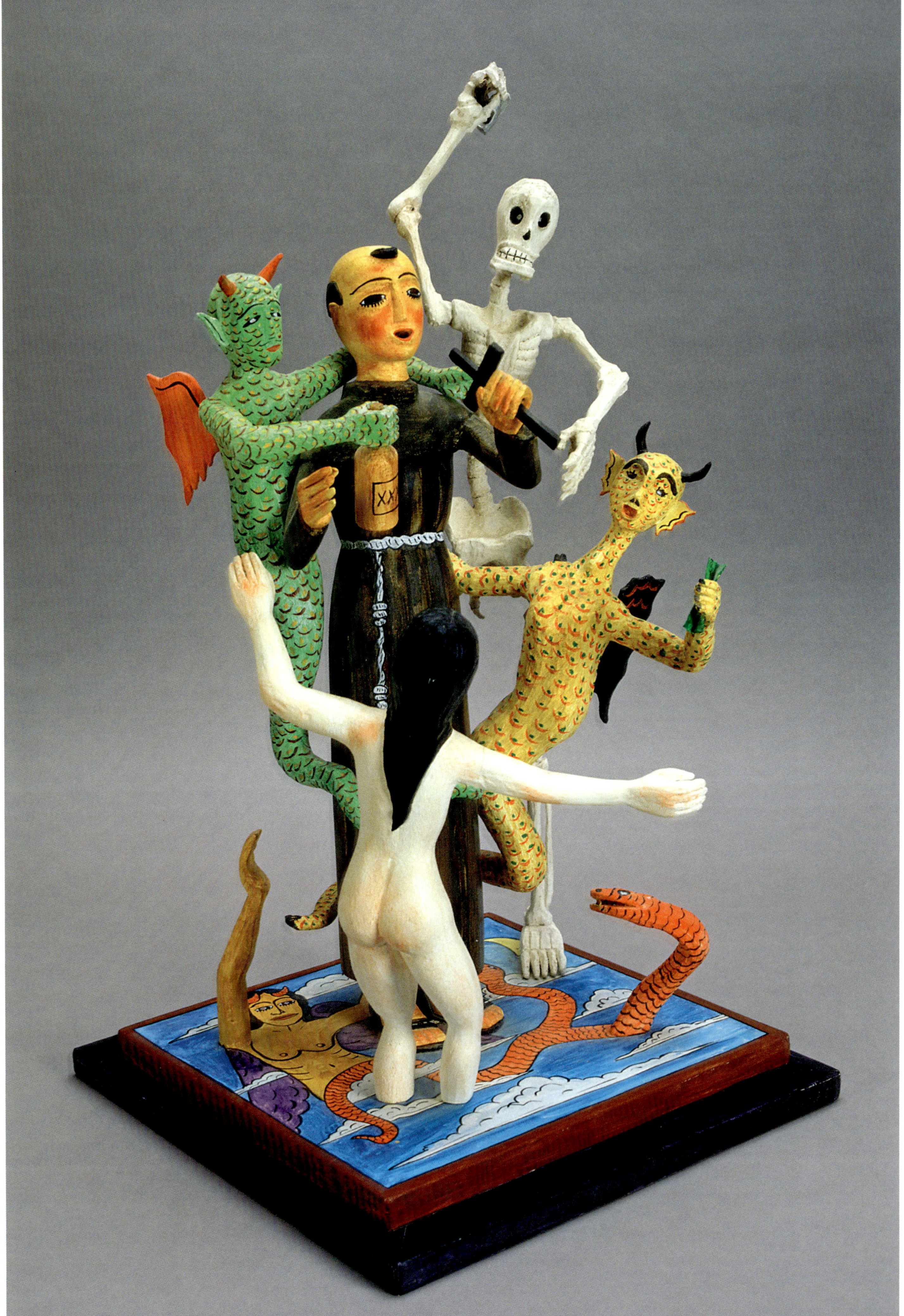

On Collectors

Cats, Sinners, Angels, and Art

Luis Tapia with Carmella Padilla

A FEW YEARS BACK I DISCOVERED A LARGE PACKAGE AT MY DOOR, addressed to "Artist Luis Tapia." It came from New York, Ohio, or some other far-away state I now forget and it had an unfamiliar name as a return address.

I carried the box inside—it was heavy—and anxiously used a pair of scissors to cut through its thick layers of packing tape. The top popped open and I reached inside, pulling out sheets of multicolored tissue paper that covered a most unusual stash: tee shirts, sweaters, candy, books, paints, brushes, all sorts of puzzling items. It also included a letter from a teacher who wrote that his students were learning about my work in class and that they liked it so much they wished to send me a gift. I was overwhelmed, a little suspicious, but ultimately flattered. I mailed a thank-you package back with a few signed posters of some of my better-known work and other information about my long career as a sculptor.

Soon another letter arrived from the teacher, who wrote that he and his wife (who was also a teacher) couldn't afford much but would love to own a piece of my art. They were collectors of art that features images of cats, he said. Would it be possible for me to carve them an affordable cat?

"I'm sorry," I wrote back, "I don't do cats."

The Temptations of Saint Anthony, by Luis Tapia, 1991
Carved and painted wood
Partial Gift of the
Diane and Sandy Besser Collections
MOSCA

OPPOSITE:

Santos y Diablos,by Nicholas Herrera, 2002

Pine, natural pigments and watercolors

Gift from the Diane and Sandy Besser Collection

IFAF

Three weeks later another package came. Return address: the same. This time the box was filled with books on various subjects, including one titled *The Secret Life of Cats.* As the jacket copy described it, the book featured photographs of artworks depicting "cats in various guises throughout the ages." These cats were of every breed, color, and stripe, from stone feline sculptures and porcelain cat busts to a line drawing of a snoozing kitty curled at the feet of a fig-leafed Adam and Eve. The package also included another plea for me to consider carving an inexpensive cat for the cash-strapped couple. Again I responded, more forcefully this time: "I don't do cats." With that, the correspondence stopped.

Looking back, the case of the cat collectors was completely harmless, even a little humorous. But it perfectly illustrates the unique interactions that can take place between an artist and a collector. The Ohio gift box could have come from anywhere—from a multimillionaire collector who wants a particular piece carved in his or her own colors and themes, or from my wife who might want me to make another piece exactly like her favorite one that I sold last week (though she knows better than to ask me). At its worst, collecting can be an act of not-so-gentle persuasion and pressure, and some collectors will go to questionable lengths to acquire an artist's work. At best, it's a nurturing, positive, respectful exchange that results in art that rises above the earthly concerns of artist and collector alike.

The artist-collector relationship is a world unto itself, and I feel immensely privileged to be part of this world. I know I need collectors: an artist without a client is just a hobbyist. But as positive and flattering as the collector relationship may be, it can also be challenging. I can't speak to collectors' motivations, only to my own experience. And if there is anything I've learned during my thirty-plus-year career, it is that maintaining the creative freedom I need to be the best artist I can be while building fruitful connections with my collectors is a delicate balance. Compare it to a dance where the dancers must agree early on who is in the lead. Is it the collector who has the financial wherewithal, the connections, and the interest to carry an artist's work to the next level (that is, to other collectors, to a more successful career, and best of all, to a museum)? Or is it the artist whose skill and inspiration are what brought the artist and collector together to begin with?

A FEW ART SINNERS I'VE KNOWN

In the world of art collectors, there are sinners and there are angels. I've dealt with both. From the time I began working as a sculptor in the early 1970s, I was keenly

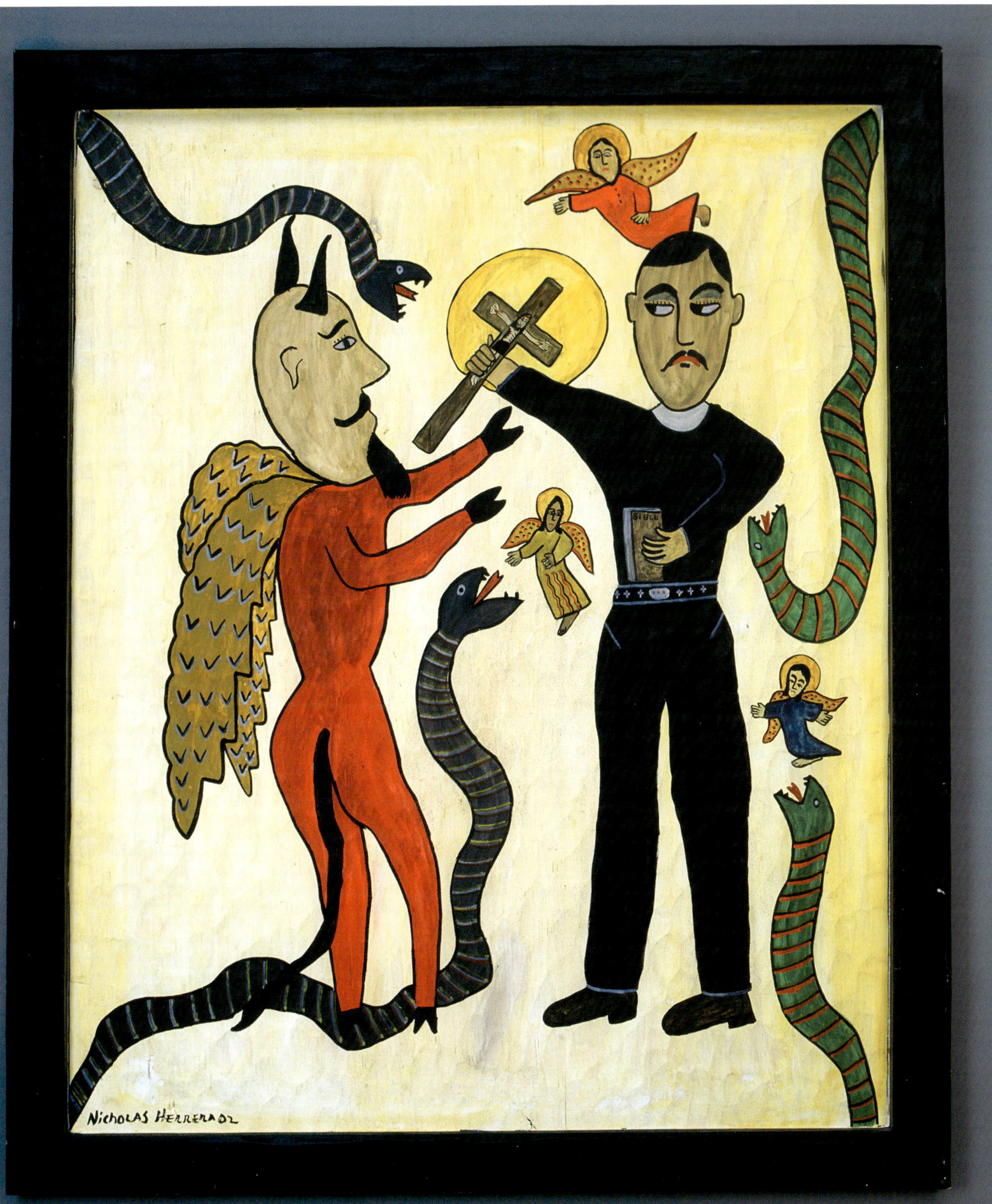
BIBLE
NICHOLAS HERRERA 02

aware of the importance of collectors. I spent those early years trying to carve out my own style and identity as an artist, trying to show my work and make a name for myself. Ultimately, I hoped that my name would become synonymous with a high quality of work, not with the number of collectors it attracted. Of course, I knew I'd have relationships with collectors, especially if I achieved what I wanted to achieve. But I wanted those relationships to be about art, not about me. I wanted people to look to my art if they wanted to learn about me.

Nonetheless, as my work began to gain some degree of renown, I began to feel a subtle pressure to accommodate other people's needs. I was proud of and overwhelmed by the attention the work began to receive in the art community, as well as pleased by people's desire to learn about it. I made every effort to be available to clients, but as more attention shifted to me, the boundaries I had drawn in my mind between myself and my clients got confused.

As a young artist with a wife and two kids, at the time I didn't have much. I had no telephone but had to pick up messages at my mother's house. However, I soon learned what could happen if I didn't immediately return a prospective client's call. People began showing up at my mother's front door, asking where I could be found. When she wouldn't tell them, these would-be clients would find other ways to track me down. One person went so far as to find out where my grandmother lived. At that time my grandmother was in her late eighties, but she still lived alone and didn't speak English. When she related the story of the strange visitor who kept asking for her grandson, the artist, I was amazed and annoyed.

Early in my career, I also felt financial pressure to accommodate collectors: not only did I have a family to support, but I had given up a full-time job—with benefits—to pursue my art. Every sale counted. My earliest works were modeled after the religious *santos,* the woodcarvings and paintings of saints that came to New Mexico during the Spanish Colonial period. This work not only helped me hone my carving skills, it also brought me my earliest sales and commissions. In the colonial tradition, specific santos possess certain iconography and other attributes, so it wasn't uncommon for a client to request a favorite saint. This soon led to requests either to make exact duplicates of my previous works or to create pieces that incorporated the collector's own designs and attributes, which often included the family pet.

I did this at first. After all, it was a sale, and the work was mine. However, in these works my imagination was absent. The process didn't feel right from the

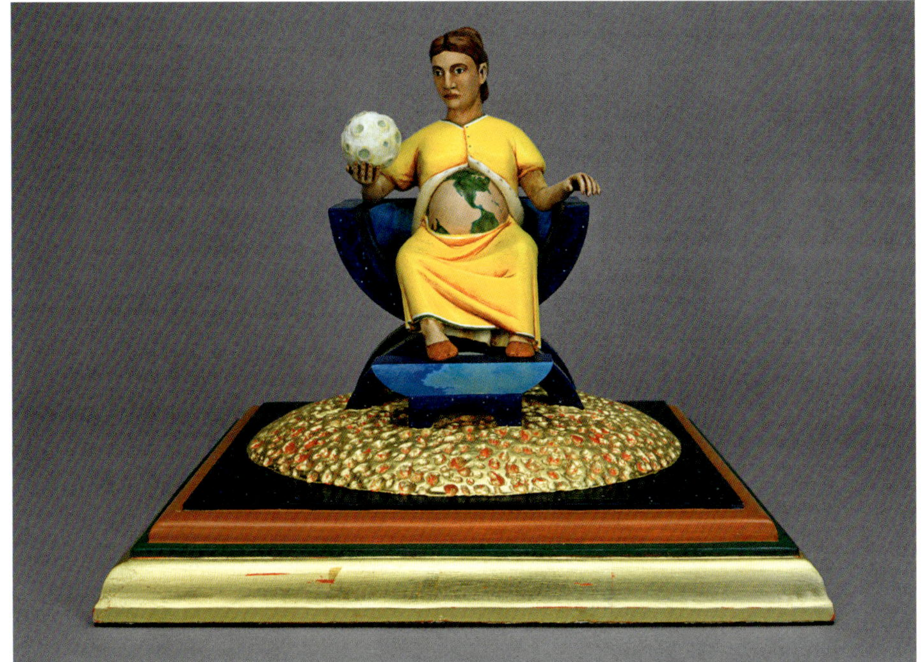

Mother's Love, by Sergio Tapia, 2001

Carved and painted wood

Gift from the Diane and Sandy Besser Collection

IFAF

start, and, in fact, the result rarely met the client's expectations. The color might have been a bit off, or my rendition of the family pet was not exact. I couldn't even duplicate my own work well. It was a completely frustrating exercise for both my clients and me. I decided never to accept that kind of commission again.

Financial pressures took other forms as well. One particularly negative collector experience came in these early years when a pair of major folk art collectors came to my home to see my work. They admired one particular santo but made it plain they wanted a better price. They were extremely complimentary about the work yet insisted they deserved the piece for less money. By the time the visit was over, I had sold the $75 santo for $35, but my emotions were mixed. Naturally, I was excited that my work was going into a major collection, but I also felt defeated: the piece was clearly worth more than they had paid. In the end I felt I had no choice—$35 bought a lot of groceries in those days.

About six years later, the two came to call again. By then I had progressed much farther in my career and had become known for innovative contemporary interpretations of traditional colonial works. The couple asked to interview me for a book, and though I rarely invited guests into my creative space, I welcomed them into my work studio. I regretted that move as soon as the interview began. They wanted to put words in my mouth, wanted me to say things I didn't want

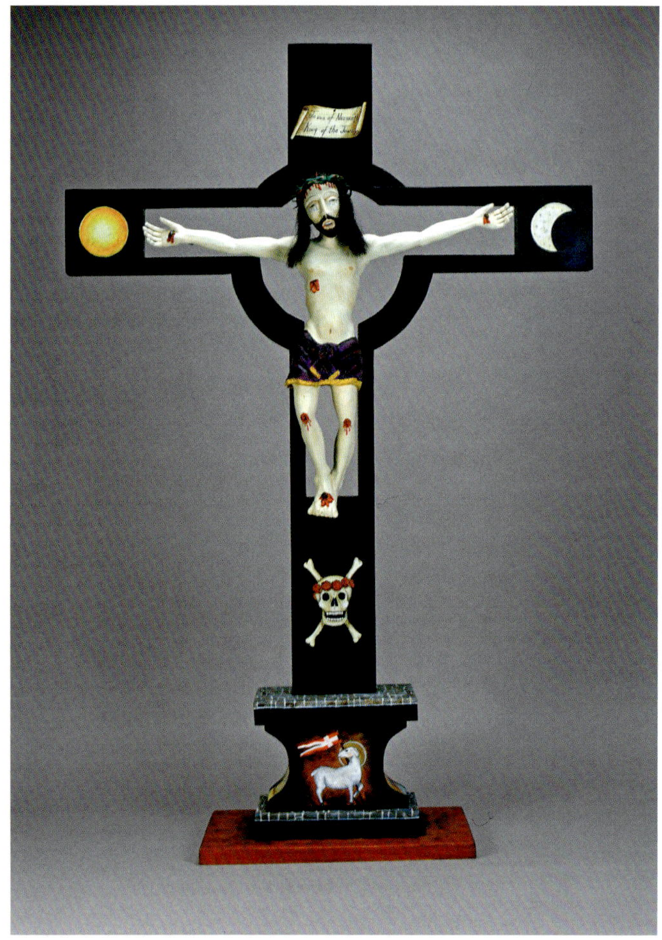

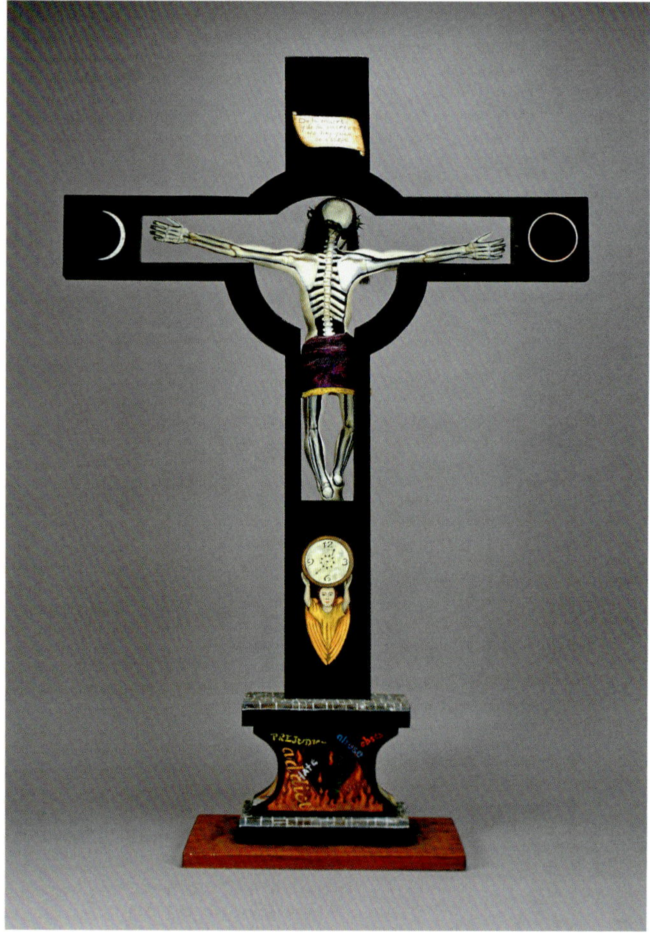

LEFT:

The Passion of Christ, by Luis Tapia, 2002

Carved and painted wood

Partial Gift of the
Diane and Sandy Besser Collections

MOSCA

RIGHT:

Reverse of Luis Tapia's
The Passion of Christ

to say; and they tried to make the article more spectacular than it might otherwise have been. I resisted that approach but, again, they insisted. As the interaction got increasingly tense, I held my temper. But when they began rifling through my work cupboards for additional details to color their story, they crossed the final line. I exploded and threw them out.

Amazingly, the story did not end there. Many years later, I had signed on with a well-known gallery. In addition to the benefits the gallery could provide in promoting my work, the move had been a conscious decision to help me create a more structured way to interact with clients. Knowing this, the pair called the gallery to schedule an interview for another project they had underway. As long as the interview would take place in the gallery, I agreed. This time the interview went well. When it was over the two browsed my current gallery work. When they had selected a favorite, they approached the gallery director: Could they have it at a significantly reduced price?

Ironically, though, my exasperation with the couple turned into inspiration. Shortly after the gallery visit, I carved what is now considered one of my seminal works, "The Folk Art Collectors." The polychrome sculpture is a not-so-subtle commentary on the ill-mannered methods of some collectors. In the piece, a couple clad in the Santa Fe style proudly display two santos, their latest acquisitions. Dollar bills bulge from the pockets of the man's flowery Bermuda shorts, while money fills the woman's left hand, each eager to buy their next folk art find. It's a completely satirical sculpture, though obviously carved with my past experience in mind. The irony here is that, unaware that they had been the inspiration for my work, the same two people tried their best to purchase the piece, to add to other works of mine they had purchased through the years. Eventually "The Folk Art Collectors" went to another, much different kind of collector—an art angel, if you will—who later donated it to a museum.

AND SOME ART ANGELS, TOO

For someone who depends on the support of collectors, I realize it might seem ungrateful of me to criticize any collector's enthusiasm for my work. But while I'm humbled by many people's support, there have definitely been times in my career when clear lines of courtesy and good behavior have been crossed. These unfortunate experiences are often the first to come to mind, but in reality they have been few and far between. The upside is that I've learned a lot from these experiences. I've learned that I can be naïve about collectors, and about human nature in general. More than anything, I've learned to appreciate the many wonderful relationships I've enjoyed with collectors through the years.

If I were to identify an ideal collector, it would have to be people like the "art angel" I earlier described. These are collectors who buy an artist's work not only for their personal enjoyment but with the clear intention that one day they will donate the work to a museum. Their support of an artist's work is not as much an effort to build or promote their own collection as an attempt to build and promote the career of the artist they believe in. Art angels push your work and expose it to the public; they do everything they can to show their enthusiasm about what you are doing and are persuasive about why others should be enthusiastic, too. There is no pressure involved in the relationship, no attempt to control any part of the creative process, only sincere good will and good faith in what the artist can do.

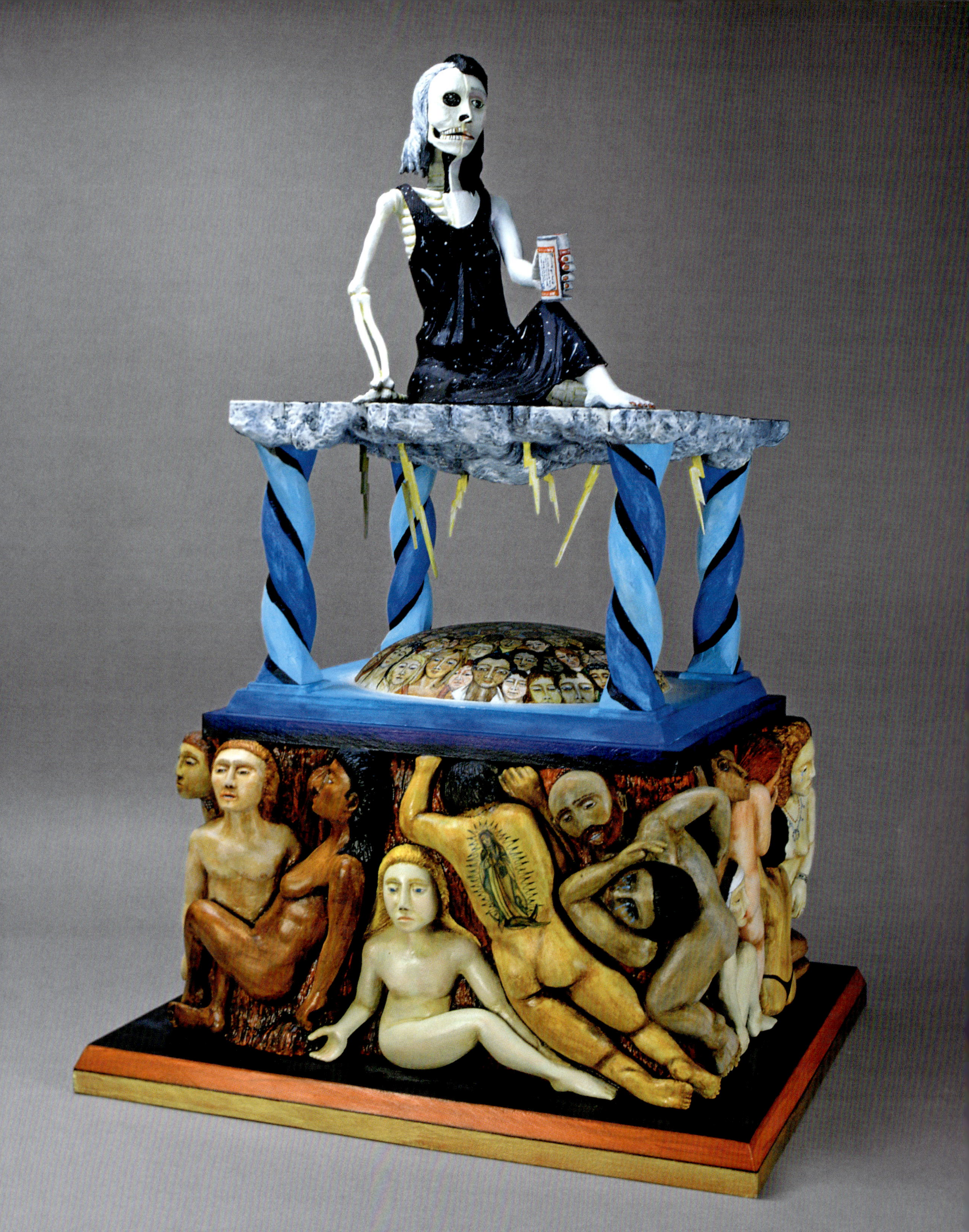

I've had many doors opened for me through the kindness and support of the art angels in my life. When the doors to museums swing open, this is the best thing I or any other artist can achieve. It is not only an immense compliment, it gives your work credibility and confirms that your work is good enough to attract serious interest in the art world. This also increases your exposure and makes your work even more collectible. Having work in a museum collection or exhibition gives artists a longevity that they might not otherwise achieve: I could be dead for fifty years and people would still be seeing, and hopefully enjoying, my work. What more could I ask for?

Art angels are rare, and I cherish those who have taken on that role in my life. Some are among my closest friends, though I admit those friendships did not just happen overnight. Just as I'm selective about my friendships in general, I'm also selective with my collector friendships. I take these relationships very seriously; I work very hard at them and never abuse them. Thankfully, the relationships are reciprocal. Collector relationships that are grounded in mutual respect and true freedom of expression are some of the most rewarding relationships I have. Even if I weren't an artist, these are the kinds of people I would want in my life.

And what about the collectors who fall somewhere between the art sinner and the art angel extremes? Of course, not all collectors want to be closely connected to an artist's life, and there are collectors with whom I have no relationship at all. A few of my most prolific collectors I've never even met. Even so, we share a rich relationship. For them, the work is the relationship. We communicate through my sculpture. All that is unsaid between us in terms of traditional conversation is expressed through art.

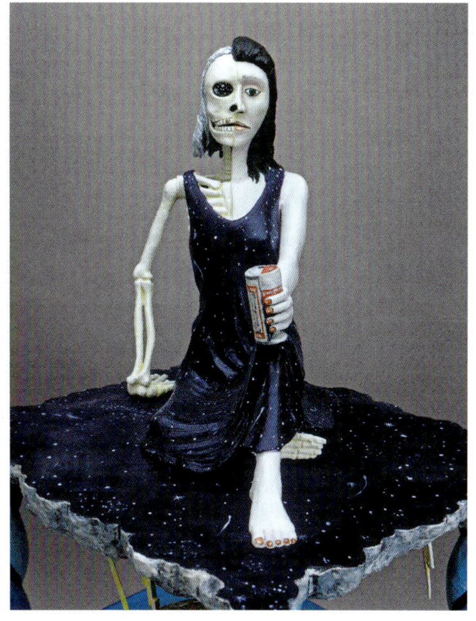

Detail of *Doña Sebastiana*,
by Luis Tapia, 2003

Partial Gift of the
Diane and Sandy Besser Collections

MOSCA

OPPOSITE:

Doña Sebastiana Relaxes After a Hard Day at the Office, by Luis Tapia, 2003

Carved and painted wood

Partial Gift of the
Diane and Sandy Besser Collections

MOSCA

ARTISTS AND COLLECTORS

I admit I'm somewhat of a recluse, as those who know me would likely agree. I have an unlisted telephone number, no cell phone, and no phone in my work studio. I have a wonderful gallery that is willing to act as a go-between for my clients and others who want to be in touch.

Some might view my approach to the art world as arrogant. I call it self-preservation. Without these types of boundaries, an artist finds it hard to work. Without the unlimited space to imagine, dream, and create, my art would go nowhere. I treasure my creative space and guard my privacy fiercely. Given the choice, I'd rather be unavailable than uncreative.

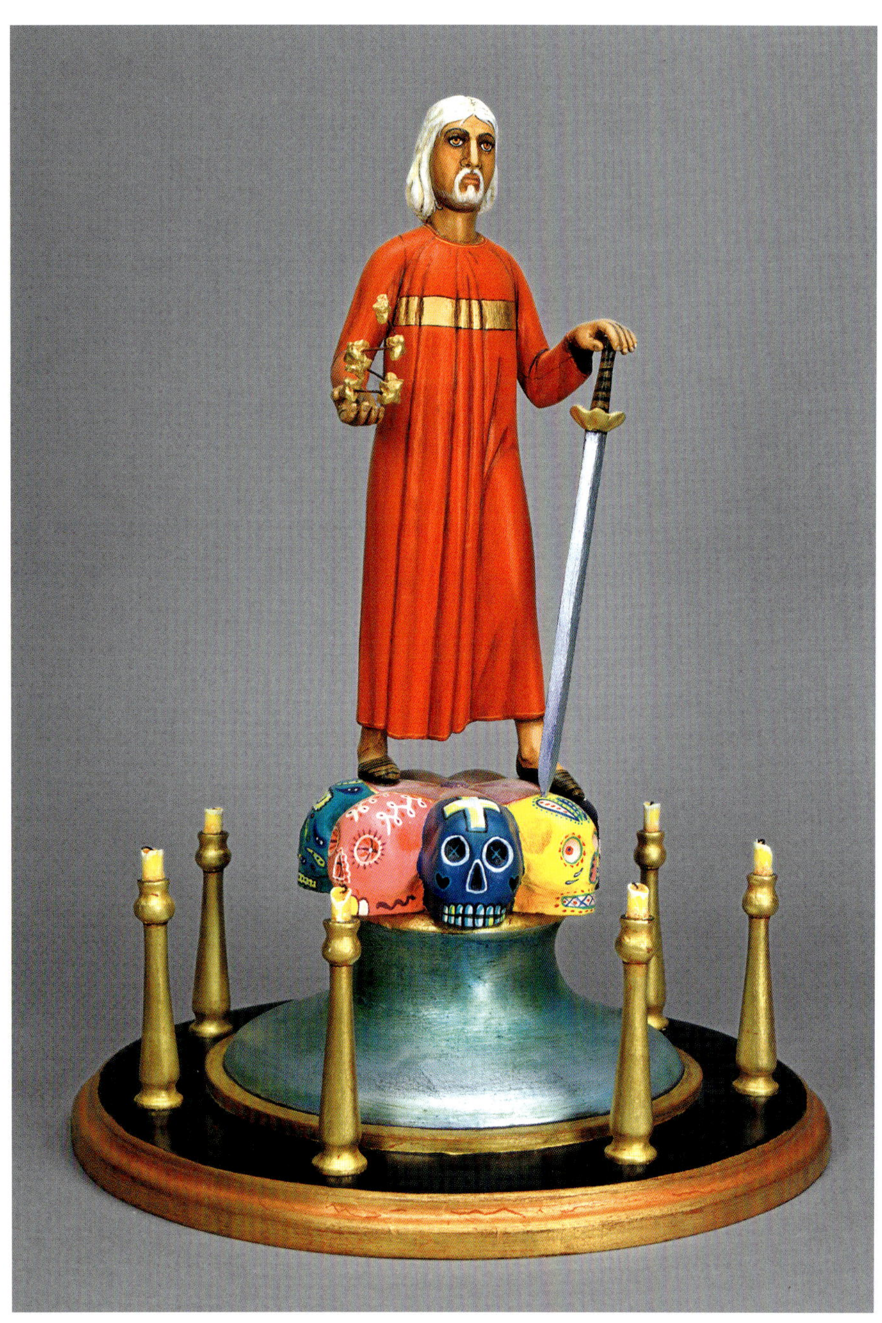

Judgment, by Sergio Tapia, 2001

Carved and painted wood

Partial Gift of the Diane and Sandy Besser Collections

MOSCA

Of course, I realize that art is a business, and I know that my resistance to interacting with every client who calls has not always been my most-appreciated quality. I'm sure that my finances have suffered because of my inaccessibility. On the one hand, I understand that the ability to support myself with my work is central to my artistic and personal survival, and that this often requires making the time for those who might be interested in buying my work. But on the other hand, a lot of baggage can come with this, and an artist like me can suddenly find himself putting the needs of his clients before his own. Some artists fall into the money trap. They do well financially, but by focusing on finances, they lose the focus of their own work. Their art suffers in the end.

Long ago I made a vow to myself that I would never make something because I thought it would sell. Ironically, the few times in the past when I made something I thought would be particularly appealing to collectors, the work never sold. Today, thoughts about finances or sales potential don't enter the picture. The only work I put out there is work that I believe has something to say.

While I occasionally undertake commissions for collectors, I'm very discriminating about which projects I agree to. Again, I always try to keep in mind who is leading the creative dance: Am I working to create the collector's vision of what the work should be or my own vision? Early in the process I work closely with the clients to determine what aspect of my work is especially appealing to them, and what general thoughts they have about the kind of work they would like to see. Later, I'll make a presentation of what I imagine the work to be. If they accept my interpretation, fully understanding that the work could still change as it evolves, we continue. If not, we're done.

I've been fortunate to create a long-term relationship with a gallery whose clientele understands and believes in my work. The gallery allows me the advantage of attracting collectors who accept the way I work. The gallery also accepts my approach and style, never asking me to bend to market demands, and giving me the autonomy to pursue my own artistic inclinations, no matter how saleable—or not—my sculptures may be.

In the end, regardless of the kind of relationship that exists between an artist and a collector, artists need collectors—sinners and angels both. Collectors play a vital role in an artist's creative and professional journey. Collectors deem an artist's work important, giving it validity and meaning beyond the artist's own mind. Collectors teach an artist how to let go, how to transfer one's work from the very private space in which it was created to a public venue where it can be seen and, in the best-case scenario, admired. Even if a work flops in the public arena, collectors remain loyal. In good times and bad, collectors support you—they "have your back."

Thanks in large part to my collectors, I've been able to achieve many things as an artist, both in my personal and my public life. Among my proudest moments are the times when collectors have donated my work to museums, and I've been grateful for the professional opportunities that this provided. But perhaps my greatest achievement is the freedom that my most committed collectors have given me *to be me.*

Moses and the Burning Bush,
by Sergio Tapia, 2000

Carved and painted wood

Gift from the
Diane and Sandy Besser Collection

IFAF

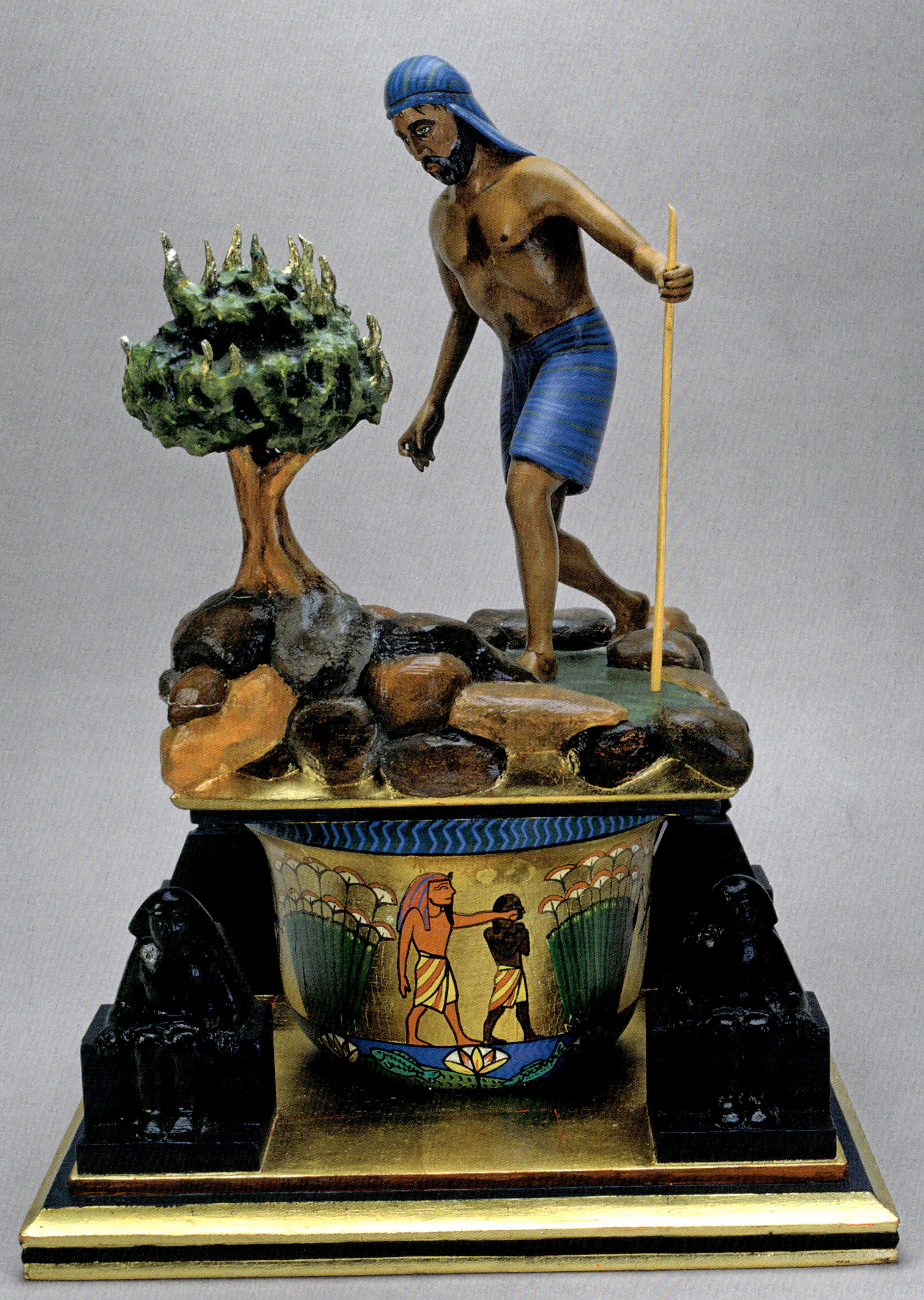

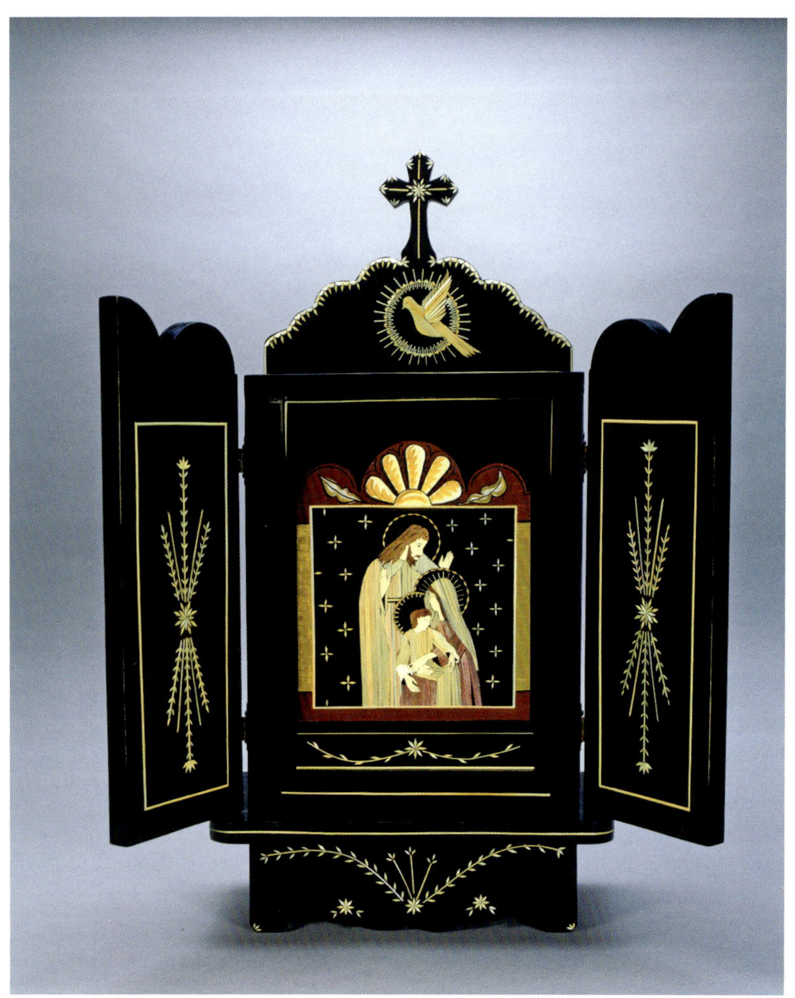

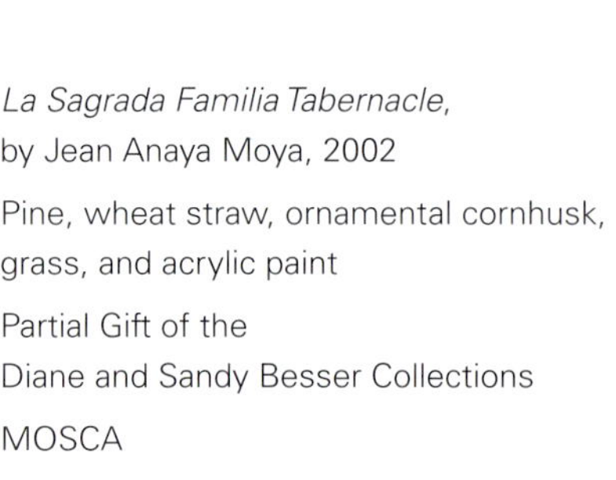

La Sagrada Familia Tabernacle,
by Jean Anaya Moya, 2002

Pine, wheat straw, ornamental cornhusk, grass, and acrylic paint

Partial Gift of the
Diane and Sandy Besser Collections

MOSCA

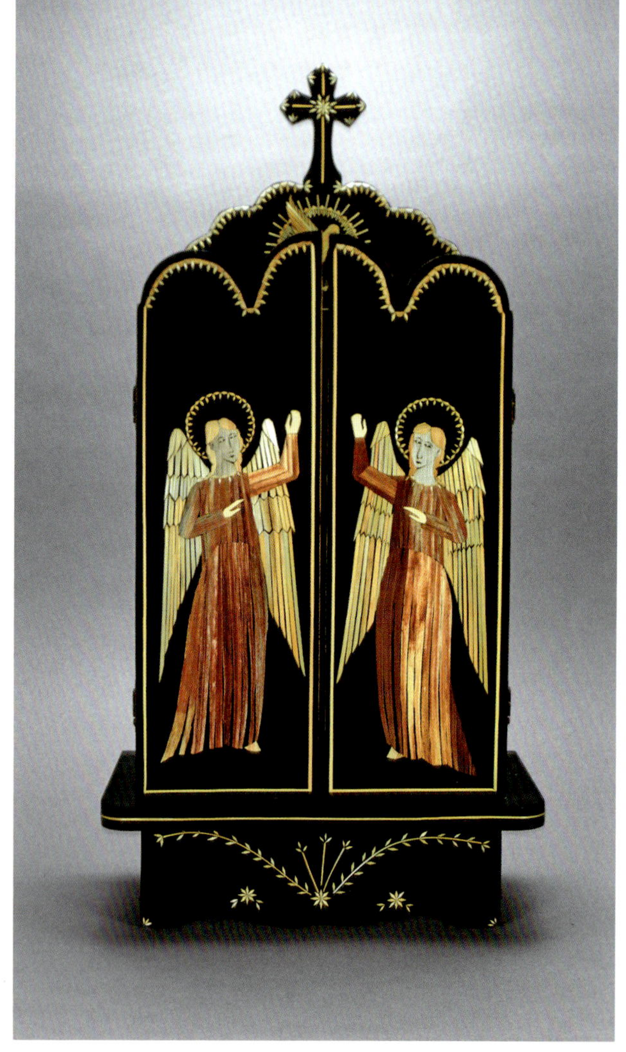

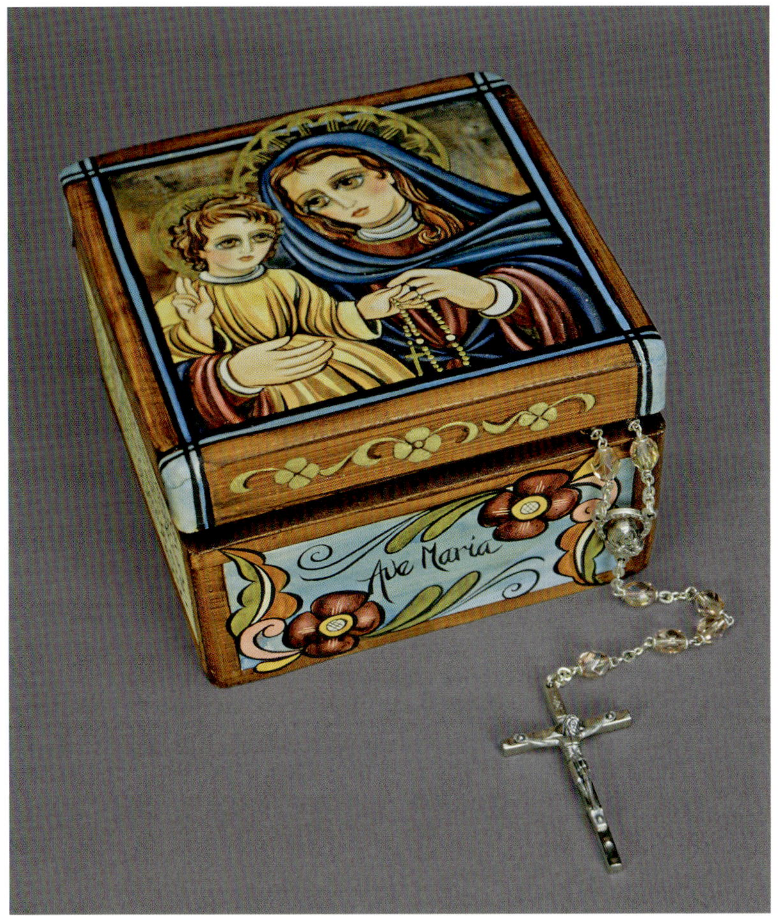

Ave María rosary box,
by Arlene Cisneros Sena, 2002

Handmade gesso, pigments, piñon varnish, and gold leaf

Gift from the
Diane and Sandy Besser Collection

IFAF

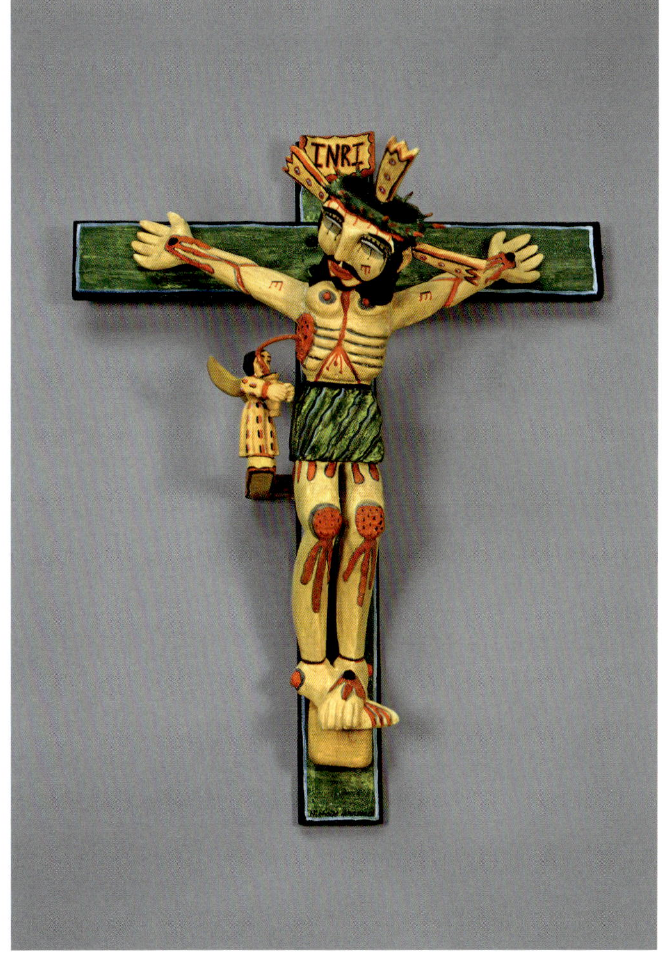

Cristo crucificado,
by Nicholas Herrera, 2001

Pine, natural pigments and watercolors

Partial Gift of the
Diane and Sandy Besser Collections

MOSCA

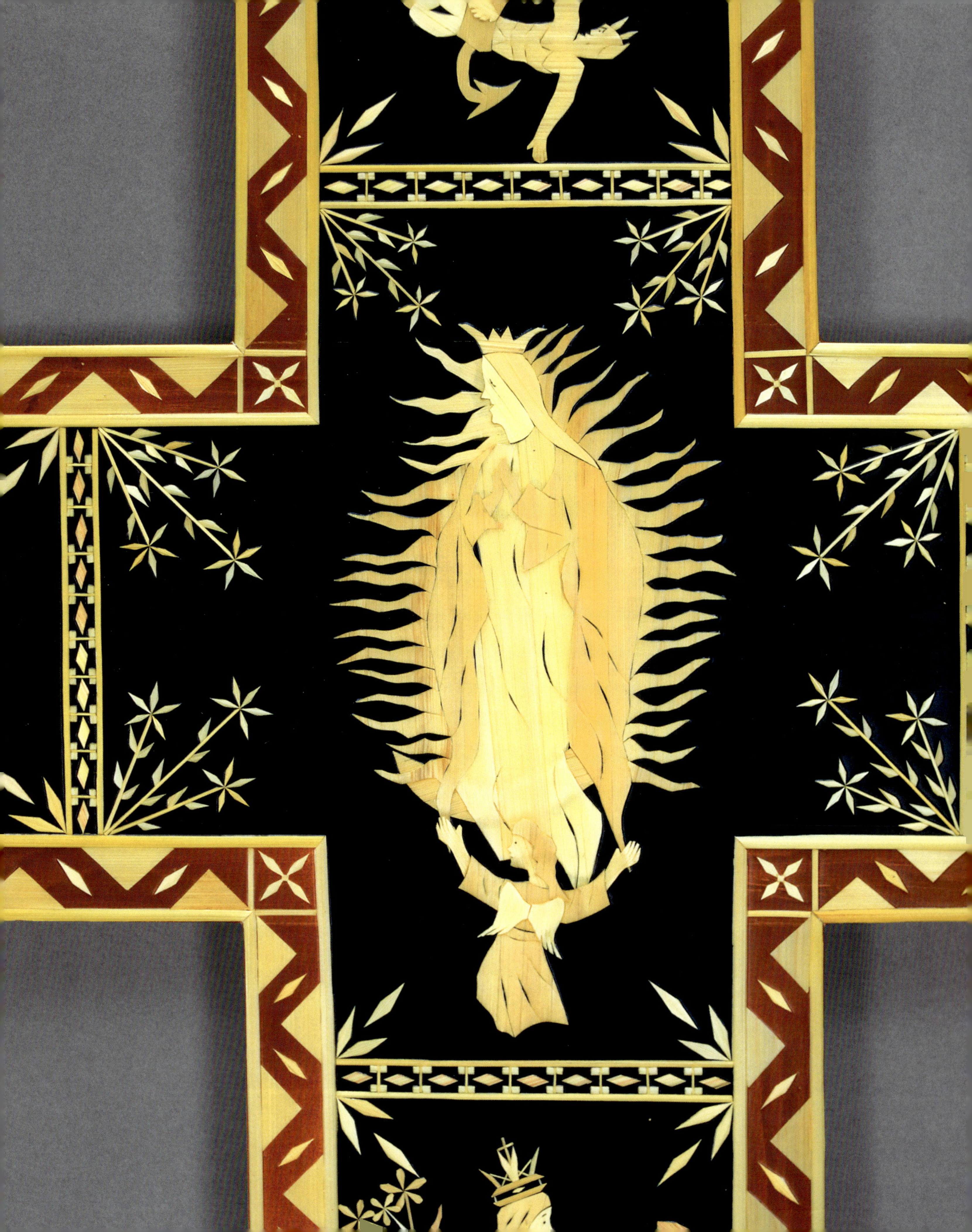

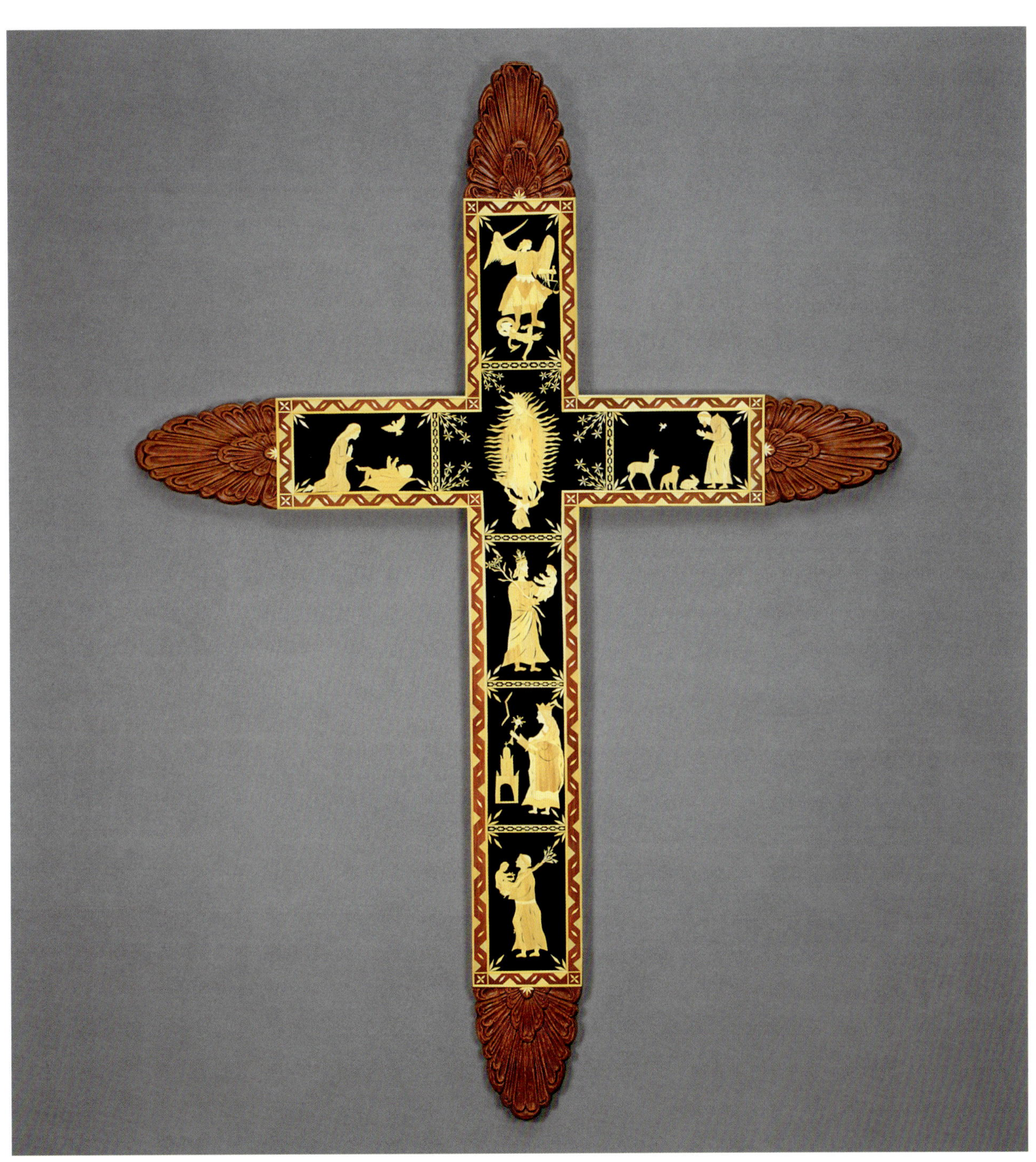

Santa Cruz, by Mel Rivera, 2002

Straw, wood, gesso and paint

Partial Gift of the
Diane and Sandy Besser Collections

MOSCA

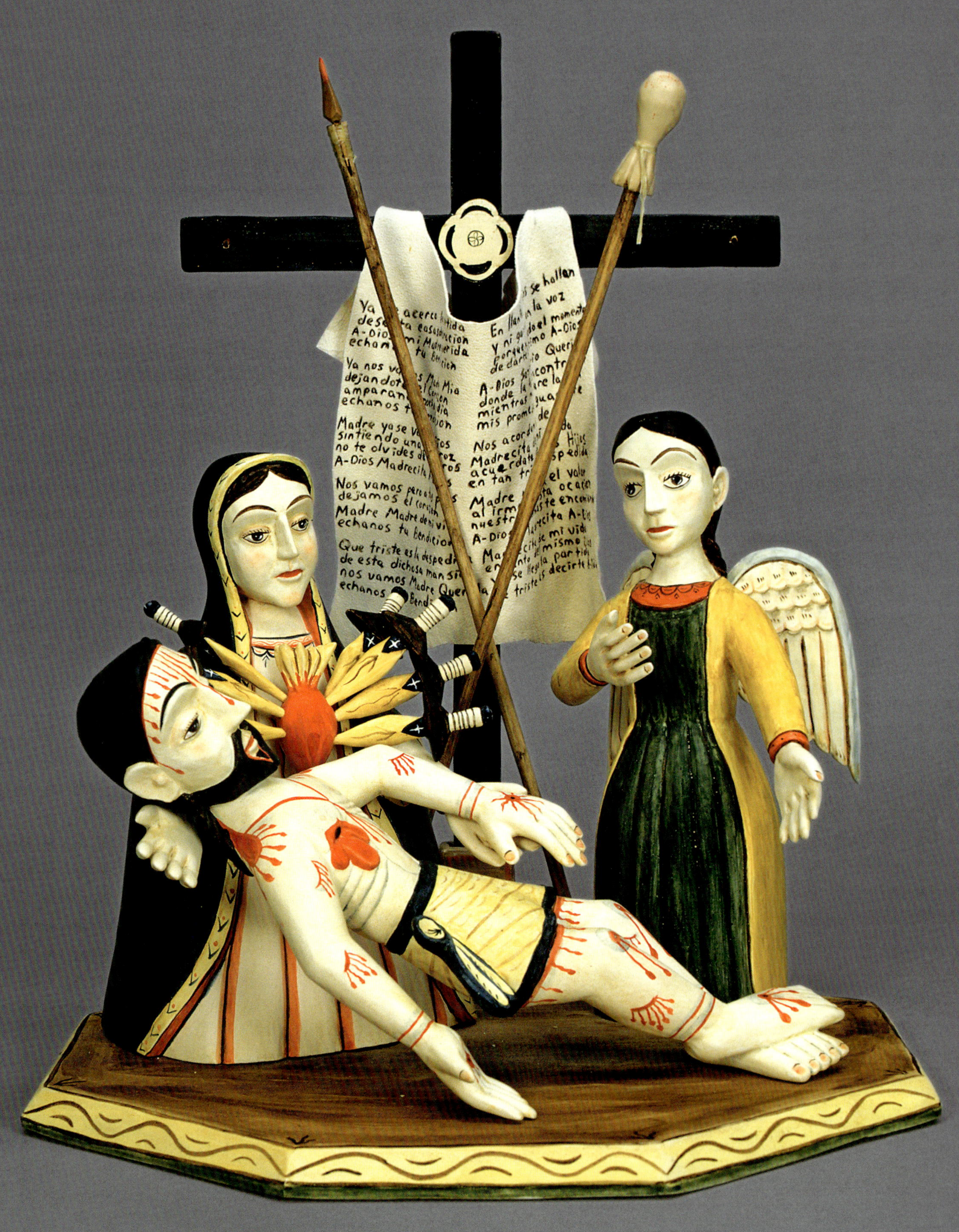
Ya nos vamos
Madre ya se va
sintiendo una
no te olvides de
A-Dios Madrecita
Nos vamos
dejamos el corazón
Madre Madre
echanos tu bendicion
Que triste es la despedida
de esta dichosa mansión
nos vamos Madre Quer
echanos
se hallan
En llanto la voz
y ni quedo el momento
A-Dios
A-Dios
donde la
mientras
mis prome
Nos acord
Madrecita
Hijos
acuerdate
en tan tri
el valor
Madre
al irm
te encomi
nuestr
A-Dios
se mi vida
mismo
triste es decirte

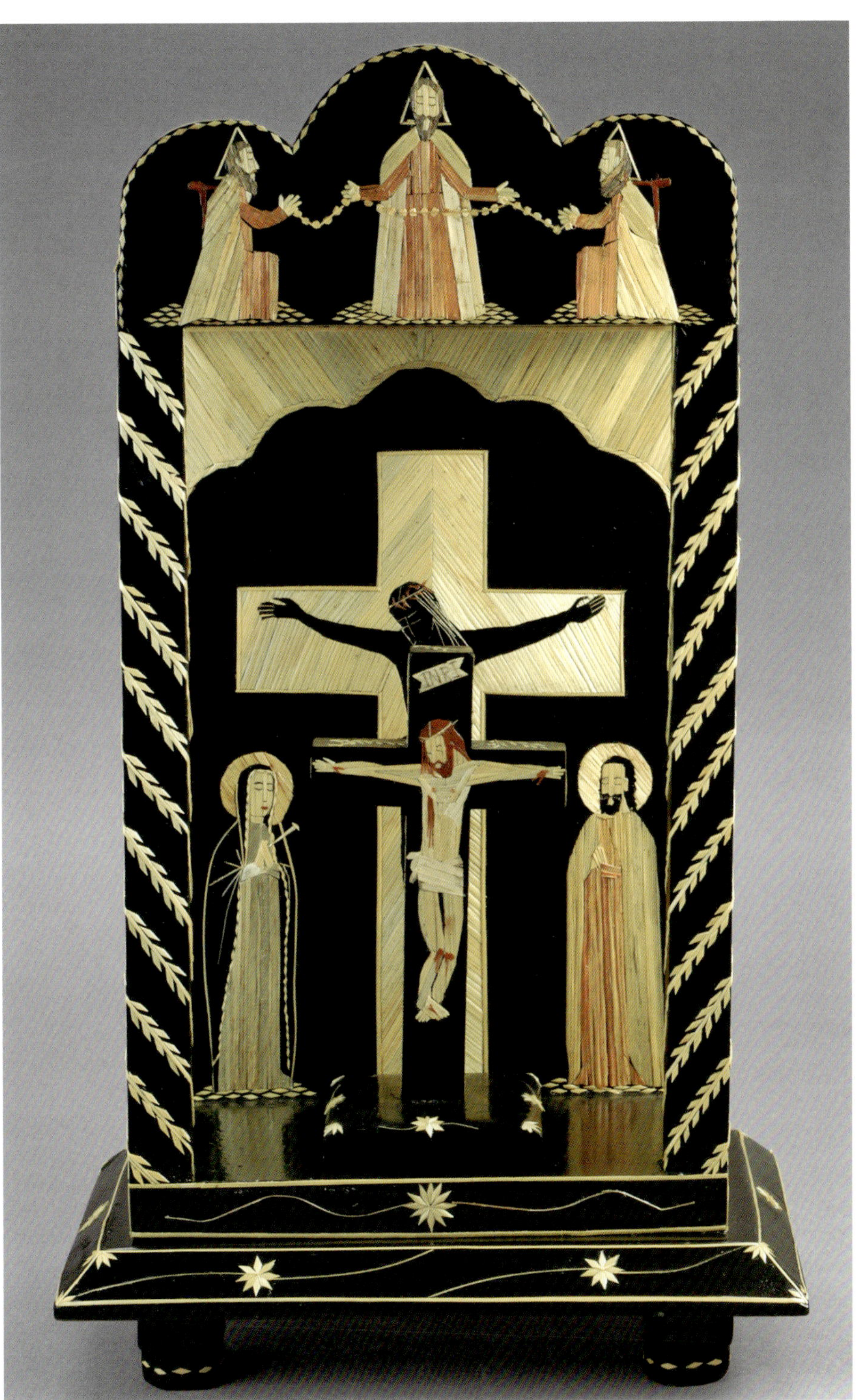

Cristo crucificado con Nuestra Señora de Dolores y San Juan Evangelista, by Diana Moya Lujan, 2000

Straw on pine

Gift from the
Diane and Sandy Besser Collection

IFAF

OPPOSITE:

Sangre de mi Jesus/Lágrimas de Maria, by Jerome Lujan, 1999

Aspen, pine, deer hide, natural pigments and piñon varnish

Gift from the
Diane and Sandy Besser Collection

IFAF

Nuestra Señora de la Immaculada Concepción, by John M. Gallegos, 2002

Watercolor on paper

Gift from the Diane and Sandy Besser Collection

IFAF

OPPOSITE:

Santo Niño de Atocha, by Gustavo Victor Goler. 2002

Watercolor on paper

Gift from the Diane and Sandy Besser Collection

IFAF

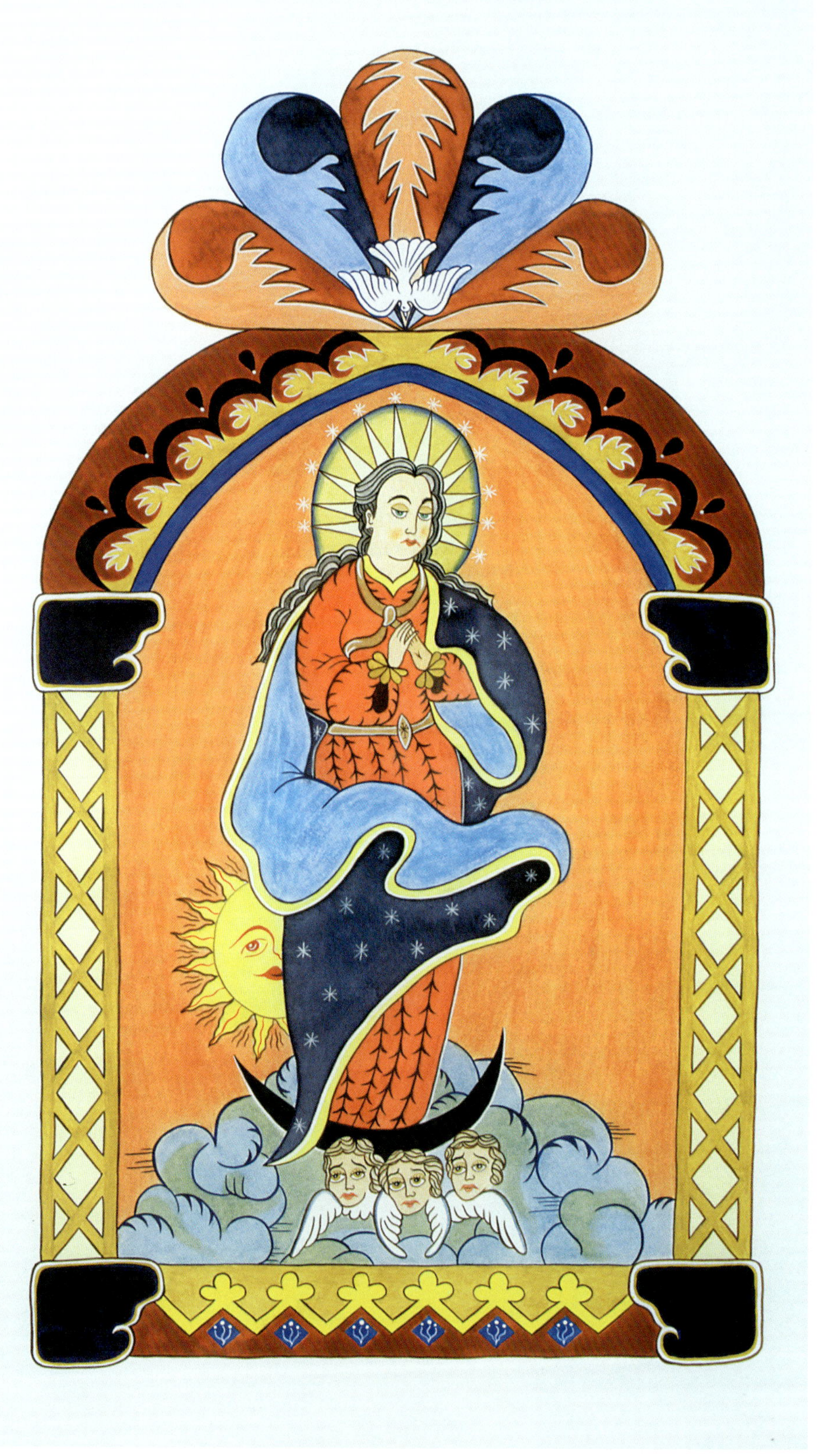

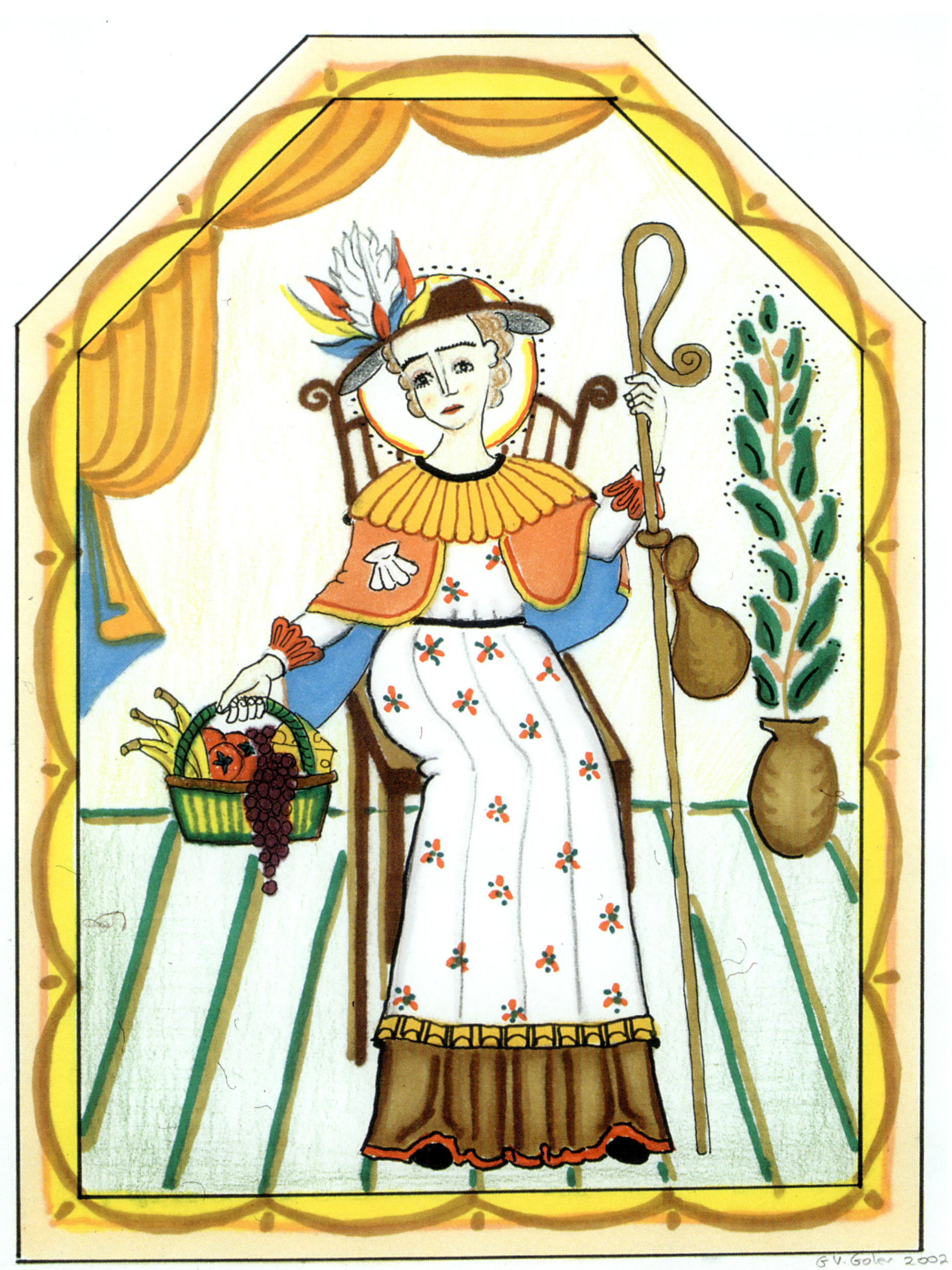

G.V. Goler 2002

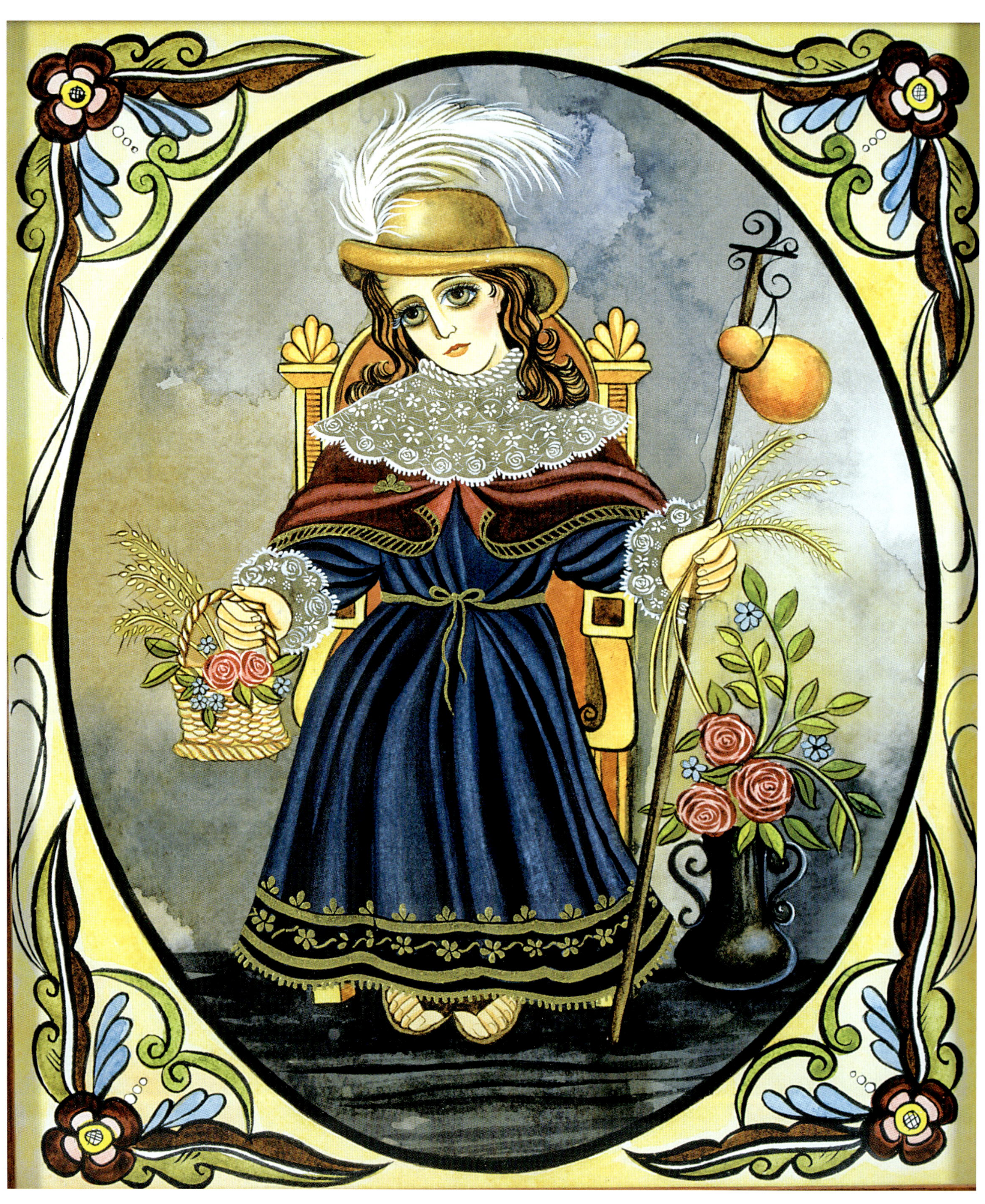

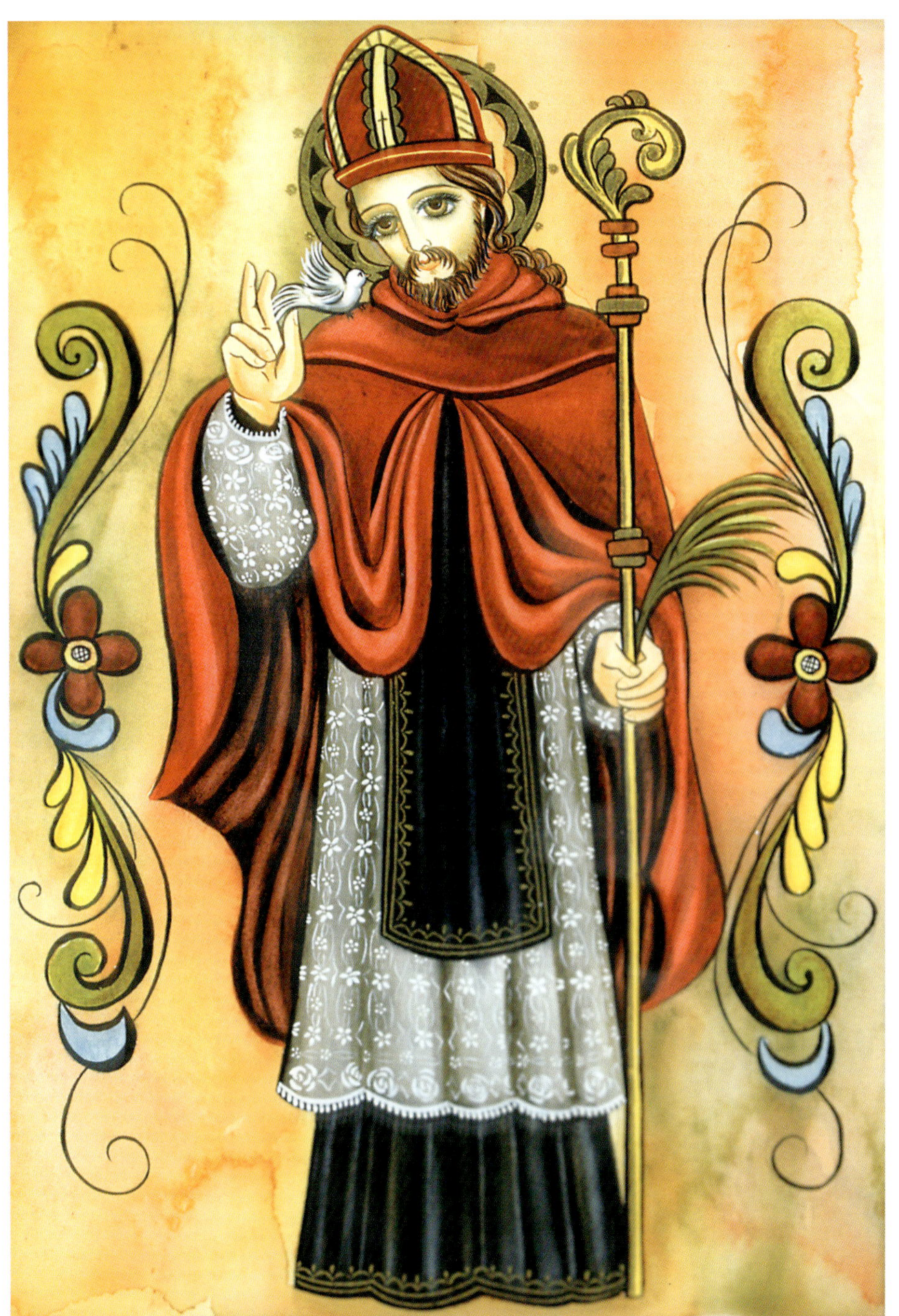

San Nicolás, by Arlene Cisneros Sena, 2002

Watercolor on paper and gold leaf

Gift from the Diane and Sandy Besser Collection

IFAF

OPPOSITE:

Santo Niño de Atocha, by Arlene Cisneros Sena. 2002

Watercolor on paper and gold leaf

Gift from the Diane and Sandy Besser Collection

IFAF

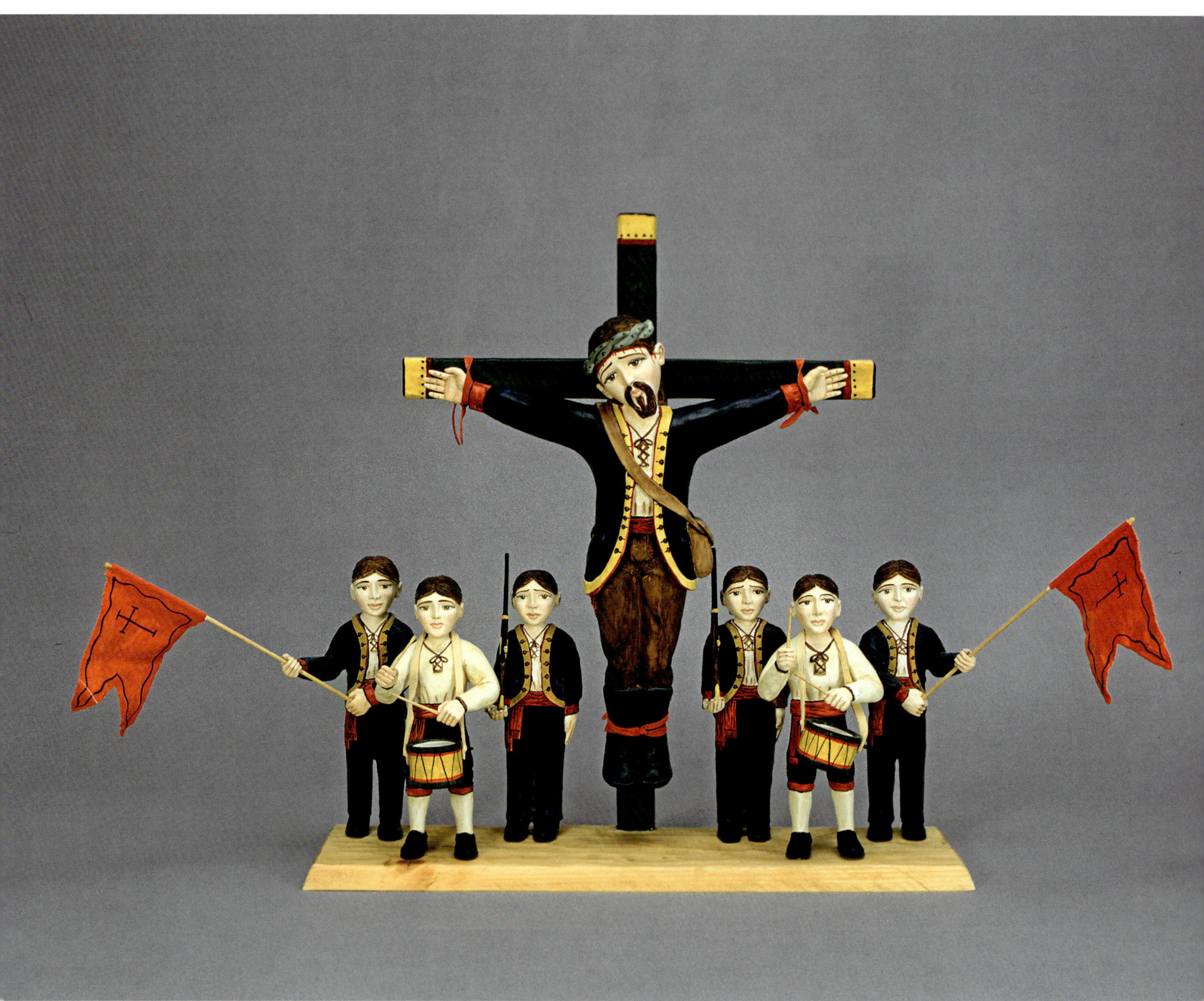

I Beat the Owl Lady

A "Collection" of Personal Anecdotes on Collecting

Tey Marianna Nunn

This essay will address my predisposed genetic attraction to collecting and collections. As someone who has gone through life with an intense need to amass objects and who is now (at the time of this writing) a curator in charge of the contemporary Hispano and Latino collections at the Museum of International Folk Art (MOIFA), I am in a unique position to examine this intriguing behavior. I will explore the nature and phases of my personal collections since childhood; the family lore and humor surrounding my collections; and finally how, now that I am an adult academic, my collections have spurred my research.

The title of this essay, "I Beat the Owl Lady," refers to the time when I won first place for "Collections" at the Arizona State Fair in the mid-1970s. My panda collection beat the owl collection, and I won a blue ribbon (which I still have) and a check for ten dollars (which I don't). It was a pivotal moment in my life because my collecting habits were validated and rewarded; it was also the moment when family members began to tease me about my penchant for amassing things—"Do you want this for your shopping bag collection?" "Are you saving this for your used toothpick collection?" "I thought you might want this for your dirty Kleenex collection." I've heard it all, but it hasn't stopped me.

OPPOSITE:
San Acacio, by Arthur López, 2003
Jelutong, pine, gessoed fabric, and natural pigments
Gift from the Diane and Sandy Besser Collection
IFAF

From purses to pandas, from miniatures to floating pens; from dolls to salt and pepper shakers; from things made from sugar to images of the Santo Niño de Atocha (the Holy Child of Atocha); and from "sleeping Mexican" stereotypes to Latina Barbies, my collections mark different phases in my life. Over the years, my interest in these objects has led me on physical and intellectual journeys that I might not have taken otherwise.

I STARTED YOUNG

Apparently it started early. My father remembers working in his study and hearing me make my way down the hall toward him, arms laden with purses—all of them—hanging off my little outstretched limbs. "Cathunk, Cathunk." as the numerous purses brushed the walls. My father refers to this as my first "conscious" collection. At that point I was not yet five years old.

From there, my penchant for assembling objects into collections broke loose—or, was set free—depending on how you want to look at it. Of course, I had stuffed animals, including my Bunny, whom I still cherish but whom I ignored for an entire year after I received her as a present on my second birthday. Instead, family lore says that I preferred the box she came in and they tell me that I played in the box for close to a year. The next "official" collection was dolls. Not just dolls from the good old United States of America but dolls from everywhere my family, relatives, and friends had lived or traveled.

My mother gave me an original Madame Alexander doll, which was dressed in a red corduroy outfit with a white fur-trimmed collar and muff, and a handmade Peruvian doll with baby. Both the Madame Alexander and the Peruvian dolls were hers as a child—and, of course, I still have them. I also still have two composition dolls from the 1920s, complete with their original wardrobes, which my mother purchased from the "lady who lived next door" in Portland, Oregon. My mother also found another large antique doll at either a garage sale or an antique store. She and my grandmother spent hours sewing an entire wardrobe for this doll. I remember my mother telling stories about sewing last-minute sequins on the doll's green taffeta dress at a cocktail party one Christmas Eve so that the doll and her outfits would be ready for me to open Christmas morning.

In addition to these heirloom dolls, I also owned the "usual suspects"—Raggedy Ann and Andy, and Barbies—but my doll collection became more and more international. My grandfather traveled around the world, always bringing me a doll from his trips to places like Japan, England, Ireland, and Australia. My mother, father, and I traveled to Mexico and Latin America, where we had family and where my parents did research. Although I took my Barbies with me on those trips, I still amassed a collection of handmade rag dolls and other types of dolls from each region or city that we visited. I think collecting these dolls, as well as miniature doll accessories and dollhouse furnishings, was a way for my parents to keep me entertained—but it was also a way to remember the experience and to learn about the culture and communities that created the dolls.

My father brought me dolls from his trips to Brazil, Argentina, Chile, and Bolivia. When queried about his recollections for this essay, my father replied: "I think you started collecting when we went on trips, then Barbies and clothes, and the little plastic cartoon characters that came with ice cream in Peru. Travel seems to have a lot to do with children collecting things. The idea of having one example of an item may come from Noah's ark, don't you think?" He also remarked that collecting occupies extra time. "When I collected stamps, I could think of nothing else. This went on for nearly two, maybe three years. And, I learned a lot of geography and history from it."[1]

Objects gathered on travels can also be tourist items and souvenirs—symbols of having "been there," much like the tokens of pilgrimages to holy religious sites that were probably the original souvenirs. Patssi Valdez, a Chicana artist and costume-and-set designer, who worked on the movie *Mi Familia,* often includes objects collected during her travels in her paintings, which are mostly of rooms. She once remarked to me that she likes to hang onto the feelings and memories she gets from her trips and experiences. And Patssi likes to surround herself with those reminders. For me as well, more often than not, collecting is about preserving memories and experiences. It is about immersing oneself in that moment in time.

In an interview with my mother and stepfather, more clues forced me to the comforting conclusion that a path was laid out for me early on and I had no choice but to collect. My mother said that I had been collecting for a long time: "Just one isn't good enough—you have to have five, six, or seven." She also said I was always careful with my things but that I was reluctant to get rid of my collections (ahh! the making of a good museum curator). My mother did admit that she is a shopper, like my father, and she felt that I collected "as a release, not a compulsive thing." Luckily, both my mother and stepfather admitted that they "supported, aided, and abetted," and to some extent they still do. I asked them about their collections and noted that my stepfather had a lot of cookbooks. "Isn't that a collection?" I asked. "No, he replied, "it's a library."[2]

In the early 1970s, my passion was panda bears—a collection that not only beat the owl lady but which at one point numbered over 500 objects. This collection may have been one of the key factors that started me on my road to being a curator and scholar. I was caught up in the "panda-monium" when, following President Richard Nixon's visit, China made a gift of two pandas (Ling-ling and Hsing-hsing) to the National Zoo in Washington, D.C. I read all the available books about pandas. I saved my money to buy panda things. I vividly remember dusting my panda shelves on the weekends, rearranging the pieces, and cataloguing the objects. With each addition I would announce the new total of objects. I visited my first live pandas at the London Zoo and then in Washington, D.C. I can remember stocking up on new acquisitions at the zoo gift shops. For me the excitement can only be compared to that of Christmas Day. Although most of my panda collections have been boxed up for years (first stored in my mother's garage and then in my own garage), my family, despite their protests and teasing, still adds to this collection every once in a while. A few years ago, after I had survived a traumatic car accident, my stepfather traveled to Washington, D.C., where the zoo had just obtained two new pandas. My stepfather returned with a panda sweat shirt, a panda float pen, and other panda items—not to mention the panda-embossed shopping bag from the shop that held all the other items. It was one of the most touching presents I had ever received, especially since my stepfather has been the person who has teased me the most about my collecting habits.

FLOATY PENS AND OTHER USEFUL COLLECTIBLES

When I was writing my doctoral dissertation, I became obsessed with the pens known as float pens (or floaty pens), made by Eskesen in Denmark. At that point, the collection had long been around in my house, numbering in the hundreds, but had not yet been formally recognized as a major collection. In fact, I can't even remember how my collection started: again, I think the pens were small items to be gleaned from travels that wouldn't take up too much room. I love these colorful pens with floating objects that move up and down against a scenic backdrop in the specially concocted mineral water. The floating pens—as well as the floating tooth brushes, letter openers, and key chains (not to mention the new "twist and click" style pens, which retract or open with a twist of the barrel)—are well-designed, and kitschy with a slightly retro flair. Essentially they are a smaller version of snow globes.

In a classic case of dissertation avoidance syndrome, I began to catalogue my floating pen collection. I searched the fledgling (at the time) World Wide Web for pens. I joined floating pen fan clubs and traded with other collectors. You'd be surprised at how many museum professionals collect floating pens! I even joined others to commission our own collectors' pen (one with a float pen passing between the hands of collectors).

My collection now numbers close to 4,000. I have one pen from Lourdes with the Virgin Mary floating up and down. I have one from the D-Day Museum in New Orleans, where a big D floats past the troops landing on Normandy Beach. I have a pen from Kellogg's Cereal City in Michigan. I have a variety of Star Trek designs, and I have the Buenos Aires floating pen with a couple tangoing up and down. I am currently after the Marshmallow Peeps fiftieth anniversary pen.[3] I also heard that there was a Chichen Itza (Mexico) floating pen about five or six years ago. At this point the Chichen Itza pen is my Holy Grail. Although I store my collection in boxes, I do take my pens out every once in a while and tilt them to watch the objects move. I actually find it very relaxing to take a moment and focus on the little things.

A sub-category of the floating pen collections is a very small pencil collection—mostly unsharpened. Unsharpened pencils have always held a fascination for me for two reasons. When I was little, my mother told me a story about my grandmother and her brother, who grew up in El Oro, Mexico. There, my great grandfather had a general store, and he received a shipment of beautiful Italian pencils wrapped with handmade paper. My grandmother and her brother sold the pencils to get money to see the movie *The Last Days of Pompeii.* As a kid, there was something magical, romantic, and adventurous for me about that story, and I imagined the pencils were very beautiful. The second reason I like these items is that when I was in elementary school we would sell pencils to raise money for school projects. I remember they were in primary colors, and I can also recall the sound they made as they clicked together in the pencil box outside the classroom door. I think the price was five cents each for red, blue, green, and yellow pencils.

A CURATOR-COLLECTOR

Now, as a museum curator, I often find myself reflecting on collecting and collectors. The personal has become the professional. I collect objects that become part of the permanent collection at the Museum of International Folk Art. I am responsible for the acquisition, care, exhibition, and research of twentieth- and now twenty-first-century Latina/o, Chicana/o, and Hispanic art, as well as pre-twentieth-century Spanish Colonial objects. My area of expertise also crosses over into our Mexican, Latin American, and Caribbean collections. On a daily basis, I work with artists (who often have the best collections because of their interest in a subject and because they trade art with other artists) and with collectors to arrange loans and gifts to the museum. I also receive general inquiries from collectors about objects in their collections. I lecture to individuals and groups about what a curator in charge of a collection does. In getting to know these kindred spirits, I always ask the following questions: "Have you always been a collector?" and "If so, what was the first thing you collected?"

One unusual example was the young girl, a member of an organization called Girls Inc., who came to visit the museum. I was giving the tour and asked if any of the participants collected anything. There were the usual answers from this pre-teen and teenage group: shells, rocks, toy horses, and dolls. But one young lady answered, "I collect dryer lint." Trying not to crack too obvious a smile I remarked that she was the first person I had ever met who collected dryer lint and then I asked her why. She answered enthusiastically, "Because it comes in so many colors." Right then I knew she would grow up to be creative, aesthetically inclined—and perhaps even a scholar and curator.

The Museum of International Folk Art is the home of the Alexander Girard Collection. Girard was a designer who, among other things, was responsible for the mod makeover of Braniff Airlines in the 1960s. He amassed an incredible collection of folk art from all over the world, but especially from Mexico and Latin America. Girard's gift helped to build a new wing on the museum. The exhibit, which took two years for Girard himself to install, features thousands of objects, set up in village scenes with plazas, markets, pueblos, stores, meals, religious processions, and Día de los Muertos (Day of the Dead) altars. But the story doesn't stop there. Girard only showed, at most, 15 percent of his collection in MOIFA's permanent upstairs exhibit gallery. Downstairs, in collections storage, there are thousands of additional objects. As a true collector, Girard

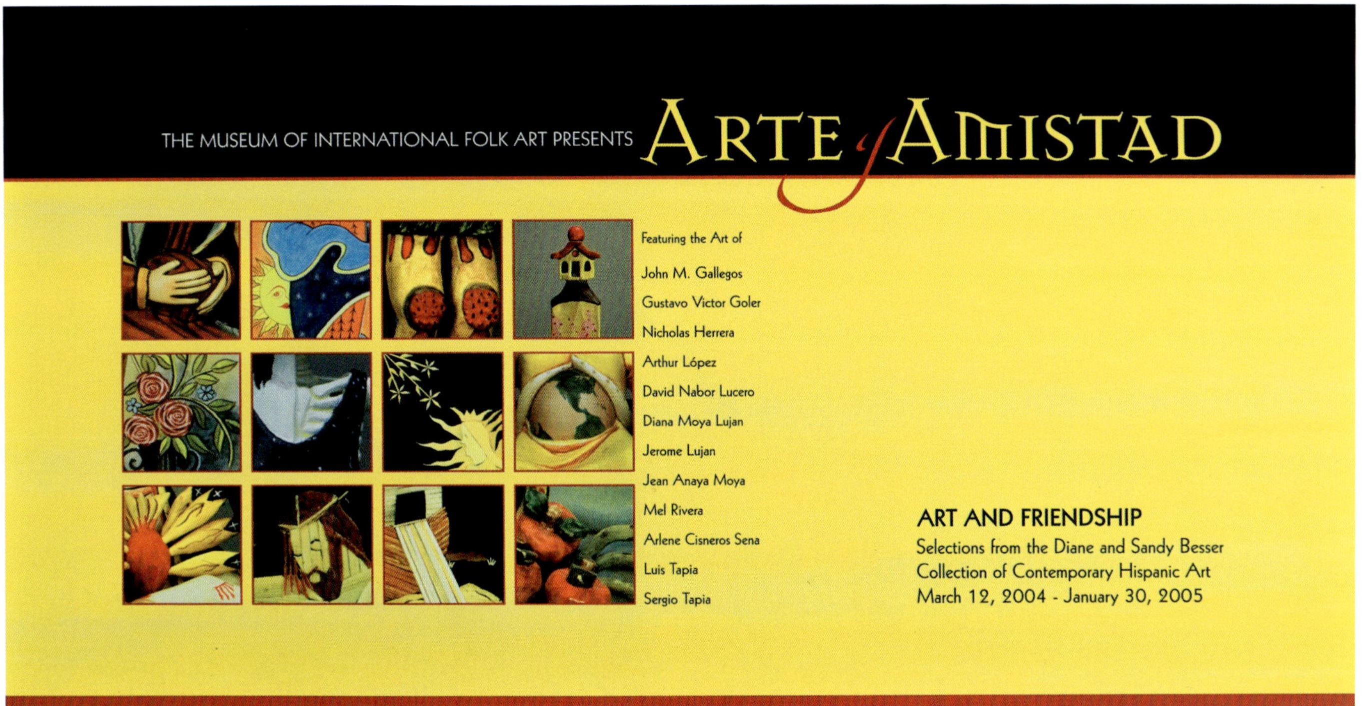

Arte y Amistad, Exhibition announcement, 2004; design by Anita Quintana, Media Mantis

couldn't just stop at one. Recently, a museum visitor told me that he had once visited Alexander Girard in his Santa Fe home. Although Girard had a storage unit, his house was filled with his treasures. The visitor told me about the armchairs in the Girard living room: one could only perch precariously on the seats, as the arms of the armchairs were covered with tiny objects.

In March 2004, I curated the MOIFA exhibition, *Arte y Amistad* (art and friendship): Selections from the Diane and Sandy Besser Collections of Contemporary Hispanic Art. The show featured thirty-two masterpieces made by twelve Nuevomexicana/o artists.[4] In addition, much of the overall Besser Collection is a promised gift to MOIFA. In my essays for the gallery guide, I focused on the Bessers as collectors. Sandy Besser started out collecting swizzle sticks and matchbook covers, moved on to postcards, and then to drawings and Hispanic art. My gallery guide also gave the biographies of the twelve participating artists, along with a brief statement about what each artist in the show collected. Only one of the artists didn't really collect anything; the rest did, and I was interested in the role collecting played in their lives and their creativity. For example, as a child, Arthur López, a relatively new, groundbreaking artist, collected car-shaped Avon bottles. (Actually, he blames this collection on his mother who

Our Lady of the Immaculate Conception altar screen, by John M. Gallegos, 2001

Sugar pine, natural pigments, and gouache

Gift from the Diane and Sandy Besser Collection

IFAF

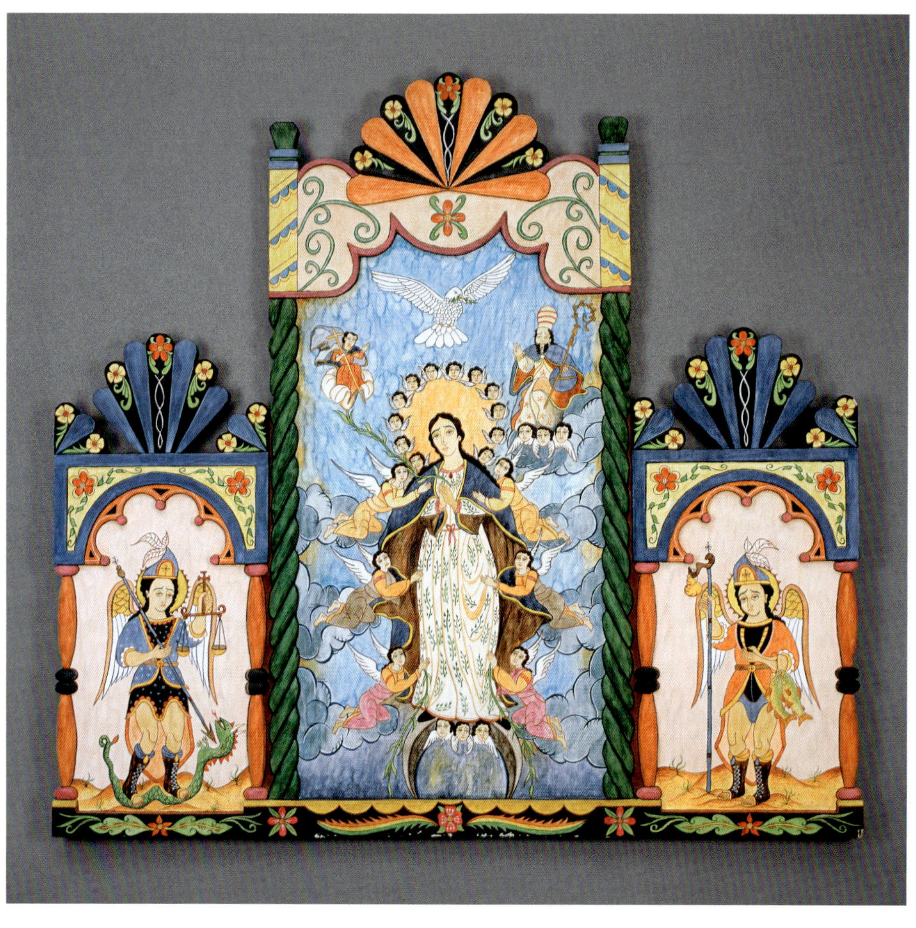

bought the bottles for him at garage sales.) Now, López collects art by fellow New Mexican artists. David Nabor Lucero collects works by fellow Hispanic artists, but with a twist. He buys from the new artists who aren't selling anything at Santa Fe's annual Spanish Market. As a child, Arlene Cisneros Sena used to collect holy cards because of the gold and lace elements. The influence that these delicate aesthetic details have had on her work is obvious.

My office has served as a venue for my collection of Latina Barbie Dolls—some by Mattel and some Barbie look-alikes from Mexico. The official Mattel dolls include Puerto Rican Barbie, Chilean Barbie, Peruvian Barbie, Inca Princess Barbie (in blue taffeta), Spanish Matador Barbie, and the most recent acquisition, Princess of Ancient Mexico. The unofficial Latina Barbie collection includes China Poblana Barbie, Yucateca Barbie, Xochimilco Barbie, and Tarahumara Barbie. I am now in search of Adelita Barbie and Aztec Princess Barbie, both of whom I once saw in Juarez.

OPPOSITE:

Folding altar screen, by Arlene Cisneros Sena, 2000

Handmade gesso, pigments, gold leaf, and piñon varnish

Gift from the Diane and Sandy Besser Collection

IFAF

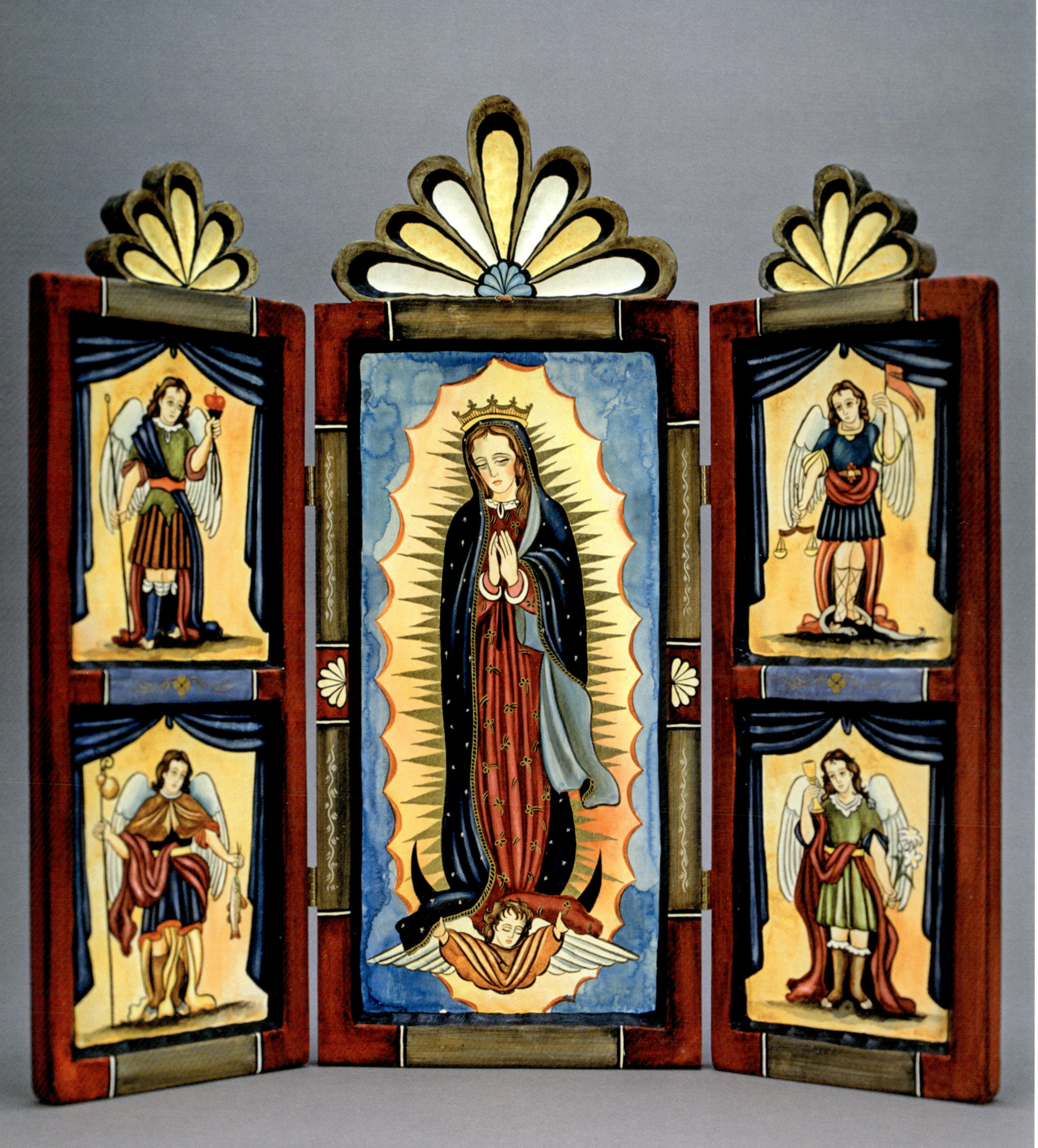

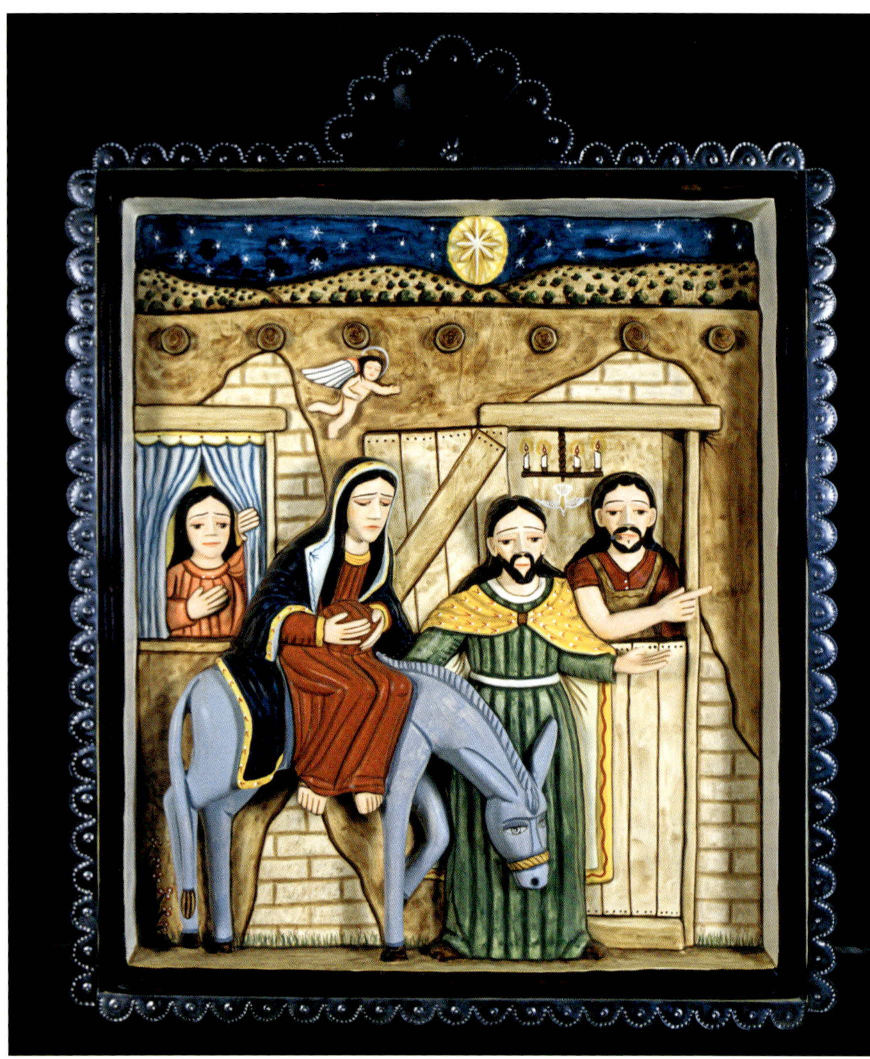

No Room at the Inn,
by David Nabor Lucero, 2002

Gesso relief with natural pigments, tin and wood frame

Partial gift of the Diane and Sandy Besser Collections

MOSCA

My office also contains my collection of unusual religious votive candles, including "Ajo Macho" (macho garlic), Martin Luther King (purchased in Ybor City, Florida), and the "lucky bingo" votive candle. More recently, I acquired an "Our Lady of the Garage Sale" candle. The explanation on the back of the candle tells the user to light the candle on Friday night and to repeat a prayer that includes the phrases "Ensure that I will know the difference between treasure and trash. And keep the best deals hidden from my competitors. And with your great power keep me from risking my retirement fund on tchotchkes!"

The other objects in this personal and public space are my collections of Chicana/o and Latina/o posters, the Chicano action figures known as Homies, and lots of examples of religious kitsch given to me by friends and family. Among the examples of the last category are my Virgen de Guadalupe (Virgin of Guadalupe) rose-scented aerosol spray room deodorizer and my pope soap on a rope. The general observer might gasp (or be awe-inspired) at such a display of popular culture and religious commentary, but I can assure you that they are all work-related and genuine objects worthy of academic study.

The collections came from my scholarly interests, or perhaps my scholarly interests developed so that I could justify these collections. I am deeply intrigued by popular culture and its connections to art history and social commentary, and this focus has been combined with my area of expertise in Latino arts. Most recently my research interests have led me to collect vintage China Poblana dresses[5] from the 1930s and 1940s, as well as hand-painted Mexican circle skirts from the 1950s.

These works showcase some amazing artistry, as they are all hand painted and incredible examples of wearable art. Many of them have hand-sewn sequins and others are painted on black velvet. A few were signed by the artists. They feature exquisite artwork and design, laying the groundwork for a future research project on the makers of these skirts and their role in shaping Mexican tourist fashion.

Collecting is a part of who we are and who we want to be. Surrounding yourself with things and amassing multiples of objects are considered by some to be a sickness. But I think exactly the opposite. Collecting helps you feel alive—because there's the thrill of the hunt, the zest in the quest (a term coined by two friends who are also collectors), the educational component of buying locally on trips, the magical attraction you have for something, and the affinity you can feel for an object from another culture. All of these factors, and more, help to retain a memory—and these memories become part of your life, your identity, your very self. As far as I'm concerned, one object is not enough to tell a story (you need at least three). But all collections have a story to tell; and perhaps the most important story is the one they tell about the collector him- or herself.

Notes

1. Frederick M. Nunn, e-mail message to Tey Marianna Nunn, 25 November 2003. Collection of the author.
2. Tey Diana Rebolledo and Michael M. Passi, interview by the author, Fall 2003.
3. Peeps® are the marshmallow candies in the shape of chicks and bunnies that are sold at Easter.
4. Nuevomexicana/o: a Spanish-speaking resident of New Mexico.
5. China Poblana, a style of dress from Puebla, Mexico, is said to have originated with an immigrant from China. China Poblana is characterized by embroidered peasant-style blouses and colorful skirts, which often display the national symbols of Mexico.

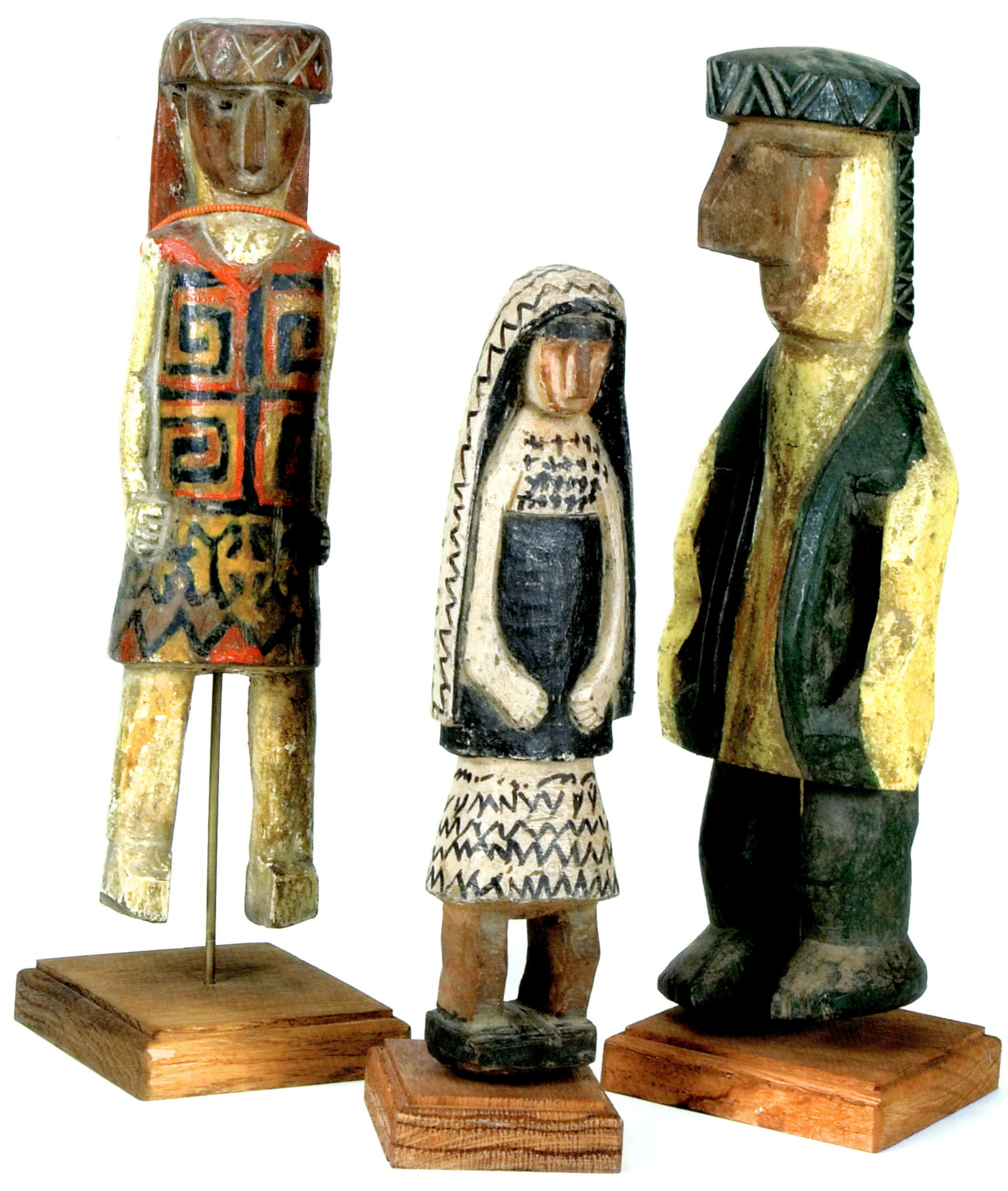

On Collecting

The View from the Director's Office

Joyce Ice

Museums, as stewards, hold in their collections objects and works of art that are deemed to be of significant cultural and artistic value and that express the great range of human creativity throughout history. Donations from private collectors have enhanced, expanded, and strengthened museum collections, both at the time of the gift and over the years, as the collections create a legacy that future generations can learn from and enjoy. With the transformative gift of a significant collection, an individual collector can help a museum to realize its full potential and to achieve higher stature as an art institution. Museums carry on the legacies of donors by safely housing and caring for collections, and by making the art works available to a wide public audience. As cultural institutions, museums value research, interpretation, stewardship, care, maintenance, and conservation of their collections—all of which are major responsibilities central to their primary mission.

OPPOSITE:
Curing dolls (*nuchus*), 20th century
Wood and paint
Kuna people, San Blas Islands, Panama
IFAF Purchase from the Diane and Sandy Besser Collection

COLLECTOR-DONORS AND MOIFA

The Museum of International Folk Art (MOIFA) in Santa Fe is one public institution that has benefited since its beginning from the generosity of private collectors. Museum founder Florence Dibell Bartlett was an avid collector who traveled widely and who assembled the collection that was to become the core of the museum's holdings. Concerned by the threats that global industrialization and urbanization posed to the sustainability of folk art, she obtained examples of traditional art from many different regions of the world that expressed the makers' artistry, function, and cultural identity.

In Santa Fe, Bartlett found a receptive climate in which to establish a museum that would house and exhibit her collection and share it with the public. Her hope was that the museum would attract additional donors who would give their own art to the collection—and she chose the name Museum of International Folk Art to encourage a wide range of future donations, rather than incorporating her own surname into the museum's name (as her sister and brother-in-law did when they founded the Heard Museum in Phoenix).

After the museum opened to the public in 1953, twenty-five years passed before it again captured the country's attention with the news of an important donation; the Girard Foundation Collection, given by Alexander and Susan Girard in 1978, was a transformative gift for the museum. When the museum opened a 10,000-square-foot exhibition, Multiple Visions: A Common Bond, in 1982, it drew national attention for the exhibition's ground-breaking, unconventional design, and for the sheer immensity of the Girard Collection. Characterized by multiples, miniatures, ephemera (including mass-produced, manufactured objects as well as the handmade), this vast collection quintupled the size of the museum's holdings. Staff and volunteers spent years in accessioning and cataloging the contents of this collection, much of it having been stored in boxes neatly labeled in Alexander Girard's hand.

The Girards were talking with other museums, too, and negotiations that stretched over several years finally resulted in a gift that transferred the enormous collection of 106,000 pieces to the state of New Mexico. The terms of the agreement with New Mexico delegated control over the design and contents of the permanent exhibition to Alexander Girard. He installed the exhibition in the gallery of the newly built Girard Wing, the first major addition to the original museum building, which had been designed by noted Santa Fe architect John Gaw Meem.

Tensions ran high as the opening date neared and the exhibit installation was running behind schedule. With time running out, the relationship between the collector/donor/designer and the museum director was strained. Both were strong-willed individuals and as a result of the tension between them, their communications flowed through other staff members. Nevertheless, the exhibition proved a huge popular success. Today, museum visitors continue to be enthralled by the exhibition and to be fascinated with Girard—the man who was responsible not only for collecting the vast number of objects, but also for designing an exhibition that displays approximately 10 percent of the total Girard Collection. Along with the visiting public, members of the museum profession also respond to the enormity of the collector's vision and the challenges posed by the level of care and the time required to maintain the exhibition.

In 1995, inspired in part by Alexander Girard's creativity and great sense of curiosity, Lloyd Cotsen, former CEO and President of the Neutrogena Corporation, donated the extensive Neutrogena Collection of some 2,600 objects and textiles to the Museum of International Folk Art. As had been the case with the Girard donation, a number of other museums were also interested in obtaining the Neutrogena Collection. However, strong support from then Governor of New Mexico Gary Johnson and his wife, the late Dee Johnson, from board members, and from private collectors affiliated with the museum helped convince Mr. Cotsen to choose MOIFA. Again, the donor's understanding with MOIFA was based on the commitment of the New Mexico state legislature to appropriate capital funds for the construction of a new wing, which would be used for storage and exhibition purposes.

This major collection required both additional space and additional staff to store, care for, and exhibit the artworks; and the terms of the gift agreement required the museum to show 80 percent of the collection in the first five years after the opening of the Neutrogena Wing. In keeping with the vision of the museum's founder, Mr. Cotsen also generously established an endowment to provide funds for care, curation, and exhibition of the Neutrogena Collection, as well as for the educational programs related to it. The Neutrogena Wing opened in 1998 and was able to meet the 80 percent goal; the second five years of the Wing's operation were designated to showcase textiles and costumes in the Cotsen Gallery exhibitions.

Like the collections that have come to the Museum of International Folk Art in past years, the Diane and Sandy Besser Collection represents a significant addition to the museum's present collection and establishes a legacy that will continue to be appreciated for generations to come. The 2006 donation from the

Besser Collection has already helped to prompt other gifts to MOIFA's overall collection and has attracted interest from other collectors. No doubt the Besser donation will encourage still others to consider making their own gifts of artwork and monetary contributions to the museum.

THE COLLECTOR-MUSEUM RELATIONSHIP

Collectors, dealers, artists, and museums enjoy symbiotic relationships that can be described as cooperative, competitive, combative, beneficial, and detrimental—often all at the same time. Some people become collectors by happenstance—falling into it by accident through a chance encounter or by coincidence—and have gone on to build eclectic and wonderful collections. Some individuals may begin collecting in childhood and bring a clear focus to their collecting from the very earliest stages; others discover their zeal for collecting later in life, but they, too, are hooked on collecting forever after, unable to help themselves.

In my observation, serious collectors speak a common language, half in jest and half in serious tones. When they describe the appeal that collecting works of art holds for them, they use a vocabulary of illness and addiction as symptoms of their condition or affliction—words like craving, obsessive-compulsive, incurable sickness, tortured passion, and unrequited love—all reflecting the power that this activity holds over its adherents. If humans are genetically predisposed to collecting, then it may be difficult, if not impossible, to give up this behavior. And few collectors, in my experience, express any desire to do so. Ownership brings intense pleasure and further attests to one's good taste, trained eye, and skill in negotiating, and achieving what one wants. Collectors are devotees to a cult of art and beauty, practicing rituals of pursuit and possession. And while they may moan about the amount of time and money they have spent over the years amassing their collections, it is a half-hearted complaint that is more than offset by the sheer delight they derive from their collections and from the process of collecting.

The exciting process of discovering and obtaining desirable objects calls forth an aesthetic high, not unlike a runner's endorphins or a gambler's rush—a habitual response that is at once satisfying and yet never fully satiated. The process of collecting, the thrill of discovery, the hunt, the competition, all drive many collectors in an unending quest.

Sandy Besser describes his collecting philosophy in baseball terms: "Hit 'em where they ain't." In other words, look to areas where the field is relatively

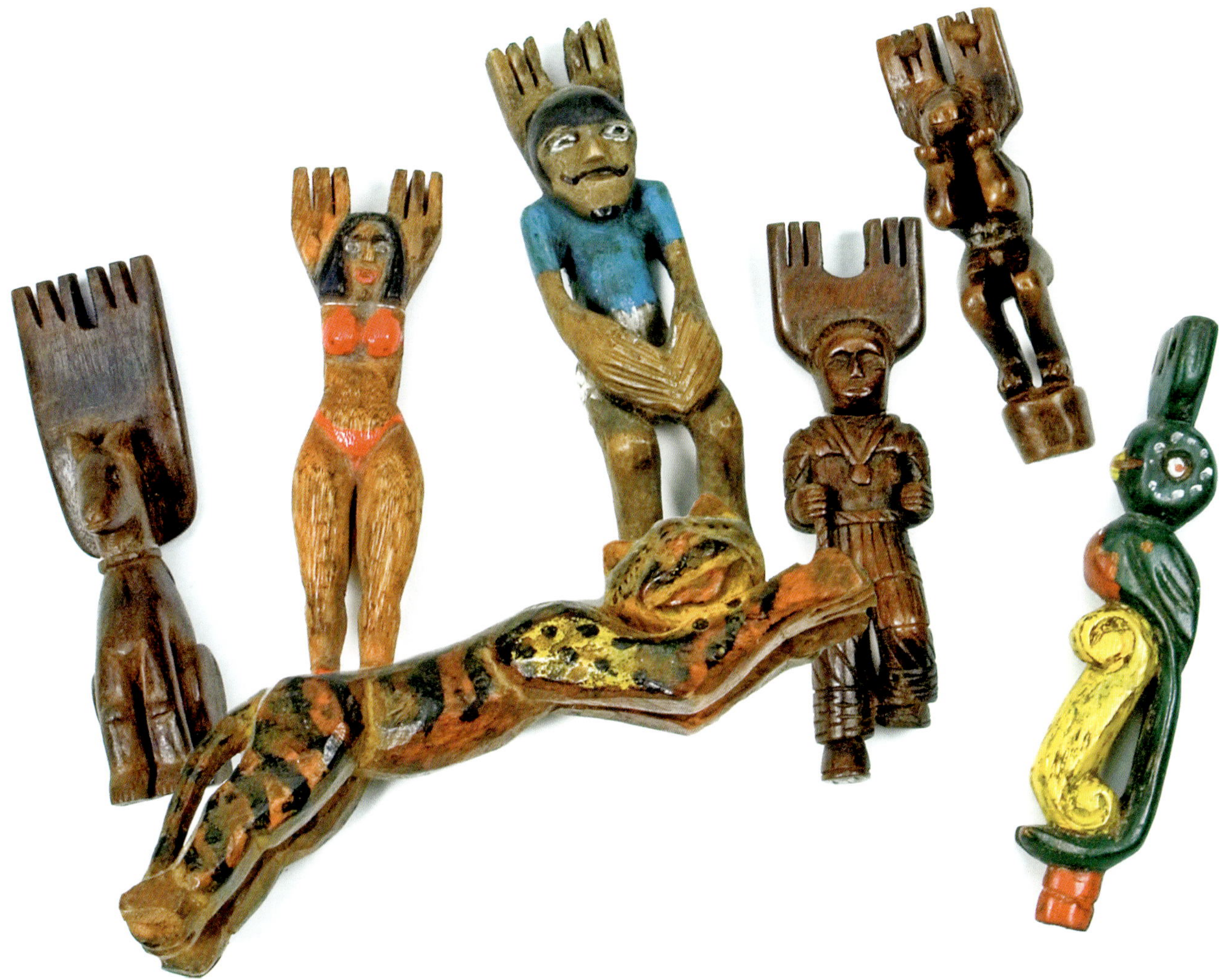

Slingshots, ca. 1950

Used by farmers to kill birds and rodents, these carved wooden handles demonstrate the varied images used on a single form.

Guatemala

Wood and paint

IFAF Purchase from the Diane and Sandy Besser Collection

empty and collectors are nowhere to be seen. Every collector fantasizes about finding and acquiring outstanding pieces that increase the value of a collection in terms of its worth and significance, but at less than the going rate for the pieces. With a keen eye and strategic purchases, such collectors can find objects of high quality without having to pay the high prices commanded by sought-after pieces in other categories that have higher art world profiles.

A parallel approach for Besser has been to discover an unknown or little recognized artist whose work represents a new find on the artistic frontier. Sandy Besser enjoys being able to support and promote living artists by helping raise their profiles in the art world, boosting the artist, and making an impact on the market.

Collectors in specific geographic or cultural areas and/or genres of art are well aware not only of where specific works of art are located, and who owns them at any given time, but collectors in a specific area or genre also follow the acquisitions, holdings, donations, sales, and trades. Once the majority of the best material is either privately held or has entered museum collections, the further growth of a particular type of collection may be stymied. Over time, if an individual has patience (and survives other private collectors), pieces may eventually enter the marketplace again as estates are dispersed and sold.

Collectors can visualize others reacting to the collection with an anticipation akin to that of a violinist rehearsing alone in a great concert hall and imagining a huge audience responding to his virtuosity with admiring and enthusiastic applause. Similarly, the process of collecting can be regarded as a performance art, an act of creativity, and an art form in and of itself. Collectors make artistic, aesthetic, and financial choices when they interact with dealers and artists about what works of art are to be collected. Such collectors continually refine their eye and expand their knowledge about specific genres of art as they seek out the best examples of the forms that speak to them. Collectors tend to have a strong visual memory that allows them to recall salient details of their own objects as they consider the purchase of other pieces and to assess how the objects will look together. This keen visual sense is also key in deciding how to best display pieces in relationship to one another so that the individual pieces call attention to the aesthetic properties within a grouping.

After building a collection and developing it as far as possible, a collector may need to change direction because of a changing market with rising prices. Pieces similar to those acquired in the early stages of the formation of a collection may no longer be obtainable. Despite having a reputation as an astute collector who is sought after as a client by dealers and gallery owners, a collector may be forced to change direction because of a worldwide unavailability of specific forms, for example, because of the displacements of war, natural disasters, economic upheavals, or degraded environmental conditions. Whether specific types of art are no longer being produced, or the quality of what is being made has deteriorated, the ultimate effect is to slow or halt the circulation of high-quality objects. In addition to these considerations, the process of selecting which pieces will be traded, sold, or donated involves still more choices that affect the quality of the collection, while at the same time providing additional funds with which to buy new works of art and freeing up more display space for the collection.

Regardless of market circumstances, at some point most serious collectors begin to realize that if they desire their collections to remain intact beyond their lifetimes, they must make plans for the future. Children and other heirs may appreciate a collection and all that it represents but may not share the same passion for collecting and/or are unwilling or unable to (or not interested in) taking on the expense and responsibility for the care and keeping of a major collection.

Collectors may then approach museums as they begin to think about a permanent home for their collections, and the process of moving a collection from a private owner to a public institution begins. From the museum's standpoint, the process by which a museum acquires a collection must begin with a discussion about whether a specific collection is appropriate for the museum within the framework of its mission. A collection may be one of the finest of its kind and still not be the right match for a specific museum. In these cases, museum staff may refer the potential donor to other institutions that might be a better fit for the collection.

If the collection is in keeping with the mission and collecting priorities of the museum, the next step involves assessing how well the collection meets certain criteria for museum acquisitions. And the criteria for adding to a museum's collection are often different from a collector's own criteria for acquiring new pieces. By design, the decisions made by museums regarding the acquisitions of collections are more difficult to reverse than the choices made by collectors about pieces for their private collections. De-accessioning pieces from a museum collection is a slow, deliberate process that requires that the objects proposed for removal from the collection meet strict criteria. The number of objects that need to be de-accessioned can be reduced by making thoughtful and intentional acquisitions in the first place.

Ideally, museum acquisitions should strengthen existing collections by providing additional examples of specific art forms that allow comparative studies, as well as fill in gaps in the story of a culture or artist. But if a donor's primary interest in the objects is not closely related to a museum's research priorities—for example, if the donor is interested only in the formal properties of the objects themselves and not in their history—then the documentation that accompanies the gift of a

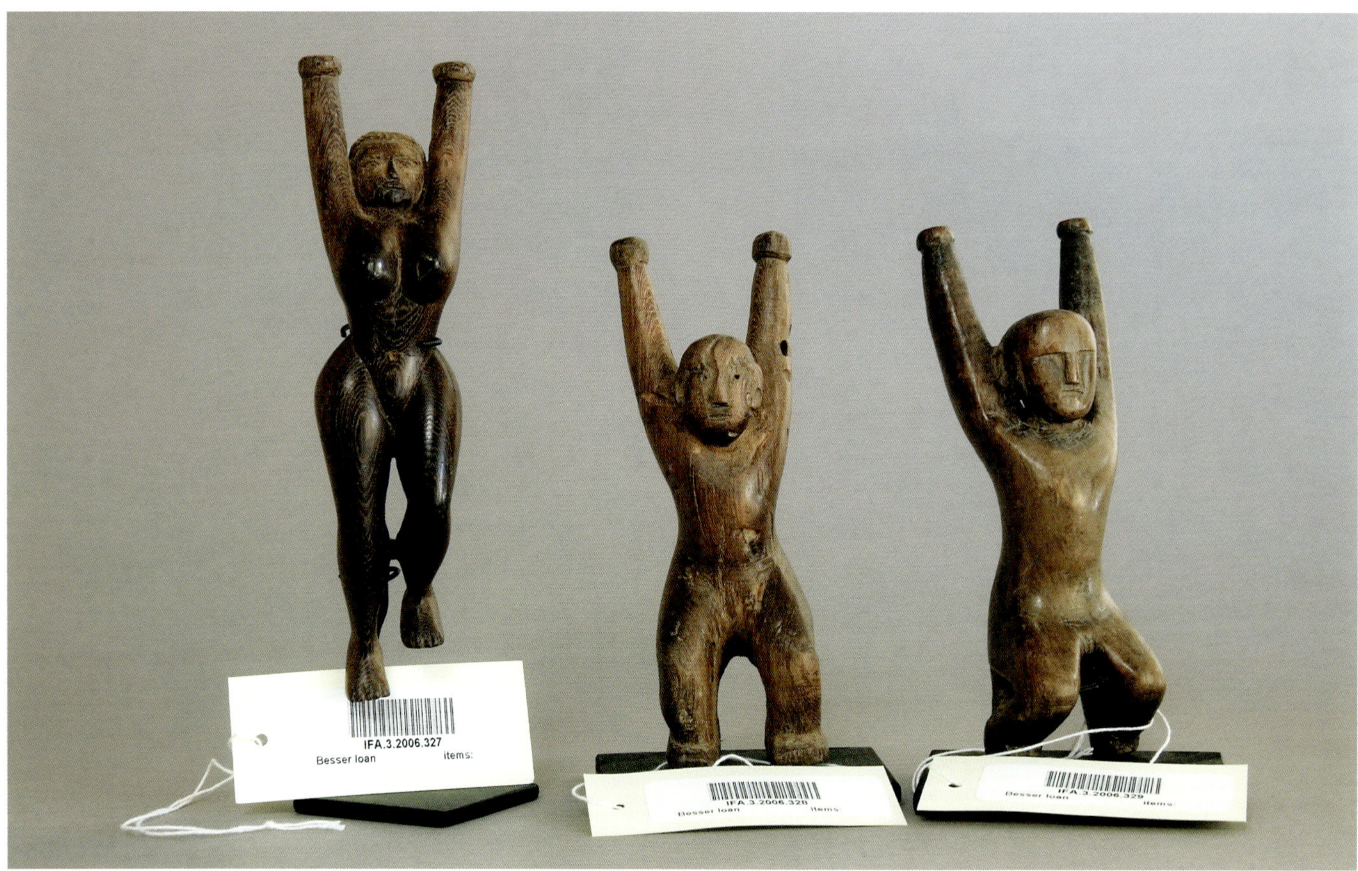

Slingshots, mid 20th century

Burma

Wood, paint, twine, and rubber

IFAF Purchase from the Diane and Sandy Besser Collection

collection may not meet the minimum levels of professional museum standards. A proposed donation is more valuable to a museum (for purposes of research and exhibition) if the donation is accompanied by as much information as possible: for example, information about the artist/maker, culture group, date, origin, dimensions, and materials; where the artwork was obtained or purchased and from whom; the price, if applicable; and an appraiser's valuation. In addition, museums prefer that collectors provide photographs and/or digital images of the art objects.

The condition of a piece is another determining factor in the museum's decision-making process, as is the overall level of conservation treatment needed for the collection. After a conservator surveys the artworks, the museum will consider all this information in determining whether it has adequate resources to care for the collection.

Some private individuals are able to house their collections in climate-controlled galleries and storage areas that rival or are better than the collections storage rooms and vaults of many museums. Other collectors live quite comfortably

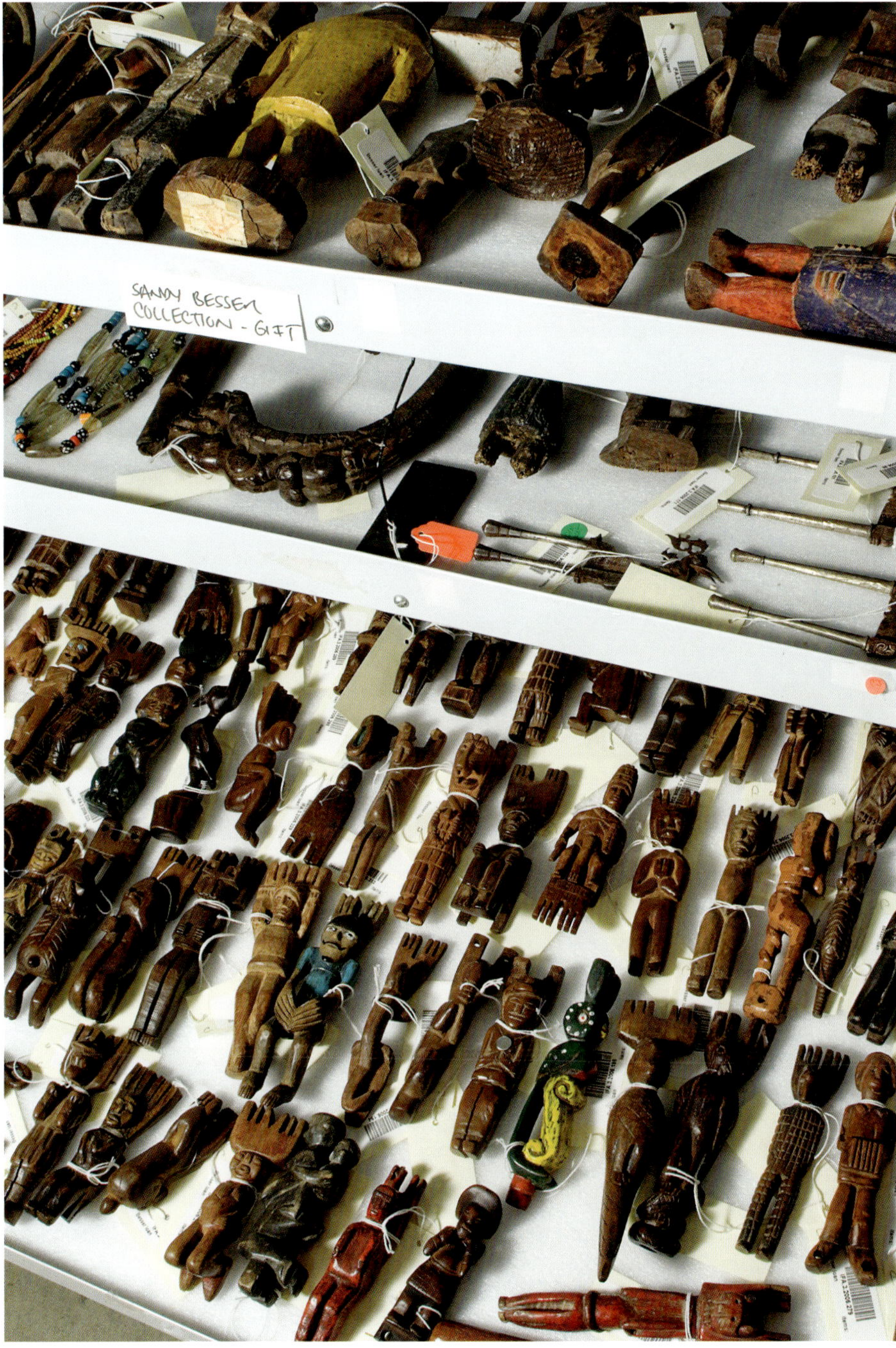

Slingshots, ca. 1950

Storage drawer with bar-coded inventory tags

Guatemala

Wood and paint

IFAF Purchase from the Diane and Sandy Besser Collection

with their collections displayed in their homes, integrated with their daily living; however, this choice may subject pieces to various threats: high light levels, dust, food, beverages, pests, excessive vibration, exposure to fireplace and cigarette smoke, and the shifts of temperature and humidity that place fragile and more vulnerable types of artworks at risk. Regardless of where and how the collection has been kept, when the objects enter the public space of a museum, the way in which they are regarded and their treatment will undergo drastic changes. Most likely, they will be placed in isolation to ensure that no pests have piggybacked a ride into the storage areas. The artworks will be handled with gloves (literally), tagged, catalogued, recorded, and monitored.

Although professionally run museums have specific policies and procedures that guide and regulate their acquisition and management of collections, interpersonal skills are also essential to the process. Discussions between collector, museum director, curator, and board members may continue over a series of meetings and visits that can take weeks, months, or even years to reach their conclusion. As one of my colleagues has said, it is easy to accept a donation for the museum collection but much more difficult to gracefully decline a proposed gift and still remain on good terms with the collector.

Even when the collection is a good match for the museum, not every piece in the collection may be appropriate: a piece may lack adequate provenance or may not be considered of sufficient quality to warrant its inclusion; the condition of the work may be unstable; or pieces may duplicate those already in the museum's collection. Collectors may take an "all-or-nothing" stance when they initiate a discussion offering a collection to a museum for purchase or as a gift. "Cherry-picking," which refers to selecting only the best pieces and declining others, for whatever reason, is greatly disliked by collectors, who have strong opinions and attachments when it comes to their collections. They may feel that they themselves have already done the cherry-picking in the formation and editing of a collection; therefore, the chances that a collector will feel insulted or take offense are high at this stage of negotiations.

The delicate balance of personal and professional relationships between the individual collector/family and the individuals representing the museum is one that can be easily upset by a careless word or irreparably harmed by an unintentional but perceived slight. In a heightened emotional context, the process of donating a collection to a museum is not unlike a courtship ritual or dance, and it can be a love-hate relationship in which the parties experience both attraction and repulsion as dreams are fulfilled and/or disappointed. During the process the parties may have to come to terms with unrealistic expectations, resolve hurt feelings from past encounters, stroke egos, and untangle legal complications.

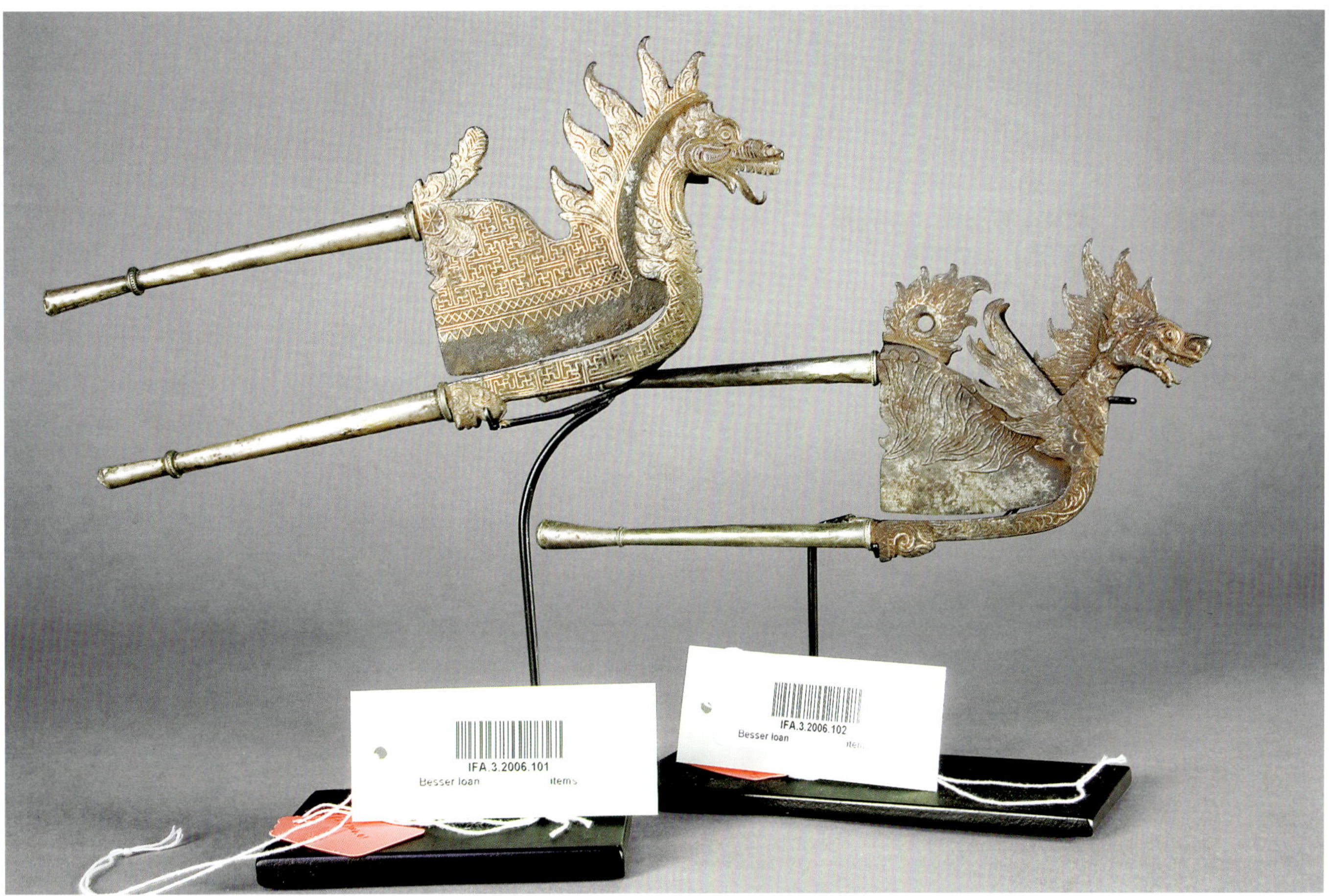

Betel nut cutters, with bar-coded inventory tags, 19th–20th centuries

Southeast Asia

Metal alloys

IFAF Purchase from the Diane and Sandy Besser Collection

Collections are shaped by the personal tastes, interests, and eccentricities of collectors. And more and more, the terms of gifts made to museums are shaped by similar idiosyncratic restrictions. Current philanthropic trends indicate that donors to museums, as well as to other charitable organizations, are placing more strings and limitations on the terms of their gifts (whether of art, cash, or both). Agreements now frequently include penalties, financial and otherwise, for not meeting a donor's expectations. The U.S. court system is dealing with an increasing number of lawsuits brought by heirs of donors claiming a museum or university is no longer complying with the donor's wishes, or suits by organizations seeking to be released from the strictures of bequests made decades before.

Like collectors, curators have their opinions and their own likes and dislikes for specific artists, art from certain culture groups, and specific forms of art. But unlike private collectors, who may take a more focused view, curators must take into consideration the museum's broader needs and goals, while they are in

Keris and a keris sheath, 19th–20th centuries

Java, Indonesia

Wood, bone, metal alloys

IFAF Purchase from the Diane and Sandy Besser Collection

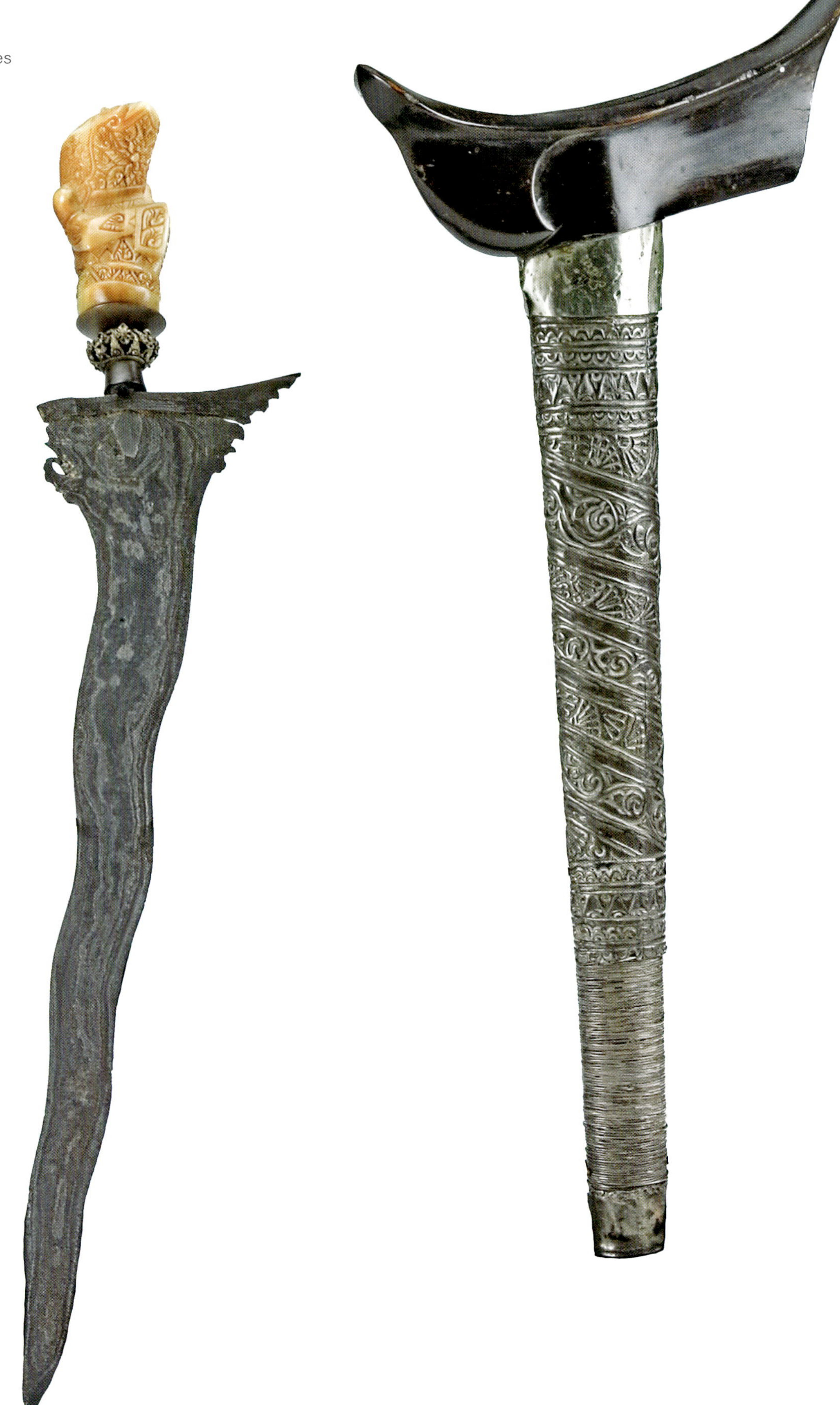

the process of acquiring objects for the museum's collections. Museum staff must consider the immediate along with the long-term good of the collection and maintain a degree of distance in the process; they must be willing to set aside their personal preferences and predilections as they evaluate potential gifts of collections that the museum may receive. Their first responsibility must be to the well being of the collection and the institution and to the ethical dimensions of their work, while keeping in mind that their decisions are likely to affect the museum long after their own tenures end.

Curators and collectors may be foe or ally, and are often both at the same time. Both groups possess specialized knowledge that may seem competitive and threatening, if only at an unconscious level. Moreover, an individual collector may feel separation anxiety about parting with a piece or an entire collection, and if challenged, the collector may distrust the intentions of the museum or devalue a curator's expertise regarding selections.

Museum curators develop their connoisseurship through years of work, combining formal training and expertise with a critical eye, while continuing their study and research in the holdings of other museums and private collectors. Curators at the Museum of International Folk Art are expected to incorporate an approach that includes, where possible, the voices of the artists and the perspective of the cultural group that makes and uses the objects. An ethnographic perspective on aesthetics in the cultural context informs an appreciation for and understanding of cultural identity and values as expressed in material form. At the same time, the curator and/or the collector may not share the same ethnic, cultural, occupational, regional, religious identity, or socioeconomic background as the artists whose work they collect, and this can present a challenge in interpreting and representing material culture in museum programs and exhibitions.

A donor's generosity in giving a major collection to a museum is acknowledged in many ways—often with an exhibition and catalogue, sometimes with an opportunity to name an endowment fund, a gallery, or even a wing of a museum. The publicity that surrounds a major donation brings attention to the collector as well as to the museum. The desire for publicity varies from donor to donor but attention, appreciation, and recognition are important to everyone. The acceptance by a museum of a collection conveys a high degree of legitimacy upon the collection and, by extension, further validates the collector's highly skilled connoisseurship. An exhibition allows a particular collection to be shared

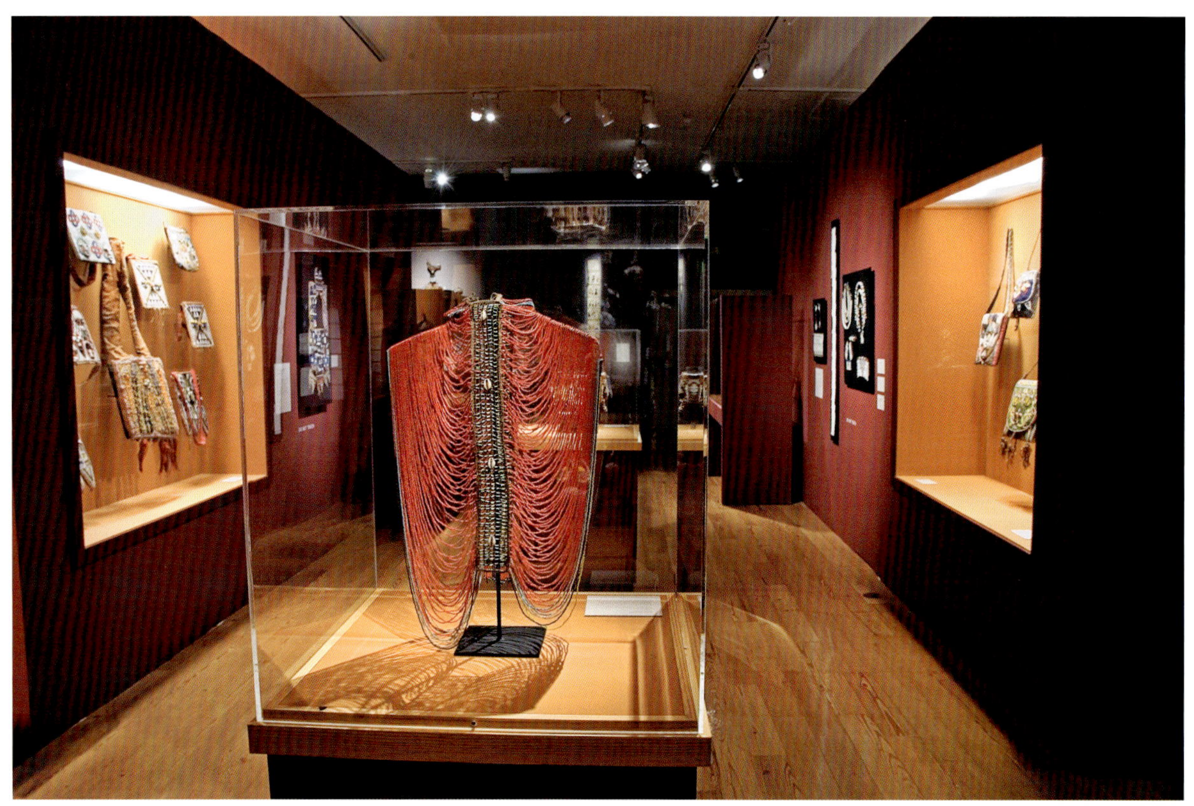

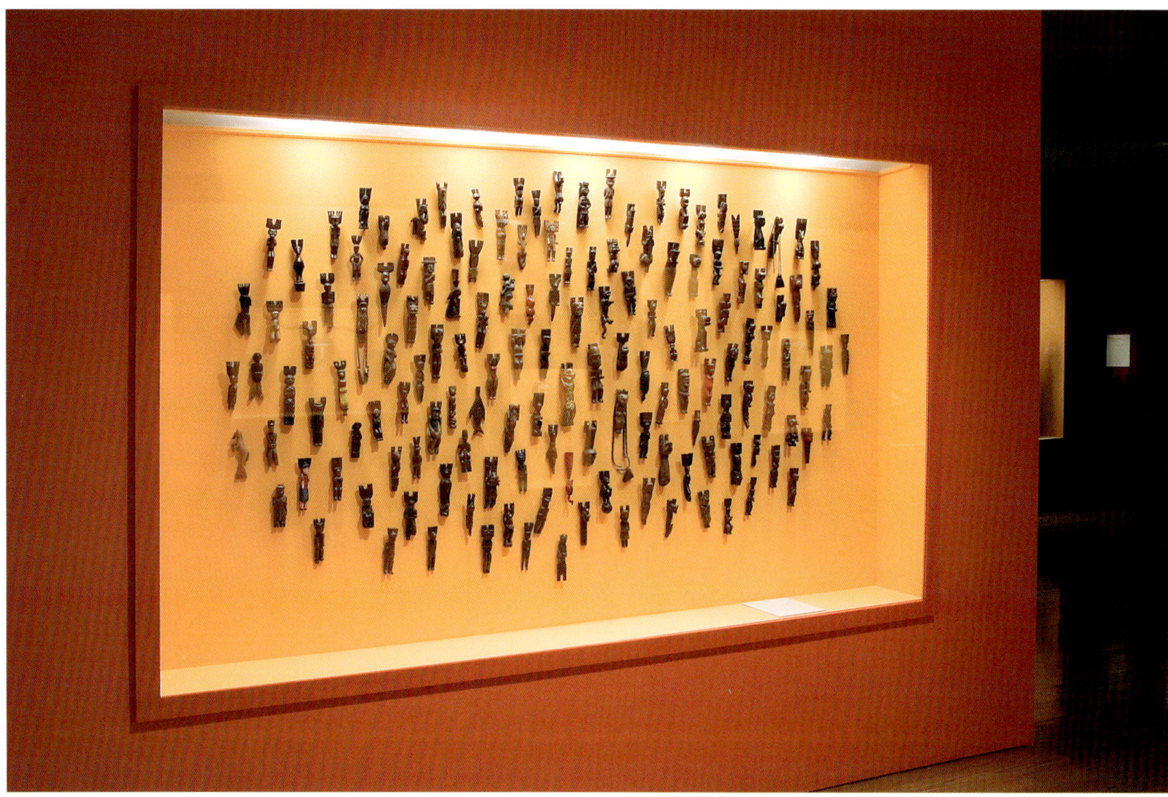

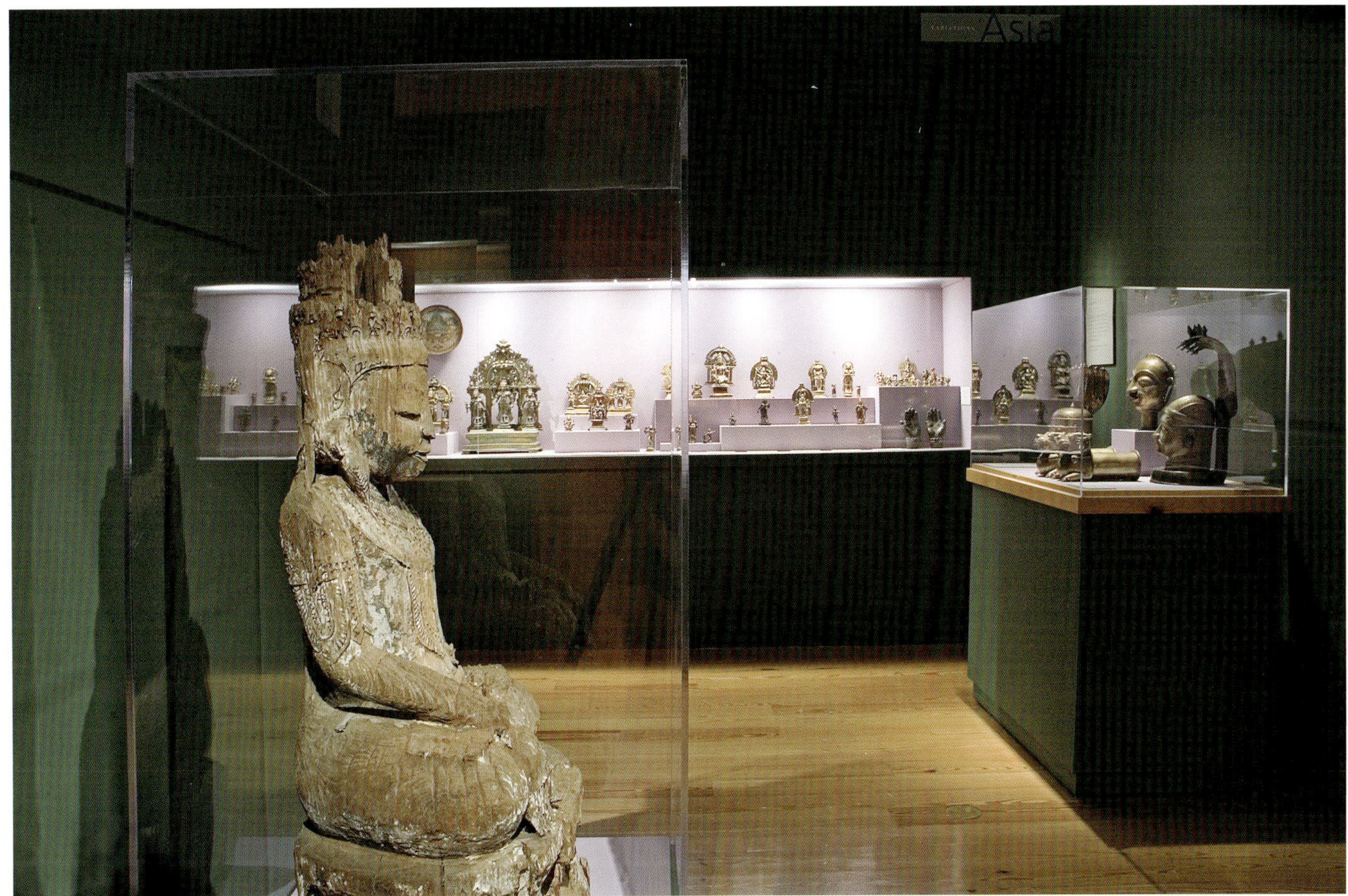

with a much larger public audience than when it was held privately, and the publication of an exhibition brochure or catalogue makes a collection available to an even wider audience. Further, the transfer of a private collection to a public institution offers this collection a permanent home that provides greater accessibility for study by present and future curators, researchers, and educators.

OPPOSITE AND ABOVE:
Variations exhibition,
October 2006 through April 2007
Bartlett Wing, Museum of International Folk Art

Private collectors have often been among the first to recognize the importance of an artist, art form, or genre, before museum curators or scholars become aware of the cultural significance of this art. Visionary collectors understand themselves to be temporary caretakers of art and, through their devotion and good will, freely pass on the legacy of their personal collections to the public arena as gifts that will continue to exist well beyond the lifespan of the collector. All of us are enriched by their generosity of spirit.

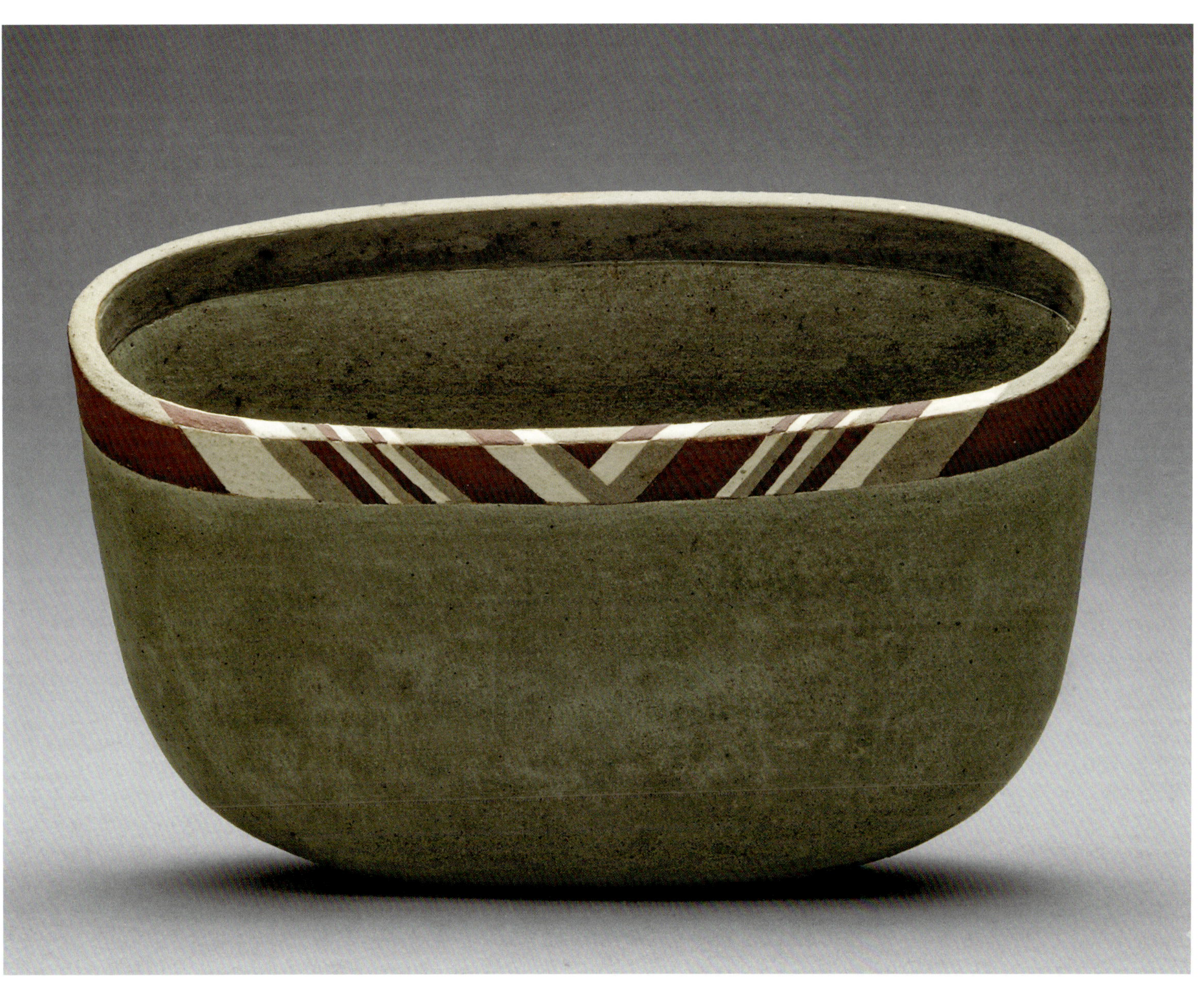

Optical pot, by Elizabeth Fritsch, 1975

Clay

Gift from the Diane and Sandy Besser Collection

MOIFA

Flanged form, by Ursula Morley Price, 1978

Porcelaneous stoneware

Gift from the Diane and Sandy Besser Collection

MOIFA

BELOW:

Round bottom pot, by Mary Rogers, n,d.

Ceramic

Gift from the Diane and Sandy Besser Collection

MOIFA

OPPOSITE:

Bowl on foot, by Mary Rogers, 1976

Porcelain

Gift from the Diane and Sandy Besser Collection

MOIFA

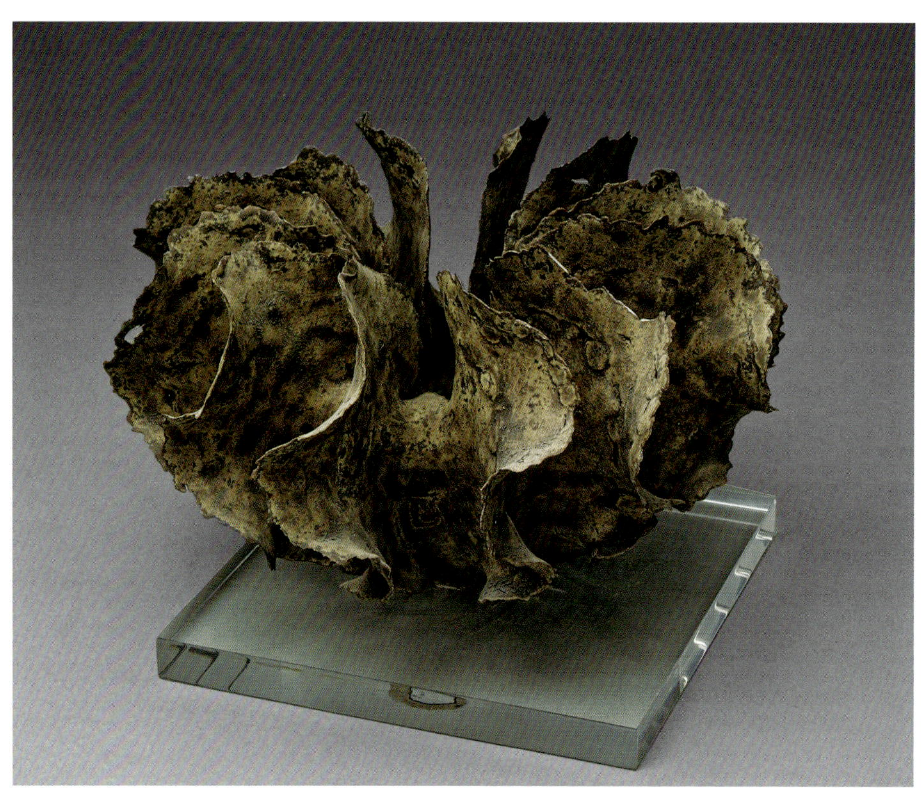

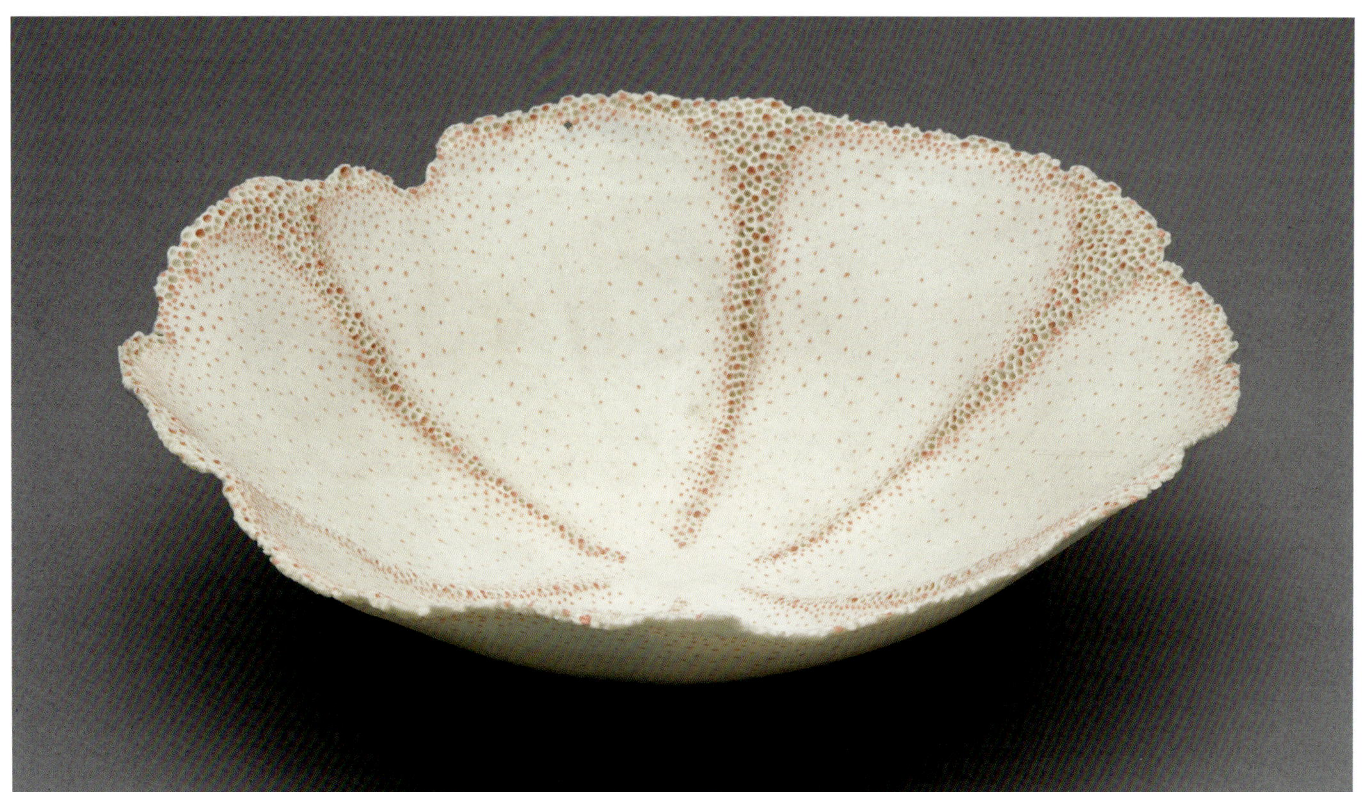

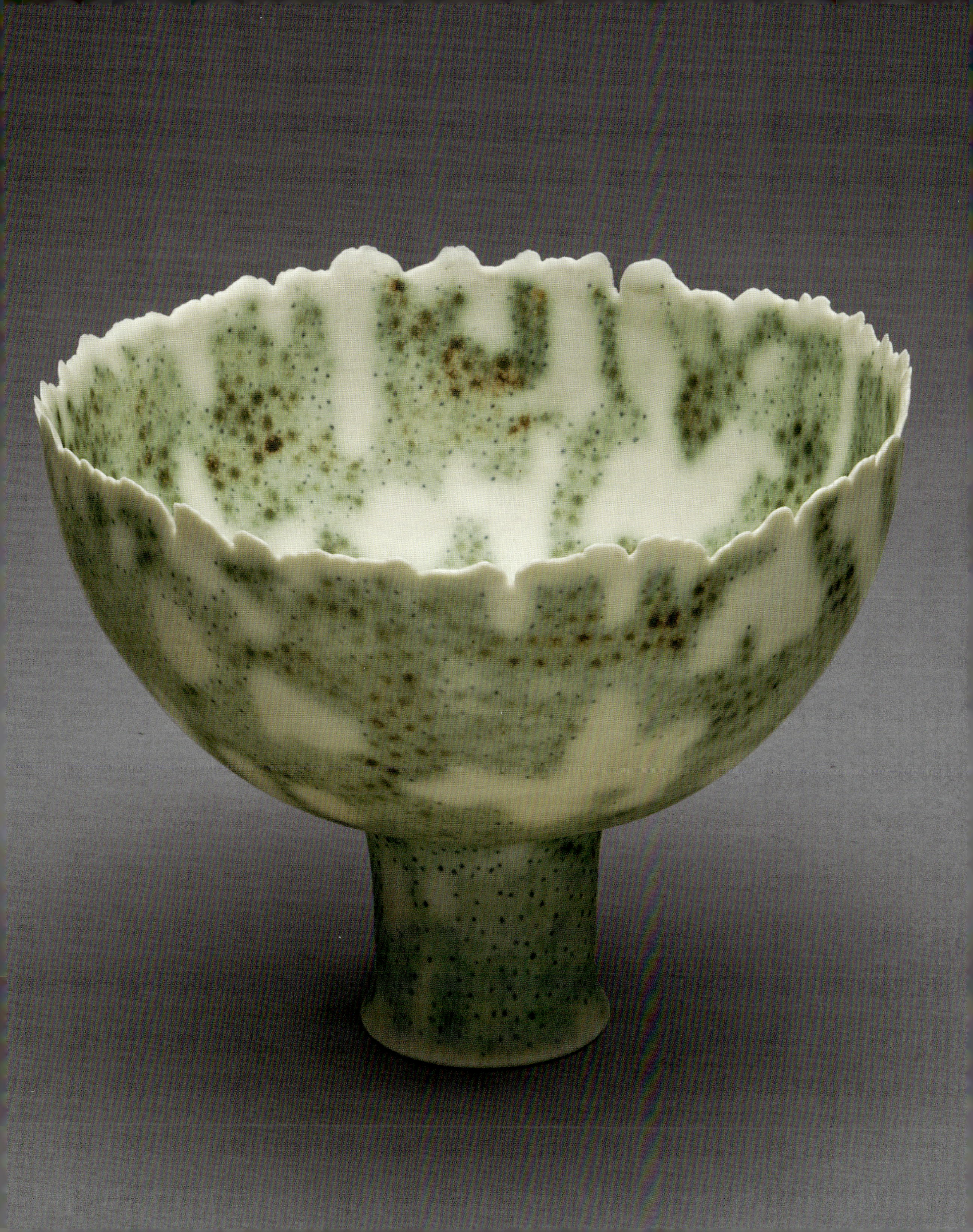

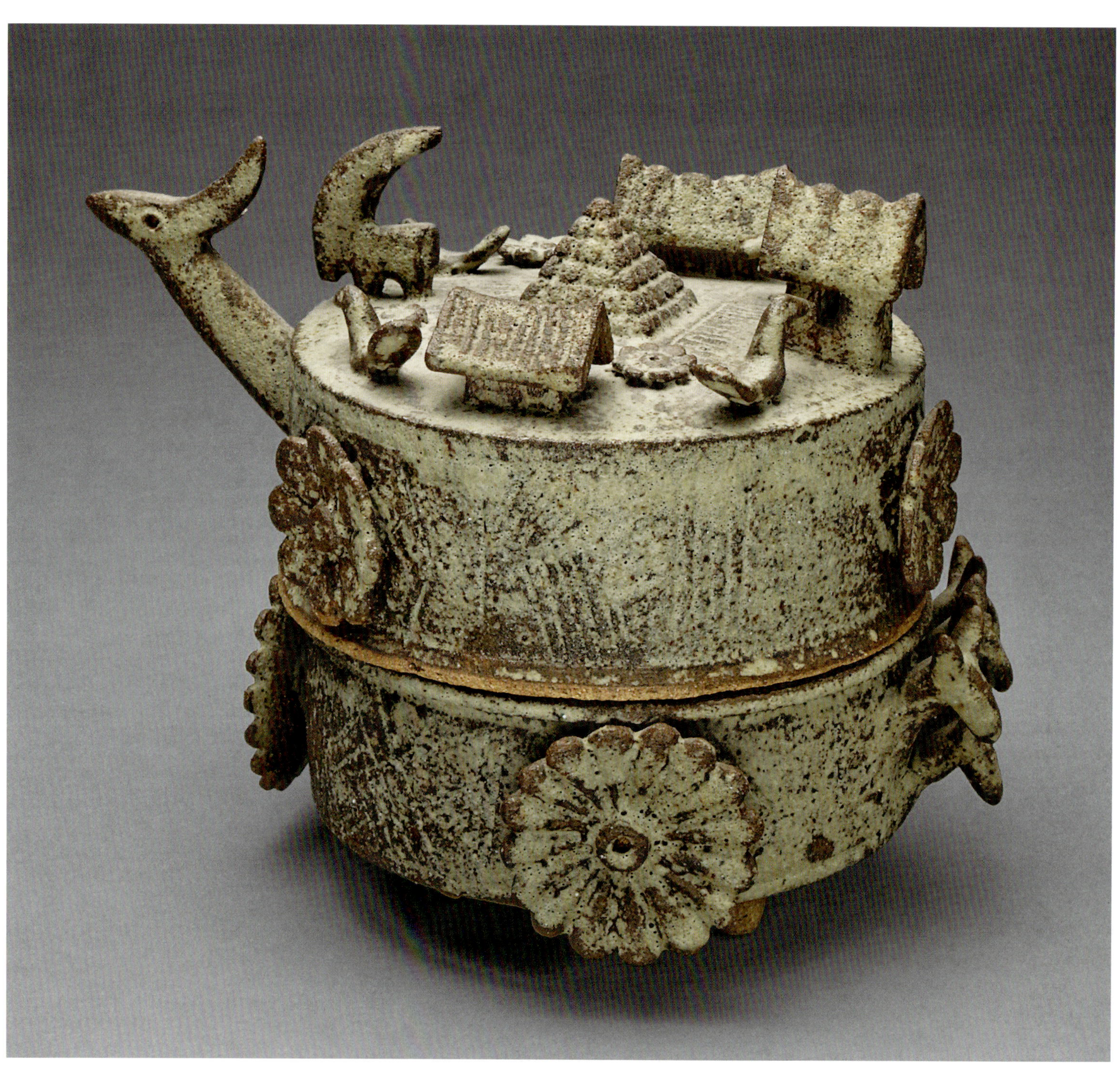

Fox Box, by Ian Godfrey, 1973

Earthenware

Gift from the Diane and Sandy Besser Collection

MOIFA

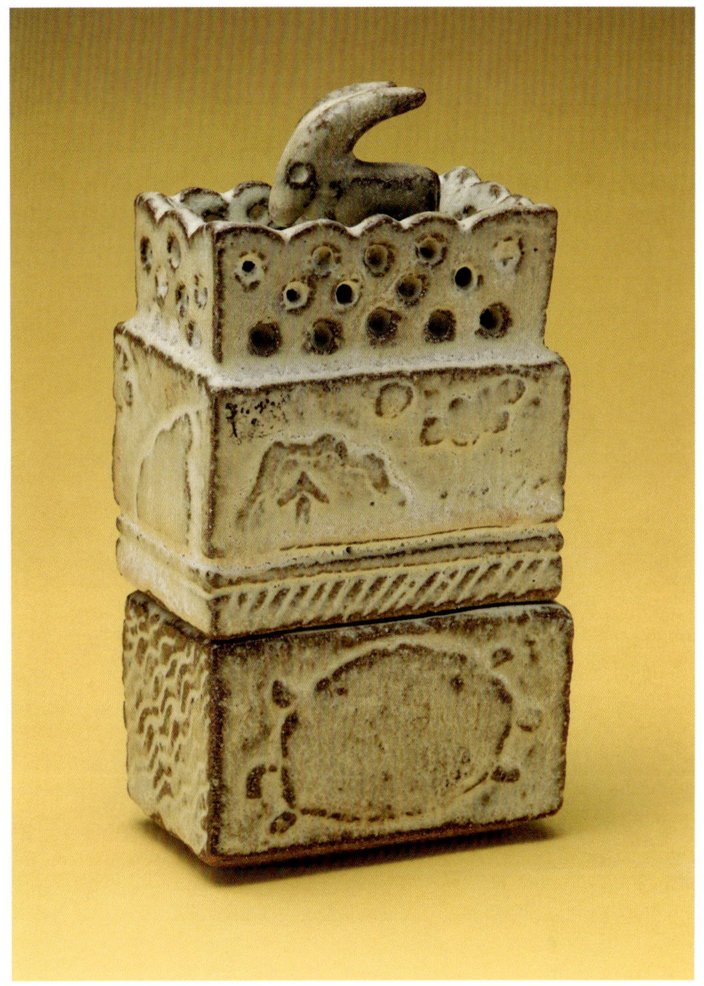

Turtle House, by Ian Godfrey, 1972

Glazed stoneware

Gift from the Diane and Sandy Besser Collection

MOIFA

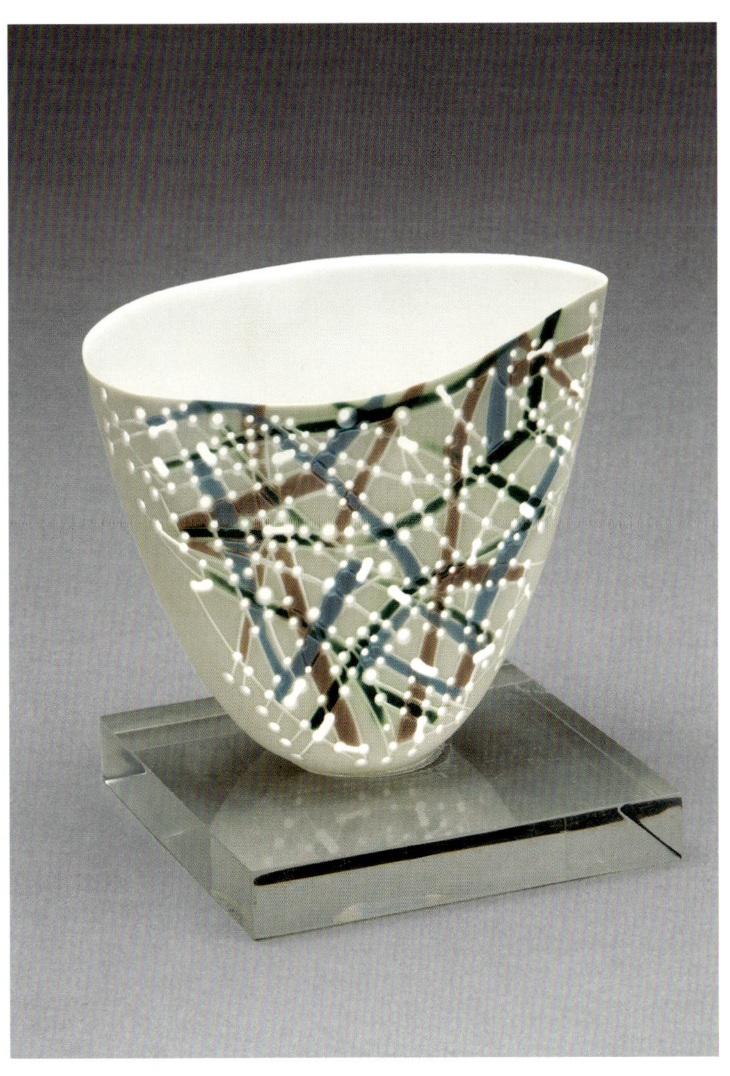

LEFT:

Bowl #7, by Angela Verdon, n.d.

Ceramic

Gift from the Diane and Sandy Besser Collection

MOIFA

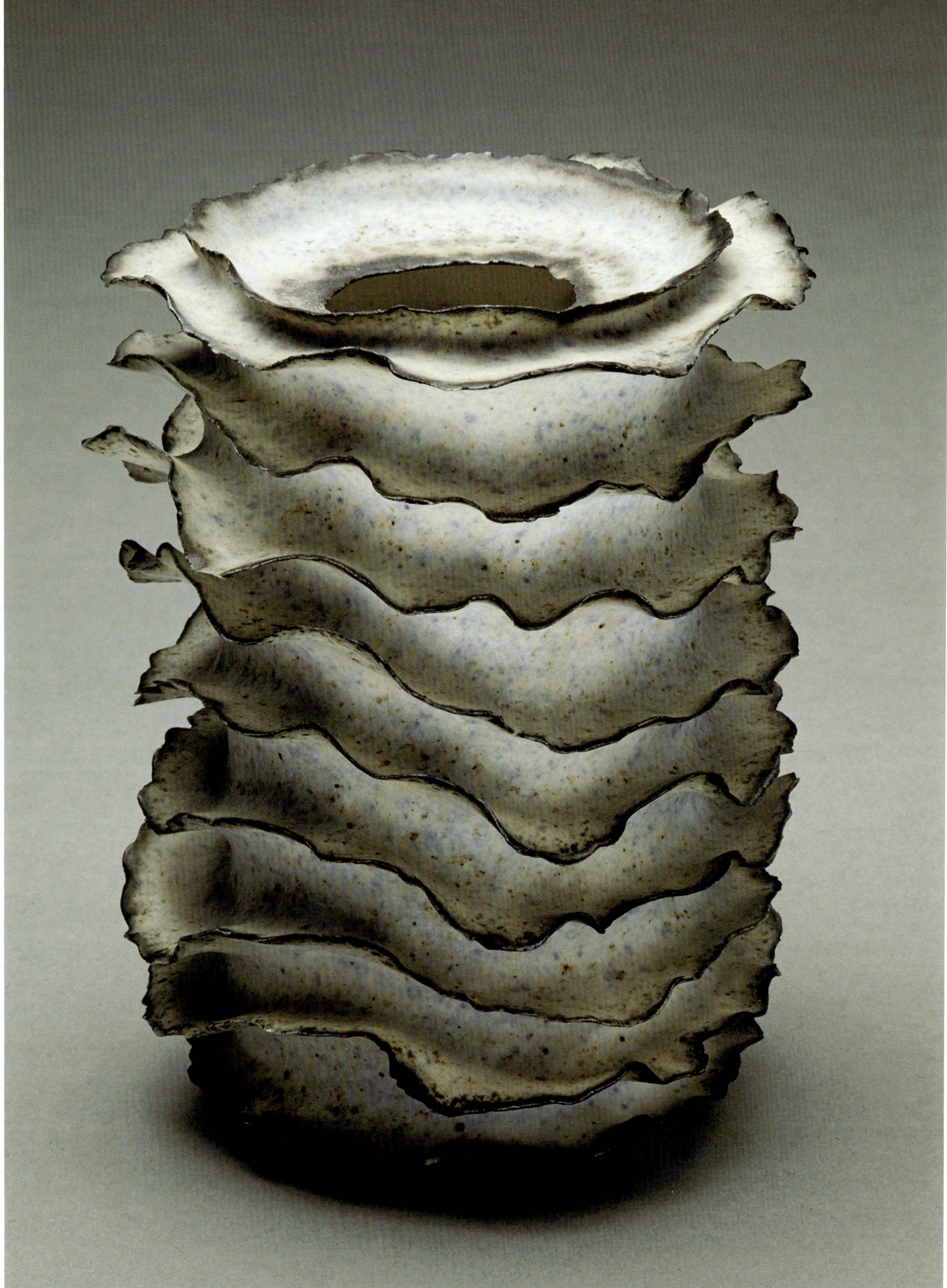

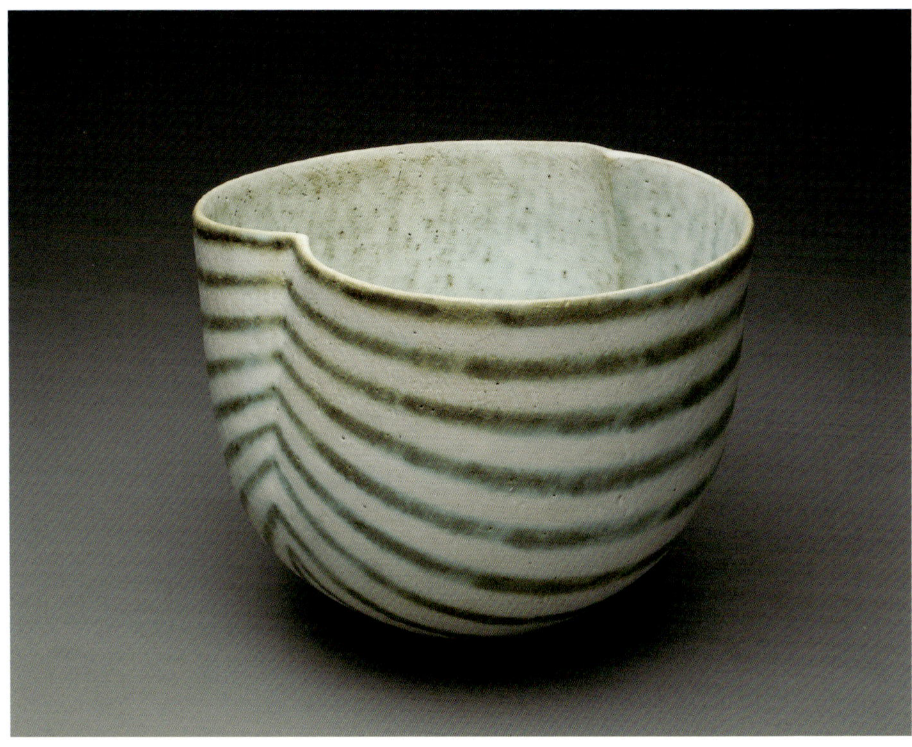

LEFT:

Stoneware, stained and glazed, by John Ward, 1985

Gift from the
Diane and Sandy Besser Collection

MOIFA

BELOW:

Bowl, by Angela Verdon, 1980

Porcelain, drilled

Gift from the
Diane and Sandy Besser Collection

MOIFA

OPPOSITE:

Flanged cylinder, by Deirdre Burnett. 2001

Porcelain with glazes

Gift from the
Diane and Sandy Besser Collection

MOIFA

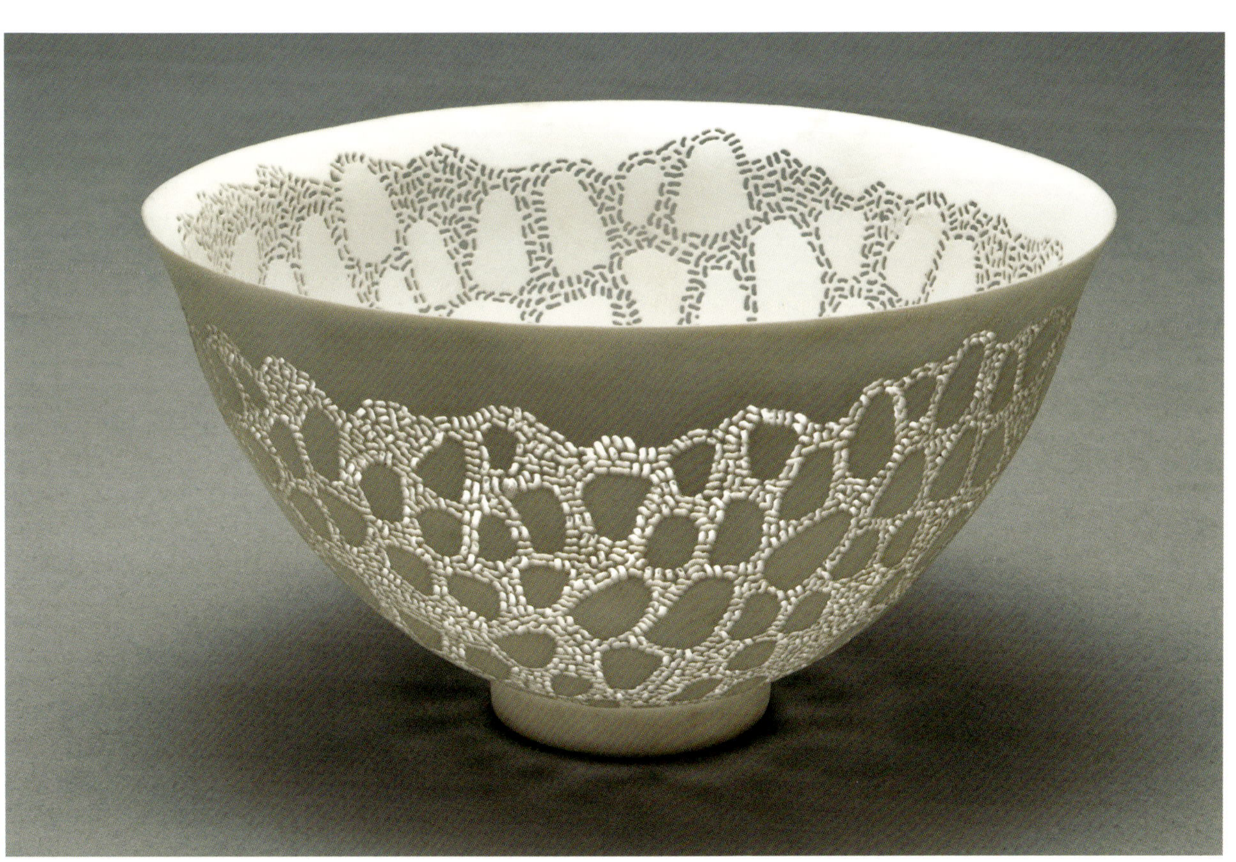

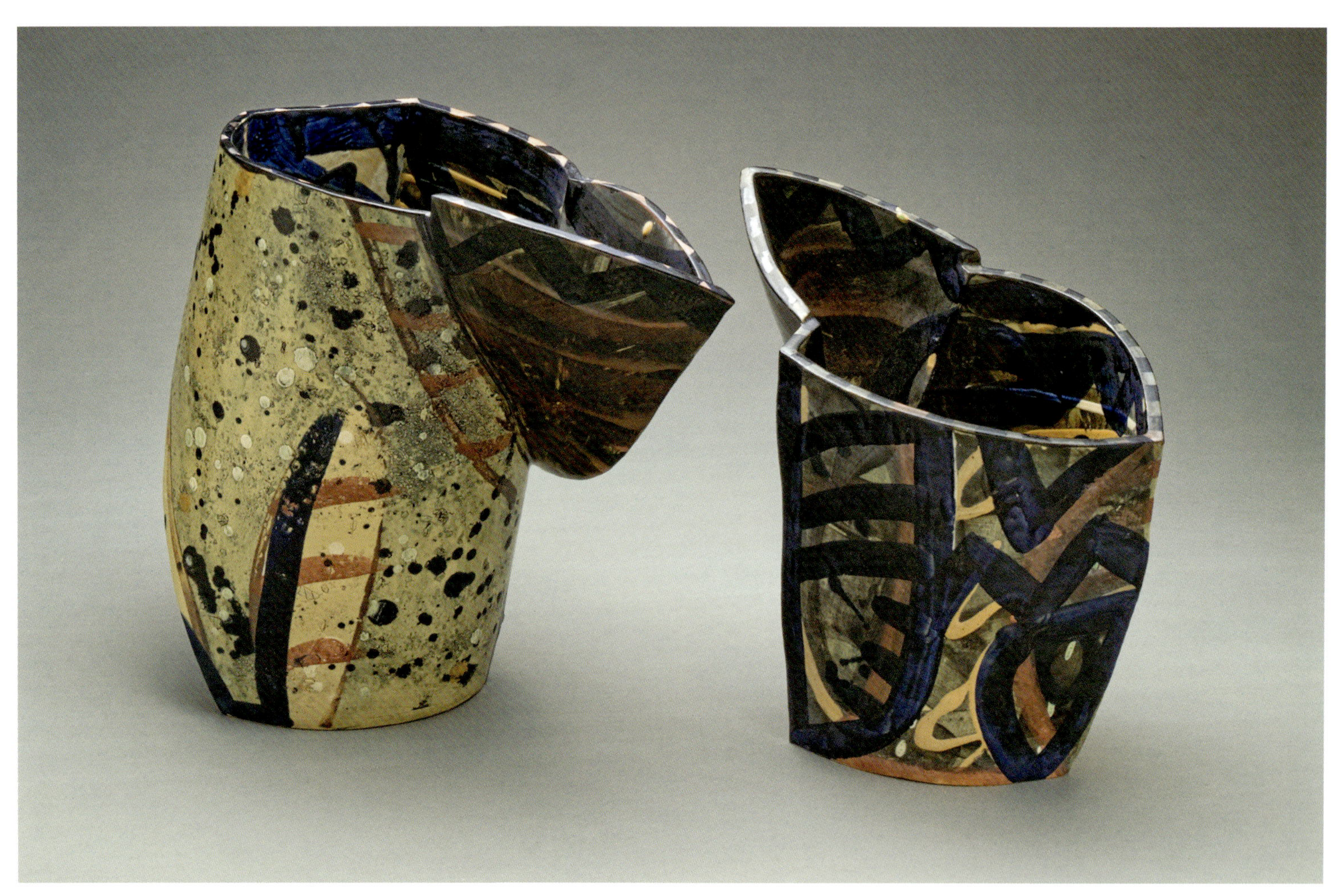

Earthenware, by Alison Britton, 1985

Gift from the
Diane and Sandy Besser Collection

MOIFA

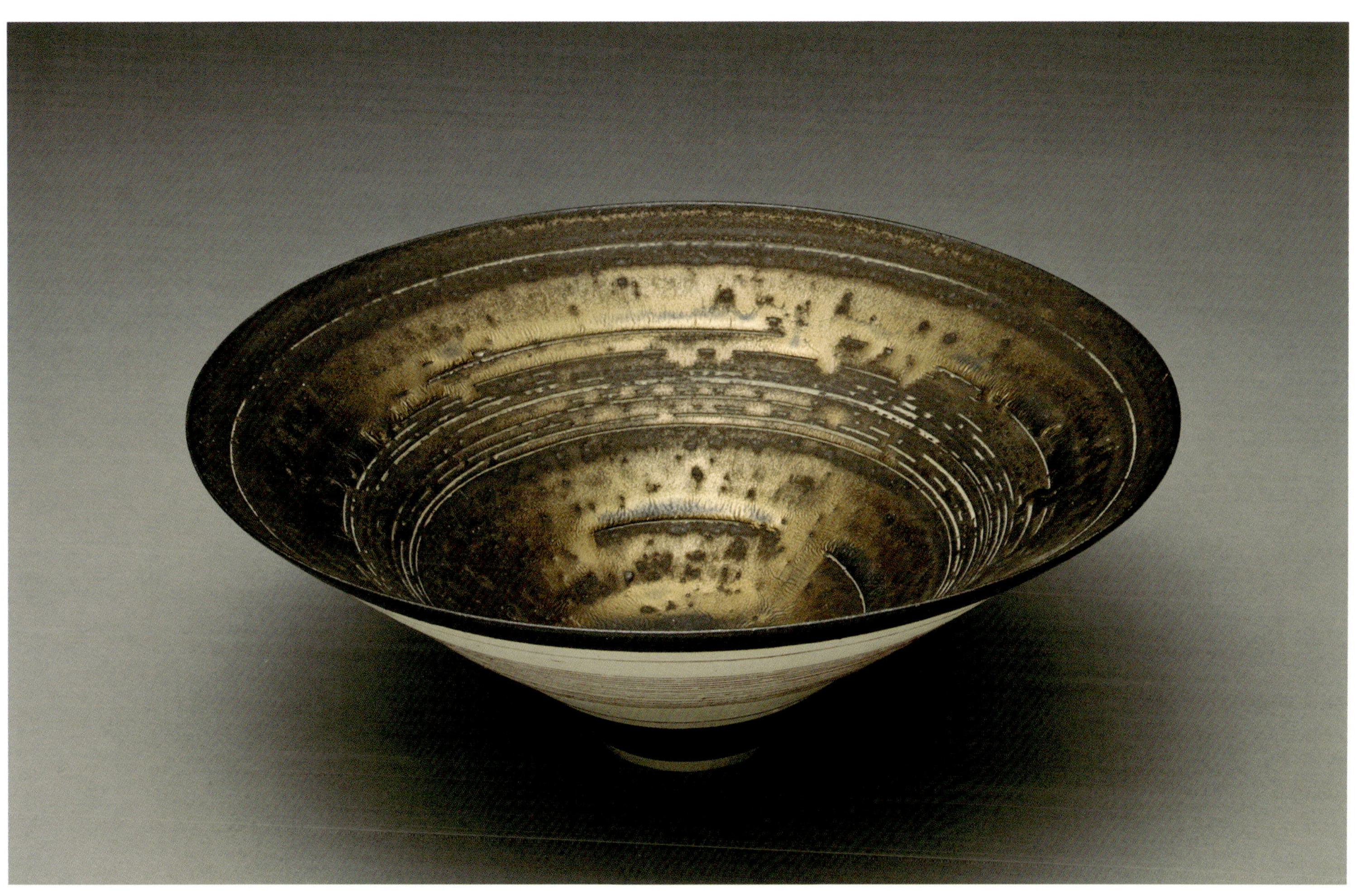

Porcelain, etched, manganese glazes
and stains, by Lucie Rie, 1975

Gift from the
Diane and Sandy Besser Collection

MOIFA

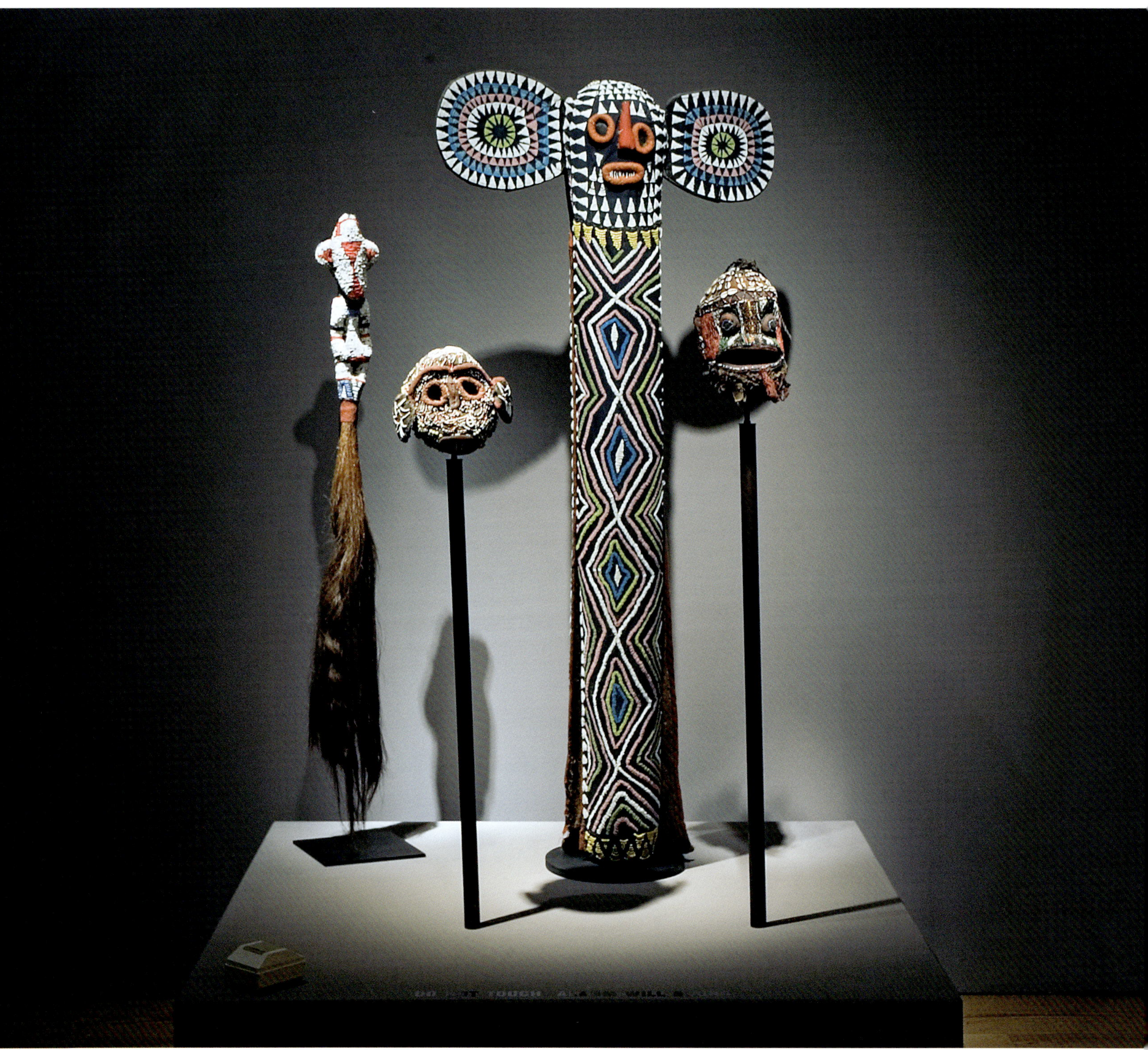

Important Legal Issues for Art Collectors

Susannah Evans

In general, the most significant legal issues facing art collectors occur upon the acquisition and disposition of their art. The transfers explored in this chapter include buying and selling and making lifetime gifts and estate bequests to charitable and non-charitable beneficiaries. This chapter serves as a primer for collectors with respect to these transactions. It does not examine artwork held in trusts and foundations, collecting art as a business or investment, effects of the alternative minimum tax and copyrights, state laws governing estate taxes, and transactions of exceptional complexity—all of which are beyond the scope of the chapter. Federal laws are constantly changing, and other laws, both tax and non-tax, vary from state to state, so legal and tax advice is recommended when a transaction involving a work of art is contemplated.

BUYING AND SELLING

Art collectors typically acquire artwork thorough purchases from the primary and secondary art markets. Whether dealing with a primary source (like a gallery) or a secondary source (like an auction house), collectors will want to ensure that the work to be acquired is authentic and that the seller has the authority to sell it. This is important for two reasons: first, collectors want to acquire

OPPOSITE:
Exhibition installation of African beaded pieces, *Variations* exhibition

authentic works not in excess of market value, and, second, upon the future disposition of the artwork collected, they must have an authentic work to transfer and possess good title to the work. In most cases, collectors are purchasing from reputable sellers and will not encounter problems, but when in doubt, assuring a work's authenticity and a seller's authority to sell are prudent measures to take.

At some point, a collector may wish to sell works from their collection—perhaps intending to use the funds to improve the value of the collection, to change the focus of the collection to another genre, or to capture the initial investment. A collector has several choices, including selling directly to the buyer (who may be an individual, a museum, or a gallery) or selling through another party, such as through a gallery dealer or on consignment. Many galleries prefer to sell works for a collector on consignment to avoid expending capital on an outright purchase. To protect his or her interests in the work, a collector (the consignor) should make sure that the consignment agreement made with the dealer (the consignee) is in writing. Such an agreement should include detailed terms regarding the arrangement between or among the parties. Recommended terms include (1) the retail price, (2) percentage of selling price each party will receive, (3) any discounts the dealer is authorized to give a potential seller, (4) when and how the collector will be paid after the sale takes place, (5) the duration of the consignment, and (6) whether or not the dealer has the exclusive right to sell that work.

If a warranty is given separately by the collector guaranteeing that he or she has the authority and good title to sell and that the artwork is authentic, it should be referenced in the consignment agreement; if not, the warranty should be included as one of the terms in the consignment agreement itself. The dealer may want an indemnification from the collector if a claim arises from a future buyer at a later date, in which case the dealer may insist that detailed indemnity provisions be included in the agreement. The party responsible for carrying insurance, paying for transportation of the works consigned, and providing repairs or restoration for the duration of the consignment should be clearly indicated in the agreement, when applicable.[1]

It may be advisable for a collector to take a security interest in the work consigned and the proceeds of the sale to secure his or her rights over the dealer's creditors.[2] For example, if the dealer uses the consigned work as collateral for a loan and the dealer goes bankrupt, the dealer's creditor(s) could have a superior claim on the art and proceeds to that of the collector—even though this collector was the owner of the art prior to the consignment arrangement. First, the consignee should be notified of the intent to take the security interest and the consignment agreement should grant the consignor the right and authority to take and perfect a security interest in the artwork. Next, the collector should, through his or her attorney, take the security interest in the artwork consigned by filing a financing statement with the applicable state authority and notify the consignee's creditors of the interest taken.[3]

Whenever a sale of artwork of considerable value is about to be consummated, it may be appropriate for collectors to consult an attorney to ensure the legitimacy of the transaction and a tax expert to determine the tax consequences of the proposed sale.

LIFETIME GIFTS TO CHARITABLE AND NON-CHARITABLE BENEFICIARIES

Art collectors can make lifetime gifts to charitable beneficiaries, such as art museums, and non-charitable beneficiaries, such as family members and friends. Gratuitous transfers by a collector during his or her life to family and friends will not result in favorable income tax benefits and may result in adverse gift-tax consequences. Collectors, as donors, are entitled to make non-taxable gifts each year not in excess of the annual exclusion (currently at $12,000 per beneficiary).[4] Also, collectors are entitled to a lifetime exemption on how much they can gift without gift tax consequences (in 2009, the exclusion is $3,500,000); but once their lifetime limitation is exhausted, gift tax liabilities will result.[5] The amount of lifetime gifts over the annual exclusions to friends, family, and non-charitable beneficiaries must be taken into account when determining the collector's future gift taxes for subsequent lifetime gifts and when determining the estate tax liability for the donor's estate at the time of his or her death. Therefore, a gift of artwork made during a collector's life to a non-charitable beneficiary in excess of the donor's annual exclusions will offset his or her lifetime dollar limitations before triggering any actual gift tax liability.

Alternatively, collectors can make gifts during their lives to charitable organizations (the "donees") without incurring a gift tax and receive various income tax benefits for doing so.[6] Transfers to museums and other charitable arts organizations serve an important cultural purpose in addition to sparing an organization's acquisition costs. For centuries, many societies have housed their visual arts in museums, which in the United States are eligible for tax-exempt status.

This tax-exempt status in turn paves the way for tax deductible donations, thereby providing an important incentive to collectors to donate art. According to one expert on art taxation benefits: "The reason behind our giving to public museums and justifying their tax-exempt status is that we, as an American society, believe that museums are necessary to our cultural existence. It is this philosophy, espoused by the government, which entitles gifts to public museums to secure special treatment under the tax code."[7]

To receive a charitable income deduction for the fully appreciated value of the artwork donated, collectors must make "qualified contributions" to "qualified organizations." A qualified contribution is any transfer of "long-term capital gain property" (property held longer than one year) to a qualified organization if the use of the property by that organization is related to the purpose or function of that organization's tax exempt status.[8] A qualified organization is any organization described in Section 501(c)(3) of the United States Internal Revenue Code (Code), except certain private foundations; art museums and art institutions with this tax exempt status are qualified organizations.[9] Thus, donations of artwork (regarded as "tangible property" in the Code) may be deducted at their fair market value from the collector's income taxes.[10] Collectors can confirm a donee's status by checking Publication 78 ("Cumulative List of Charitable Organizations") of the U.S. Internal Revenue Service (IRS), or by asking donees for a copy of their letter from the IRS approving their tax exempt status and purpose. Donors considering gifts to foundations should distinguish between "private foundations" and "private operating foundations." Those making traditional gifts to grant-making private foundations may only deduct their basis, or cost, in the work of art donated.[11]

INCOME TAX BENEFITS AND DEDUCTION RULES FOR CHARITABLE DONATIONS OF ARTWORK

The tax benefit to art collectors is that they may claim an income tax deduction for the fair market value of the donated artwork in the year in which the work is donated.[12] Such deductions generally are subject to a limitation on the amount of the deduction equal to 30 percent of the donor's adjusted gross income (AGI) for the year; amounts in excess of that limit may be carried over for a period of five years.[13] For example, if a collector has an AGI of $100,000 and donates a work of art with a fair market value of $50,000, he or she can only deduct $30,000 in the year the work is donated; the remaining $20,000 may be carried forward for up to five future years and deducted until exhausted against the same limits for the next five years.[14] Strategic tax planning is advisable to collectors making substantial contributions to maximize the benefits offered by the carryover allowance.

Collectors should retain certain information related to the artwork they donate, such as the donee's name, the date and location of the contribution, and a description of the item donated.[15] Donors claiming a deduction of $250 or more for a charitable contribution (comprised of one or more works of art) must submit a dated receipt with their income tax return.[16] If the value of the overall contribution exceeds $500, donors must make certain statements on their income tax returns. First, they must state their cost basis (the price they paid for the contribution) and how they acquired the donated property, for example, by purchase, gift, inheritance, exchange, or commission.[17] Additionally, donors must complete the applicable sections of IRS Form 8283 and attach it to their tax return.[18] Collectors are advised to retain any other relevant information and documents about their acquisitions, in the event they need to substantiate value, ownership, or authenticity.[19] They must also disclose any restrictions on the donated art, such as any prior copyright or licensing agreements held by third parties.[20] For claimed deductions on works of art valued at $5,000 or more, donors are required to obtain a qualified appraisal (discussed below).[21]

Finally, collectors should be aware of deduction rules involving artworks that they themselves received as gifts. If an artist gives a collector one of his or her works and the collector later donates that work to a museum, the collector is not allowed to deduct the fair market value of that work from his or her income taxes; he or she may only deduct the cost of the materials used by the artist.[22]

RELATED USE AND POSSESSION RULES FOR CHARITABLE DONATIONS OF ARTWORK

To qualify for the tax benefits, the donated art must be put to a "related use" by the donee organization or the fair market value deduction will be lost for the donor.[23] The related use requirement can be satisfied if the donor demonstrates that the work is not put to an unrelated use; or if at the time of donation, it was reasonable for the donor to believe that the donee would not put the work of art to an unrelated use.[24] For instance, related uses for artwork given to a museum include being exhibited or simply kept in storage for educational and research purposes.[25] If the work of art is of the general type normally held by the museum, it is reasonable for the collector to assume the use rules are met.[26] If the donee intends to sell the art shortly after it is received and the donor has actual knowledge of this intent, then the use rules will not be satisfied, thus providing a basis for the IRS to deny a deduction.[27]

In most cases, the donor may not retain possession of the donated artwork because the donee must receive the right to possession at the time of contribution.[28] The most common circumstance under which the donor may temporarily keep possession and still obtain an income tax deduction is if the donee lacks proper storage or exhibit facilities at the time of donation; if this is the case, the transfer will still be valid.[29] Another circumstance is if the collector has made an undivided partial interest gift of artwork, which is discussed later in this chapter.

APPRAISAL REQUIREMENTS FOR CHARITABLE DONATIONS OF ARTWORK

The IRS is paying more attention to deductions taken for contributions of artwork than in years past. "Gone are the days when a collector could quietly place a value on a work of art and hope the IRS wouldn't notice."[30] In 2004, the IRS reduced claimed deductions for charitable donations of artwork by 69 percent.[31] This heightened scrutiny is, in part, a result of years of taxpayers overstating the value of works donated, and the IRS is attempting to curb such abuse.[32]

Complying with the appraisal requirements imposed for charitable donations of art is more important now than ever, and art collectors and their advisors are wise to do just that. The validity given to an appraisal is dependent on the completeness of the appraisal and the qualifications of the appraiser.[33] Fine art appraisals should conform to IRS guidelines, which require that the following information be included: description of artwork (artist, size, medium, approximate date, percentage of ownership transferred), cost and manner of acquisition, a photograph sufficiently identifying the work, and factors used to determine value (such as, comparable sales close in time of the appraisal date, catalogue quotes, market conditions, exhibition lists, and artist's standing).[34]

When a donor claims an income tax deduction of $5,000 or more (whether for a single work or multiple works of art) stricter standards apply. The donor, in this case, must obtain a qualified appraisal by a qualified appraiser, attach the appraisal summary (a specific section contained in the qualified appraisal discussed later in this section) to their return, and keep records regarding the contribution.[35] While personal property appraisers are not licensed or regulated,[36] the IRS looks to the Uniform Standards of Professional Appraisal Practice (USPAP) for guidance.[37] An art appraiser's compliance with USPAP guidelines for conducting a proper appraisal is not legally required for all fine art appraisals, but many appraisers follow these standards as a matter of course.[38]

A "qualified appraisal" must include the following: the appraisal must be made no earlier than sixty days before the date of contribution nor later than the due date of the donor's tax return, and it must be signed and dated by the appraiser.[39] It must also contain the following information: a description of the donated work of art that may be understood by a person not familiar with the type of work; the condition of the donated work; the date of contribution; the terms of the agreement or understanding between the donor and the donee institution, such as restrictions on use or other persons' rights in the property; the appraiser's name, address, and taxpayer identification number; the appraiser's qualifications; the purpose of the appraisal; the date the work was appraised; the fair market value on the date of contribution; the method and basis of valuation; and an explanation of how the appraisal fee was calculated.[40] Fair market value is defined as the price at which the artwork "would change hands between a willing buyer and a willing seller, neither being under the compulsion to buy or sell and both having reasonable knowledge of relevant facts."[41]

"Qualified appraisers" are defined as those who hold themselves out as appraisers or perform appraisals on a regular basis and their qualifications are based upon their experience and background.[42] A qualified appraiser conducting appraisals for charitable contributions and perhaps other tax purposes must be affiliated with a recognized appraiser organization or have the education and experience relevant to the property appraised; and must have two years in the market of buying, selling, or valuing the type of art appraised.[43] Additionally, appraisers may not be "disqualified persons" with respect to the donated work of art. Disqualified persons are defined as any one or more of the following: a donor claiming the deduction; a party to the transaction in which the donor acquired the donated work art (unless the work of art is donated within two months of its acquisition date and the appraised value does not exceed the purchase price); the donee; employees of the person who sold the artwork to the donor and anyone related or married to such persons; and an appraiser who is regularly used by the donor, regularly used by the artwork's seller, or regularly used by the donee and does not perform a majority of appraisals for other persons.[44] In other words, the appraiser must be detached from any transaction involving the donated artwork and may not have an interest, financial or otherwise, in the work donated. Additionally, appraisers cannot base their fees upon a percentage of the value of the donated artwork.[45]

An "appraisal summary" is a summary that is consistent with the required information requested of the donor on Form 8283. It must be signed and dated by both the appraiser and the donor and must include the following information: the donor's name and tax identification number; a description of the donated artwork; its condition; how the donor acquired the artwork; the donor's basis; the donee's name and tax identification number; the date of receipt by the donee; a statement as to whether the donor received any consideration from the donee (such as if the donee acquired the artwork through a bargain sale by the donor); the appraiser's name, address, and taxpayer number; the appraised fair market value as of the date of donation; and a statement by the appraiser confirming that the fee charged is not prohibited.[46] Appraisal fees cannot be deducted as part of the charitable contribution but may be taken as a miscellaneous itemized deduction, subject to a percentage limitation based on the donor's adjusted gross income.[47]

If the value of the artwork(s) contributed is between $5,000 and $20,000, the donor may satisfy the appraisal summary requirement by simply completing Form 8283 (for Non-Cash Charitable Contributions of $500 or more) and submitting it with his or her tax return; the donor is not required to attach the whole appraisal report to the return, but must keep it in her records in the event she must substantiate her contribution.[48] If the value of donated artwork(s) is appraised at $20,000 or more, collectors must attach to their return the whole appraisal, signed and dated by the appraiser and the donee, in the year artwork was donated—failure to include the appraisal could result in a disallowance of the entire deduction.[49] Donors must also be able to provide upon request an 8 x 10 inch color photograph or a color transparency not smaller than 4 x 5 inches of all works donated.[50]

Collectors claiming a deduction for a contribution of artwork valued at this level will likely have such claims reviewed by the IRS's Art Advisory Panel, which "helps determine whether realistic appraisals of fair market value have been placed on works of art."[51] Until the creation of the Arts Advisory Panel in

1968, the IRS had no formal method to review and evaluate charitable donations of artwork.[52] The IRS Commissioner appoints members of the panel, which is composed of art dealers, museum curators, art scholars, and auction house experts who meet twice a year in closed-door sessions to review appraisals submitted with donors' income tax returns.[53] Appraisals related to estate and gift tax are also reviewed by the panel.[54] The panel's reports are only advisory, although local IRS officers often interpret their conclusions as binding, but they may be challenged in court.[55]

Oftentimes, the IRS will challenge the fair market value stated in a deduction claimed for a donated work(s) of art. In such a challenge, the IRS may argue that the donor overvalued the work and claimed a higher deduction than warranted for the charitable donation, thus creating a deficiency in the taxes owed by the donor. Some of these disputes reach the courts, with each side offering expert opinions as to the value of the donated art; however, the court itself may ultimately use its own judgment in determining the value.[56]

The courts consider a variety of factors in determining value, such as the relevant retail market of the work donated, the condition, the rarity, and the authenticity of the artwork in question.[57] When examining the relevant market, the courts recognize that several markets exist based on individual customers, wholesalers, dealers, and collectors.[58] The courts will also look at purchases of art that are made close in time to the date the artwork was donated to determine value; in such cases, the purchase price may be determinative as to the amount allowed as a deduction.[59] Courts will also look at gallery prices and auction results, neither being an absolute measure of value.[60] If there can be a range of values stated in an appraisal—as opposed to one fixed amount—the range of values, too, may be used as a factor.[61] Fair market value should not be based on forced sales, public auctions, or sales in restricted markets, especially where there is evidence that a work of art would sell for more under different circumstances.[62] Dispute and disagreement between testifying appraisers as to value can reduce fair market value.[63] To a certain extent, courts put themselves in the shoes of the appraisers. This should serve as sufficient impetus to obtain proper appraisals by reputable appraisers operating under USPAP guidelines, who may be found in appraisal association listings.[64]

The IRS imposes penalties for tax deficiencies based on overstated deduction amounts.[65] One such penalty is to hold a donor liable for interest on a substantial underpayment of tax stemming from an overstated deduction for a work of art.[66] These penalties are another impetus for donors and appraisers to ensure appraisals are performed under the IRS and USPAP guidelines. Appraisers can be penalized, too. An appraiser who knows or has reason to believe that the appraisal he or she provides a collector for tax purposes is not accurate and could result in an understatement of relevant taxes due for that collector may be fined and disqualified as an appraiser by the IRS.[67]

A donor may avoid possible penalties by requesting that the IRS evaluate the gift and its accompanying appraisal.[68] If the IRS approves the appraisal valuation, the donor can rely on the agency's approval and will not face a challenge to their deduction amount. However, this procedure is used infrequently because a donor may only make the request after the donation of artwork has taken place and must pay the IRS a fee of $2,500, making it a cost-prohibitive approach when added on top of the appraisal fee.[69]

Finally, collectors should be aware of the current trends in on-line appraisals and the IRS's response to them. Typically, the person seeking the appraisal submits information to the on-line company as to the description, condition, provenance, and title of the property to be appraised, along with digital photographs.[70] The appraisal is typically conducted by one of the company's affiliate appraisers, who relies on information submitted by the owner, without physically examining the property.[71] Should the IRS challenge the amount of the donor's deduction, an on-line appraisal may be helpful in satisfying the substantiation requirements, but it is unlikely to support the deduction claimed.[72]

ADDITIONAL BENEFITS: UNDIVIDED PARTIAL INTEREST GIFTS AND BARGAIN SALES TO CHARITABLE INSTITUTIONS

Undivided Partial Interest Gifts

In the event that collectors wish to retain part ownership of a work of art but seek a tax benefit at the same time, they can make an undivided fractional or partial interest gift to a donee museum or similar institution. Undivided partial interest gifts allow collectors to coordinate the percentage donated with their AGI and the corresponding limitation percentages and to carry over allowances to maximize the tax benefits of charitable giving for five years.[73] No deductions are allowed for future interests in tangible personal property.[74] The gift must grant a "present partial interest" equaling an undivided percentage of ownership in a work of art to a museum, thus making both parties tenants-in-common with respect to the work donated.[75]

The donee must have a right to possession of the work and exercise dominion and control over it for the allotted time period during each year following the contribution.[76] Additionally, the museum's time period for physical possession must be equivalent to the percentage of ownership it has been given.[77] For example, if the donor gifts a 50 percent ownership right in a work, the museum must have the right to possess the work for half of each year following the contribution. The rights given to the donee museum "must extend over the entire term" of the donor's interest in the work donated.[78] To ensure the validity of undivided partial interest gifts, donors should make certain with their legal consultant that any restrictions imposed will not have a negative impact on the deductions they claim.[79]

New rules for undivided partial interest gifts were created by the Pension Protection Act of 2006, which stipulates that donors must transfer the remaining interest in the work upon the earliest of the following events: (1) within ten years of the initial contribution, or (2) by the date of the donor's death.[80] Additionally, donors may only deduct the lowest of the following two values: (1) the fair market value on the date of the initial contribution, or (2) the fair market value on the date of the final contribution of the remaining interest.[81] In short, donors will not receive the benefit of any increases in value of the art when the remaining interests are transferred. And if the value decreases, their allowable deduction will be adjusted to reflect that decrease. So, if the value of the work donated when the initial undivided partial interest equals $50,000 and increases to $100,000 by the time the remaining interest is donated, the collector will only be eligible for a total deduction of $50,000, not $100,000. If the value of that same work were to decrease to $30,000 by the time the remaining interest is donated, the collector will only be eligible for a total adjusted deduction of $30,000, not $50,000.

This legislation has drawn great opposition in both art and legal circles. Many believe the legislation discourages donations, and that collectors will avoid donating until they feel the art has appreciated enough to maximize the tax deduction.[82] Others fear art will instead pass to collectors' families or will be sold to other collectors.[83] If these concerns materialize, it is likely that less art will end up in our public institutions, which in turn arguably threatens the cultural growth supported by charitable giving.

Bargain Sales

Bargain sales involve the sale of property for less than fair market value.[84] When a bargain sale, or in other words a "donative sale" (part donation, part sale), is made by a donor to a charitable organization, the excess of the fair market value over the sale may be deducted from the donor's income taxes in the year the sale is made.[85] This type of transfer of appreciated art allows the donor two benefits—the financial recapture of his or her basis and a current income tax deduction on the appreciated value of the artwork donated. Donees potentially obtain the benefit of acquiring a work for less than they would pay in the current market. In these cases, collectors must have a charitable intent and must conduct proper calculations for the bargain sale to obtain the favorable consequences this approach offers.[86]

BEQUESTS

Bequests to Spouses and Non-Charitable Beneficiaries

Generally, transfers from one spouse to another are not subject to the estate or gift tax, since properly structured transfers qualify for an unlimited marital deduction for both such taxes.[87] Husband and wife are treated as one economic unit, consequently no federal estate or gift taxes apply when they give one another property during lifetime or at death. What this means for collectors is that a surviving spouse can take title of all the artwork in the deceased spouse's estate without the burden of owing taxes on the works transferred. Additionally, when the collection is transferred to a surviving spouse in such a manner, he or she can make charitable donations during his or her life and receive income tax deductions. Alternatively, a surviving spouse can sell art from the collection with little or no capital gains because he or she will receive an income tax basis in the art sold roughly equal to the fair market value of the art at the time of the deceased spouse's death.[88]

When a collector leaves art to a family member or friend through his or her estate, it is considered a "non-charitable" bequest. Like the surviving spouse, these beneficiaries will receive a stepped-up basis on the values of the artworks in the estate; thus, income taxes attributable to any appreciation of the artwork prior to the collector's death will not be recognized when the artwork is sold after the collector's death.[89] However, any post-death appreciation in the artwork will trigger gain subject to income tax when sold by the beneficiary. Bequests also allow artwork to be removed from an estate, thus reducing estate tax liabilities and shifting the appreciated artwork from the collector to the intended beneficiary if the art is held until the collector's death.[90]

Collectors are well advised to coordinate lifetime gifts and bequests in their estate planning to maximize the various tax benefits available and avoid exceeding their lifetime gift limitations. Collectors and their advisors should also plan for how the estate will pay both federal and state estate taxes in an effort to avoid the burden of having to sell works from the collection after the death of the collector (or the surviving spouse) to pay those taxes.

Bequests to Charitable Beneficiaries

Bequests to a museum, for instance, provide similar benefits as those to friends and family in that they reduce the value of an estate, thus reducing the estate's tax liability.[91] As a legal expert on this topic underscores, because an estate tax deduction is offered for charitable bequests "qualifying for this deduction can be a central part of anyone's estate planning, as it can serve to either eliminate, or greatly diminish the estate tax owed."[92] Thus, comprehensive estate planning for art collectors cannot be recommended enough.

The dollar amount for federal estate tax exemption has varied depending on the year of a taxpayer's death. In 2009, amounts up to $3,500,000 in any person's estate is exempt from federal estate taxes—taxes are due for any sums over that amount.[93] So, a person can pass the applicable exempt amount of wealth to family and friends without tax in the year of his or her death. In 2010, the law is scheduled to be repealed.[94] If so, stepped-up basis could be eliminated and replaced with a "carryover basis" which is equivalent to the original or cost basis in a work of art and may result in built-in income tax gains on artwork given to a non-charitable beneficiary (e.g., family member or friend) upon a collector's death to be ultimately recognized upon a subsequent sale of the artwork by such beneciary.[95] Collectors are advised to watch for any repeal and be advised of any ramifications it will have on their estate planning.

Valuation for estate tax purposes can be challenging and is subject to a variety of market conditions. Appraisals will be necessary for certain estates and the IRS guidelines are the same as set forth for charitable donations, except that the criteria of a qualified appraisal for donations totaling $5,000 or more in a single year are absent.[96] The IRS will also accept sales of artworks from an estate as fair market value if sold within a reasonable time of the decedent's death.[97] Blockage discounts may apply for a substantial number of artworks bequeathed at death and will decrease the overall dollar value of the estate. The number of works to enter the market, past sales of similar works, the size of the potential market, the necessity of reducing prices to consummate sales, and the appraiser's opinion are the principal factors considered when determining if the discount should apply.[98] If the value of artworks bequeathed to a charity is high, the collector/estate benefits from the deduction on the taxes due. If the discount applies, the value of the artworks will be lower, thereby reducing the estate tax charitable deduction. The opposite is true if the beneficiary is a family member or friend. In these latter cases, the collector's estate will want the discount applied when friends and family receive the artwork, in order to lower the estate taxes. How these competing interests will be resolved may depend in part on the collector's overall estate planning.

Other discounts and factors may affect estate planning choices that are beyond the scope of this chapter. Collectors are strongly advised to consult with tax experts to ensure that they are aware of those factors, are not exceeding their non-charitable lifetime dollar limitations, understand the implications of bequests as they relate to the exemptions from federal estate taxes, and reduce any sums due over the annual exempt amount.

SUMMARY

Art collectors benefit themselves by learning more about the tax consequences of acquiring and transferring art, especially if they collect on a large scale. Establishing authenticity and good title at the time of acquisition facilitates future sales and transfers. In many cases, collectors may reduce their tax liabilities by making a combination of gifts during life and at death to both charitable and non-charitable beneficiaries. A strategic plan for all types of transfers of artwork over time can lessen the taxes due at death, reduce income tax liability in each year donations are made, and minimize or avoid the burden of having to sell works from an estate to pay the collector's (or his or her surviving spouse's) estate taxes.

Remember, the laws are ever-changing; because of this, consulting with attorneys and tax specialists are crucial steps for collectors. By identifying the current and relevant legal and tax consequences of transferring works of art, attorneys and tax specialists can protect art collectors' interests and make the most of the potential benefits available to these collectors through carefully planned dispositions.

Notes

1. Gilbert S. Edelson, *Buying and Selling Art: The Dealer's Perspective* (Aug. 11, 2004) (unpublished CLE essay, "Visual Arts and the Law," CLE International, Aug. 10–11, 2006, Santa Fe, NM, F-5).

2. Id, at F-6.

3. Steven Kimmelman and Zachary G. Newman, *Lake Tahoe* (Aug. 11, 2004) (unpublished CLE essay, "Visual Arts and the Law," CLE International, Aug. 10–11, 2006, Santa Fe, NM, G-5–G-6).

4. I.R.C. § 2503(b) (2008).

5. I.R.C. §§ 2503(b), 2522 (2008).

6. I.R.C. § 2522(a) (2008).

7. Merrie J. Webel Rockwood, *The Fine Art of Giving Art: Tax Benefits to the Donor,* 12 Exempt Org. Tax Rev., 1017, 1021 (Nov. 1995).

8. I.R.C. §§ 170(c),(e) (2008); 26 C.F.R. § 1.170A-4(b)(1) (2008).

9. *See* I.R.C. §§ 501(c)(3), 509(a), 4942(j)(3) (2008).

10. 26 C.F.R. § 1.170A-1(a) (2008).

11. I.R.C. §§ 170(b)(1)(C)(i); 170(e)(1)(B)(ii) (2008); Joseph Toce et al, *Tax Economics of Charitable Giving* § 29.02 (Warren, Gorham and Lamont of RIA) (2003); *see* I.R.C. §§ 2522, 4942 (j)(3). (If the foundation is a private operating foundation, one that uses its assets to operate a private charity, the donor may deduct the fair market value for qualified contributions made to such a foundation. A private operating foundation and various trusts may be considered "qualified organizations," if so, donors may be eligible for deductions for contributions made to them. *(See* I.R.C. §§ 170(c)(2)(B),(f)(2); 664, 642(c)(5)).

12. I.R.C. § 170(a)(1) (2008). (Donated artwork must characterized as a capital asset as defined by I.R.C. § 1221(a) to be eligible for a charitable deduction.)

13. I.R.C. § 170(b)(1),(d)(1) (2008).

14. Thus, if in the next succeeding taxable year, the collector has $90,000 of AGI and makes no further charitable contribution(s) in such year, then the remaining $20,000 may be deducted in such year.

15. I.R.C. §§ 170(f)(8); 1.170A-13(b),(f) (2008); *supra* at Toce, § 9.02(5).

16. 26 C.F.R. § 1.170A-13(f) (2008); Toce, *supra* at § 9.02(5)(c),(d).

17. 26 C.F.R. § 1.170A-13(f) (2008); Toce, *supra* at § 9.02(5)(d).

18. Toce, *supra* at § 9.02(5)(d); (See I.R.S. Form 8283 at; site accessed on October 15, 2008).

19. 26 C.F.R. § 1.170-A13(c)(3) (2008).

20. Id.

21. *See infra* note 47.

22. Ralph E. Lerner and Judith Bressler, *Art Law: The Guide for Collectors, Investors, Dealers and Artists* (PLI 3d ed, 2005), vol. III, 1558 (interpreting I.R.C. §§ 1221(a)(3)(C) and 26 C.F.R. 1.664-1(a)(5)(i), under the operation of these rules, the artwork in this case would be characterized as ordinary income property, not a capital asset).

23. I.R.C. §§ 170 (e)(1)(B)(i) (2008), 26 C.F.R. § 1.170A-4(b)(3) (2008).

24. 26 C.F.R. § 1.170A-4(b)(3)(i)-(ii) (2008); *see also* Jennings v. Comm'r, 17-18, 521 T.C. Memo (1988).

25. 26 C.F.R. § 1.170A-4(b)(3) (2008).

26. Id.

27. 26 C.F.R. § 1.170A-4(b)(3)(ii) (2008).

28. Toce, *supra* at §25.23.

29. Id, at §25.23.

30. Gregory Taggart, *Art Appreciation,* Bloomberg Wealth Manager, 27 (Oct. 2005).

31. IRS Art Advisory Panel, 2004.

32. Jerry McCoy, *Contributions of Property: Winds of Change Blowing?* ALI 19th Annual Advanced ALI-ABA and ABA Section of Taxation Course of Study, 369, 371 (Nov. 2004).

33. Lerner and Bressler, 1513, vol. III (3d ed. 2005).

34. Rev. Proc. 66-49, 1966-2 C.B. 1257.

35. 26 C.F.R. § 1.170A-13(c) (2008); Lerner and Bressler, 1515, vol. III (3d ed. 2005).

36. Jessica Darraby, *Art, Artifact and Architecture Law*, 93 (Thompson/West)(2005).

37. Id, at 93; Lerner and Bressler, 1520, vol. III (3d ed. 2005).

38. Darraby, *supra* at 93.

39. 26 C.F.R. § 1.170A-13(c)(3)(i) (2008); Toce, *supra* at § 9.03(a); Lerner and Bressler, 1516 (3d ed. 2005).

40. 26 C.F.R. § 1.170A-13(c)(4)(i) (2008); *supra* at Toce, § 9.03(3)(a).

41. 26 C.F.R. § 1.170A-1(c)(2) (2008).

42. 26 C.F.R. § 1-170A-13(c)(5)(i) (2008); *supra* at Toce, § 9.03(3)(b).

43. I.R.S. Publication 561 (April 2007).

44. 26 C.F.R. § 1.170A-13(c)(5)(iv) (2008); *supra* at Toce, § 9.03(3)(c).

45. 26 C.F.R. § 1-170A-13(c)(6)(i) (2008); Toce, *supra* at § 9.03(5)(a).

46. 26 C.F.R. § 1.170A-13(c)(4)(ii) (2008); Toce, *supra* at § 9.03(4).

47. I.R.C. § 212(3) (2008); Rev. Rul. 67-461 (1967) 1967-2 CB 125; Toce, *supra* at § 9.03(5)(c).

48. 26 C.F.R. § 1.170A-13(c)(1) (2008); Lerner and Bressler, 1518-1519, vol. III (3d ed, 2005).

49. 26 C.F.R. § 1.170A-13(c)(4)(ii) (2008); Toce, *supra* at §9.03(4)(f); Lerner and Bressler, 1519, vol. III (3d ed. 2005).

50. Lerner and Bressler, 1519, vol. III (3d ed. 2005).

51. Lerner and Bressler, 1523, vol. III (3d ed. 2005).

52. Rockwood, *supra* at 1029.

53. Anne Marie Rhodes, *Big Picture, Fine Print: The Intersections of Art and Tax,* 26 Colum. J.L and Arts 179, 197; Rockwood, *supra* at1029.

54. Rhodes, *supra* at 197.

55. Lerner and Bressler, 1523, vol. III (3d ed. 2005).

56. Chiu v. Comm'r 84 T.C. 722, 734-735 (1985).

57. Ralph E. Lerner, *Legal Aspects of Owning Art and Other Valuable Personal Property,* PLI/Tax Law and Estate Planning Handbook Series (2004), 153, 157; Ferrari v. Comm'r, 931 F.2d 54, 1991 U.S. App. LEXIS 7068, 5 (1991); Lerner and Bressler, 1535, vol. III (3d ed. 2005).

58. Anselmo v. Comm'r, 757 F.2d 1208, 1213 (1985);. Lerner, 153, PLI (2004).

59. Lerner, 154, PLI (2004).

60. Id, at 156-157; *see also* Lerner and Bressler, 1531, vol. III (3d ed. 2005).

61. Ferrari, 5; *see also* Lerner and Bressler, 1535, vol. III (3d ed. 2005).

62. McGuire v. Comm'r, 44 T.C. 801, 808-809 (1965).

63. Lerner, 159, PLI (2004).

64. American Society of Appraisers at www.appraisers.org, and Appraisers Association of America at www.appraisersassoc.org, September 17, 2008.

65. I.R.C. §§ 6662-6664 (2008); H.R. 4 § 1218 (Pension Protection Act 2006).

66. I. R.C. §§ 6662-6664 (2008).

67. I.R.C. § 6701 (2008); Lerner and Bressler, 1511, vol. III (3d ed. 2005).

68. *See* Rev. Proc. 96-15, CFR 601-201 (1996).

69. McCoy, *supra* at 376.

70. Lerner and Bressler, 556, vol. III (3d ed. 2005); *see also* Roy Kaufman, Art Law Handbook, § 10.03(F) (2000).

71. Id, at 557

72. Id.

73. Rhodes, *supra* at 195.

74. I.R.C. § 170(a)(3) (2008).

75. Winokur v. Comm'r, 90 T.C. 733, 738 (1988).

76. Id, at 738-739.

77. Id, at 739.

78. Id, at 738.

79. Rhodes, *supra* at 193.

80. H.R. 4, § 1218 (Pension Protection Act of 2006).

81. Id.

82. Kahn, Jeremy, "Museums Fear Tax Law Changes on Some Donations," *The New York Times,* Sept. 13, 2006 at E1.

83. Id, at E1.

84. 26 C.F.R. § 1.170A-4(c)(2)(2008); Toce, *supra* at § 11.01.

85. 26 C.F.R. § 1.170A-4(c)(2) (2008); Toce, *supra* at § 11.01; Lerner and Bressler, 1209, vol. III (3d ed. 2005).

86. Lerner and Bressler, 1209, vol. III (3d ed., vol. III, 2005).

87. I.R.C. §§ 2056(a), 2523(a) (2008), 26 C.F.R. § 20.2056(a)-(b) (2008); Toce, *supra* at § 18.02(7).

88. I.R.C. § 1014 (a)(1) (2008); 26 C.F.R. § 25.2512-1 (2008).

89. I.R.C. § 1014; Lerner and Bressler, 1251, vol. III (3d ed. 2005); *see also* Jennings v. Comm'r, 17-18, 521 T.C. Memo (1988). (Note: Had the appreciated artwork been sold before the collector's death, income taxes attributable to the gain appreciated would have been recognized.)

90. *See* note 89, *supra.*

91. I.R.C. § 2055(a) (2008); 26 C.F.R. § 20.2055-1 (2008).

92. Peter E. Lippett, *Estate Planning Strategies for Artists and Collectors* (unpublished CLE essay, Visual Arts and the Law," CLE International, Aug. 10–11, 2006, Santa Fe, NM, K1-17).

93. Id, at K1-14; *see also* note 6 *supra.*

94. Lippett, *supra* at K-14.

95. Id, at K1-15.

96. See Rev. Proc. 66-49, 1966-2 C.B. 1257; *See* USPAP Guidelines at (accessed October 9, 2008).

97. Lerner and Bressler, 1511, vol. III (3d ed. 2005) (interpreting Rev. Proc. 65-19, 1965-2 C.B. 1002).

98. Lippett, *supra* at K1-18; Lerner and Bressler, 1747-1748, vol. III (3d ed. 2005) (interpreting the basis of stock and bond valuations in I.R.C. § 20.2031-2(e) applicable to valuations of artwork).

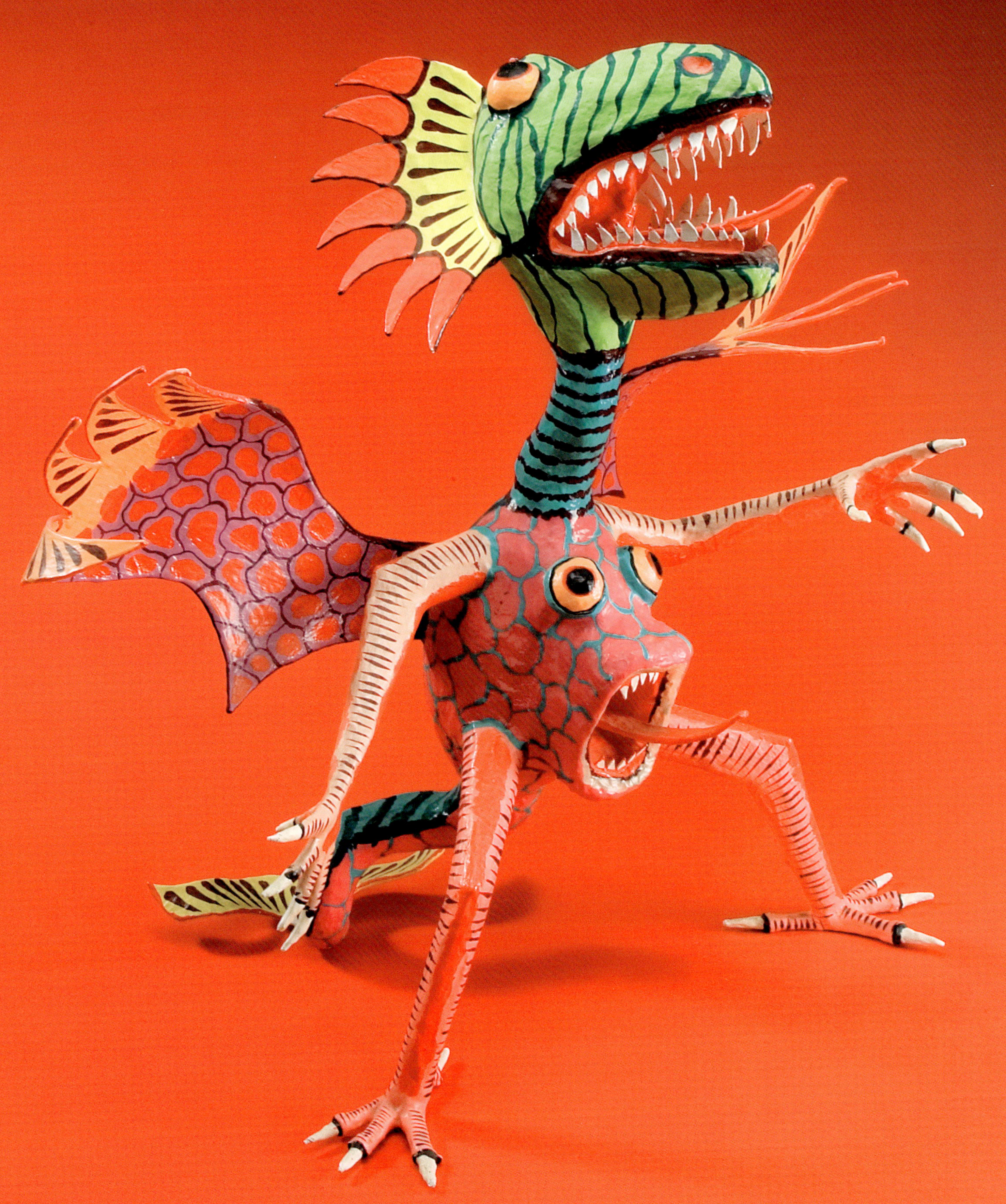

Acknowledgments

MY SPECIAL THANKS GO TO JOYCE ICE, DIRECTOR, Museum of International Folk Art (MOIFA), for her enduring friendship; John Tinker, designer, Museum of New Mexico Exhibitions, a creative genius; MOIFA collections staff members Paul Smutko, Jay Pearson, Rosemary Sallee, and Deborah Garcia-Orona, who performed the miracle of gently moving objects from my home without ever seeming intrusive; MOIFA curators Felicia Katz Harris, Barbara Mauldin, and Tey Marianna Nunn, for their tasteful and learned selection of objects to be included in the exhibition and in the permanent collection of MOIFA; and Dan Cook, Jim Barker, and Tad Dale, dealers of tribal art who are located on Bainbridge Island, Washington, and in Santa Fe, New Mexico. These three gentlemen were the key people who educated me, offered me the best material, and made that material available at a fair price, leaving me enough cash for a #3 burger at Bert's Burger Bowl in Santa Fe. Other fine dealers I should also mention are Charlie Jones (Wilmington, North Carolina), Jim Willis (San Francisco), Bruce Frank (New York), Eric Farrow (San Rafael, California), the late Teal McKibben (Santa Fe), Patricia LaFarge (Santa Fe), Mary Hunt Kahlenberg (Santa Fe), and John Strusinski (Los Angeles).

OPPOSITE:
Alebrije, ca 1990
Papier mâché, wire, and paint
Linares Family, Mexico City, Mexico
Gift of the Diane and Sandy Besser Collection
IFAF

I have deep appreciation for the many artists, both named and unknown, whose work I have been privileged to own and enjoy.

And thanks to Grant and Matthew Besser, my sons and close friends, and Stella and Ruby, my fuzzy girlfriends—we were so lucky to have had Diane Besser in our lives.

Sandy Besser

Contributors

SANDY BESSER began collecting art in 1959 and was joined in that endeavor by his wife, Diane, in 1965. Their collection of tribal and folk art had its beginnings in the mid-1970s, when they traveled to Mexico and Guatemala, and when they began attending ethnographic shows in Santa Fe. Besser has served in past years as Chairman of the Arkansas Arts Center, Treasurer of the American Craft Council, and Chairman of the Museum of New Mexico Foundation Board. He was nominated to state and federal arts councils by President Bill Clinton. Parts of his collection have been exhibited at the de Young Museum in San Francisco and the Arizona State University Art Museum in Tempe, as well as the Museum of Indian Arts and Culture in Santa Fe.

DANIEL H. COOK has assembled rare and unusual objects for both private and museum collections for over thirty years. Early in his career, Cook met the influential art collector/dealer, Albert Rudolph (known to many as "Rudi"), and the two went into business together. In 1970, Cook opened Rudi South, Inc., in Dallas, Texas, specializing in early classical art from India, China, Japan, Tibet, and Nepal, and ethnographic and tribal art from the indigenous groups of Borneo and from other islands in the Philippines and Indonesia. After two decades of owning and managing his Dallas fine arts gallery, he moved to Bainbridge Island in Washington State. Since 1991, Cook has continued to research and acquire artifacts for private clients, international galleries, and American museums. He travels widely: sometimes to luncheon with a Maharaja in East India, sometimes up river in a small cargo boat in Borneo.

SUSANNAH EVANS is an attorney in Kansas City with the Law Office of Matthew L. Hood where she focuses on estate planning and art law, in addition to assisting the firm in its general practice. She also provides fine art services and consultation for artists and art collectors. In 2005, she received her law degree from the University of Missouri–Kansas City, and in the same year she was awarded second place in the Federal Estate Planning Symposium for her legal research project, "A Portrait of Transferring Art: Important Legal Issues Facing Artists and Collectors." She holds a B.A. in Art History from Boston College and an M.A. in Applied History, with emphasis on Museum Studies and Arts Administration, from the University of Missouri–Kansas City. Evans was a graduate intern at the Museum of Indian Arts and Culture and the Laboratory of Anthropology in Santa Fe.

JOYCE ICE became Director of the Museum of International Folk Art, Santa Fe, in 1999. Under her leadership, the museum has engaged in a number of national and international projects, which have resulted in major exhibitions, programs, and publications. She received her Ph.D. in Anthropology and Folklore from the University of Texas at Austin. She serves on visiting accreditation committees for the American Association of Museums and as a panelist for the National Endowment for the Arts, for the National Endowment for the Humanities, and for state arts councils. Ice is a board member of the International Committee on Management of the International Council of Museums (ICOM), and participated in the Museum Leadership Institute of the Getty Foundation. Previously, as folklorist at the Delaware County Historical Association in Delhi, New York, she curated exhibitions on quilt-making, woodcarving, county fairs, and expressions of faith in material culture, and also developed curricula on folk arts for educational use. Her publications include *Quilted Together* and *Farm Work and Fair Play,* along with numerous journal articles.

ARTHUR LÓPEZ, born and raised in Santa Fe, is among the finest *santero* artists working in the proud heritage of northern New Mexico. His award-winning, traditional *bultos* (three-dimensional representations of the saints) are exhibited at Santa Fe's annual Spanish Market and are sought by both museums and private collectors. Equally important to López is his use of his art to transcend the bounds of the traditional santero and to express the full range of his culture and the world around him. His work is in the permanent collections of the Museum of International Folk Art, Santa Fe; the Museum of Spanish Colonial Art, Santa Fe; the Albuquerque Museum of Art and History; the Taylor Museum of the Colorado Springs Fine Arts Center; The Denver Art Museum; and The Harwood Museum of Art, Taos. His work is also published in *100 Artists of the Southwest* by Douglas Bullis. López is represented by Parks Gallery of Taos and Blue Rain Gallery in Santa Fe. He lives in Santa Fe with his wife, Bernadette, and their sons, Darean and Jeremiah.

TEY MARIANNA NUNN is currently Director of Visual Arts and Chief Curator for the National Hispanic Cultural Center in Albuquerque. She spent nine years as the Curator of Contemporary Hispano and Latino Collections at the Museum of International Folk Art in Santa Fe. She is the author of the award-winning *Sin Nombre: Hispana and Hispano Artists of the New Deal Era,* and has published numerous articles and essays, including the extended entry "Latinos and Museums," for the *Oxford Encyclopedia of Latinas and Latinos.* The curator of many groundbreaking exhibitions, Nunn is active in issues concerning Latinas/os, museums, cultural identity, and representation. She currently serves on the Western States Arts Federation Board of Trustees and is Chair of the American Association of Museums' Latino Professional Interest Committee. Dr. Nunn was voted "Santa Fe Arts Person and Woman of the Year" in 2001.

CARMELLA PADILLA is a writer and editor who lives with her husband, Luis Tapia, in Santa Fe. Her books include *Conexiones: Connections in Spanish Colonial Art, Low 'N Slow: Lowriding in New Mexico, The Chile Chronicles: Tales of a New Mexico Harvest,* and *El Rancho de las Golondrinas: Living History in New Mexico's La Ciénega Valley.*

LUIS TAPIA is a noted wood sculptor who lives in Santa Fe. His work has been exhibited and collected nationwide and is included in the collections of the Smithsonian Art Museum, the Smithsonian Museum of American History, the American Folk Art Museum, El Museo del Barrio, the Autry National Center, the Rockwell Museum of Western Art, the Heard Museum, the Albuquerque Museum of Art and History, the Museum of International Folk Art, the Museum of Spanish Colonial Art, and the New Mexico Museum of Art, Santa Fe, among other museums.

Index

Page numbers in *italics* refer to illustrations.

Photography Credits

Photographs by Blair Clark appear on the following pages:
1, 2–3, 8, 11, 12, 13, 14, 17, 18, 20, 22, 23, 24, 25, 26, 28, 30, 32, 33, 34, 35, 36, 39, 40, 41, 43, 44, 46, 54, 55, 56, 59, 60, 67, 99, 104, 109, 112, 113, 115, 116, 118, 119, 121, 122, 123, 124, 125, 126, 127, 128, 129, 130, 150

Photographs by Paul Smutko appear on the following pages:
27, 50, 52, 53, 64, 65, 66, 68, 71, 73, 74, 76, 77, 78, 81, 82, 83, 84, 85, 86, 87, 88, 89, 90, 91, 92, 100, 101, 102